Theorizing World Orders

T0384598

We need new analytical tools to understand the turbulent times in which we live, and identify the directions in which international politics will evolve. This volume discusses how engaging with Emanuel Adler's social theory of cognitive evolution could potentially achieve these objectives. Eminent scholars of International Relations (IR) explore various aspects of Adler's theory, evaluating its potential contributions to the study of world orders and IR theory more generally. Each chapter focuses on a different aspect of the social theory of cognitive evolution, such as power, morality, materiality, narratives and practices, and identifies new theoretical vistas that help break new ground in IR. In the concluding chapter, Adler responds, engaging in a rich dialogue with the contributors. This volume will appeal to scholars and advanced students of IR theory, especially evolutionary and constructivist approaches.

PIKI ISH-SHALOM is the A. Ephraim and Shirley Diamond Family Chair in International Relations at the Hebrew University of Jerusalem. He is the author of *Democratic Peace: A Political Biography* (2013), and *Beyond the Veil of Knowledge: Triangulating Security, Democracy, and Academic Scholarship* (2019), as well as editor of *Concepts at Work: On the Linguistic Infrastructure of World Politics* (2021).

MARKUS KORNPROBST holds the Political Science and International Relations Chair at the Vienna School of International Studies and is the Dean of the Master of Advanced International Studies. His articles appear in top-ranked journals and he has published seven books, most recently *Co-managing International Crises* (Cambridge University Press, 2019).

VINCENT POULIOT is James McGill Professor in the Department of Political Science at McGill University. He is the author of *International Pecking Orders: The Politics and Practice of Multilateral Diplomacy* (2016) and *International Security in Practice: The Politics of NATO-Russia Diplomacy* (2010), as well as the coeditor of *Diplomacy and the Making of World Politics* (2015) and *International Practices* (2011), all published with Cambridge University Press.

Theorizing World Orders

Cognitive Evolution and Beyond

Edited by

PIKI ISH-SHALOM
Hebrew University of Jerusalem
MARKUS KORNPROBST
University of Vienna
VINCENT POULIOT
McGill University, Montréal

CAMBRIDGE
UNIVERSITY PRESS

CAMBRIDGE
UNIVERSITY PRESS

Shaftesbury Road, Cambridge CB2 8EA, United Kingdom

One Liberty Plaza, 20th Floor, New York, NY 10006, USA

477 Williamstown Road, Port Melbourne, VIC 3207, Australia

314–321, 3rd Floor, Plot 3, Splendor Forum, Jasola District Centre, New Delhi – 110025, India

103 Penang Road, #05–06/07, Visioncrest Commercial, Singapore 238467

Cambridge University Press is part of Cambridge University Press & Assessment, a department of the University of Cambridge.

We share the University's mission to contribute to society through the pursuit of education, learning and research at the highest international levels of excellence.

www.cambridge.org
Information on this title: www.cambridge.org/9781009061001

DOI: 10.1017/9781009058193

First published 2021
First paperback edition 2024

A catalogue record for this publication is available from the British Library

ISBN   978-1-316-51228-9   Hardback
ISBN   978-1-009-06100-1   Paperback

Cambridge University Press & Assessment has no responsibility for the persistence or accuracy of URLs for external or third-party internet websites referred to in this publication and does not guarantee that any content on such websites is, or will remain, accurate or appropriate.

This book is dedicated to Emanuel Adler for being Manolo and becoming who is is

Contents

Tables

Preface

Between the three of us, we share hundreds of Emanuel Adler's hours – we being the "Junta," or "Troika," or whatever name we ran by in the past three years or so – or we, the three devoted editors of this volume. So with all those hours there was only one thing that surprised us in the upcoming business of editing this book: Adler turns seventy. We do not even remember how we came across this crucial piece of information, but we did, and it led us to two further discoveries, two unsurprising discoveries, predictable even: (1) This is an occasion to celebrate, at least the academic equivalent of celebration, which means a conference, a festschrift; (2) People were enthusiastic about the opportunity to celebrate Adler, to celebrate with Manolo.

So here we were, gathering for a conference at the University of Toronto in May 2017. Between the ten of us, the shared Adler hours now probably added up to the thousands; we being the contributors to this volume (excluding the eleventh, being Adler himself): his students, colleagues, and mostly colleagues who were also his students (who, in every context other than academic, would here be called friends). And with those thousands of shared Adler hours, we found ourselves unsurprised yet again: Adler is an unending theoretical treasure trove, and what was supposed to be a mere ritualistic and amicable festschrift turned out to be a fully fledged academic and scholarly inspiring conference. Furthermore, Adler was just polishing his long-expected monograph on cognitive evolution, which turned out a year and a half later into his seminal *World Ordering: A Social Theory of Cognitive Evolution* (Cambridge: Cambridge University Press, 2019). We all found the draft a rich source for fruitful scholarly discussions, so much so that the idea of reconvening for a follow-up workshop came up naturally to all of us; there were just too many ideas, insights, themes, theories that were budding in each of the participants following the engagement with Adler and his book manuscript. On this occasion, as on so many others before, we all felt again how

Manolo has the gift of making us think for ourselves in, through, and against his own ideas and theories; or to put it in Adler's theoretical terminology (see in the introduction): *becoming* our own scholarly selves. But there was always also a second face to that gift, and it is Manolo thinking for himself, becoming his own scholarly self, in, through, and against his students and colleagues. Yes, all of us, including Manolo, benefitted tremendously from what was supposed to be no more than an academic gathering with benefits.

As Adler put it himself, back in 1991, "the idea of 'becoming' considers everything to be in flux, as a permanent process of change and evolution, even that which appears to be static." And in an intense intellectual flux – some might even say boiling – we have all been thanks to his mind-blowing *opus magnum*. So a date and place were set again, the times being pre-COVID, and it was relatively easy and tempting. In May 2018 we reconvened in Vienna for a series of dialogical discussions with Adler and his advanced manuscript. During this second workshop critical engagements and theoretical extensions were ripening into a stand-alone academic project, which you now read: *Theorizing World Orders: Cognitive Evolution and Beyond*. Each of the participants turning contributors took one of Adler's themes or ideas, understanding how it shapes their own academic work as well as broader debates in the discipline, and yes, also how it could improve Adler's own ideas and chart a path-breaking theoretical agenda for International Relations. To put it differently, with the help of Adler's work, we were all opening new vistas, through which to understand the ever becoming of world orders. We hope you will find it inspiring as we did.

Jerusalem, Vienna and Montreal, January 2021

Note on the Cover Image

A sankofa, which means "reach back and get it" in the Akan language of Ghana, is an Asante Adinkra symbol composed of a bird with its head reaching backward to an egg. It expresses the need for us human beings to look back to the past in order to understand how we become what we are and continue to improve into the future. We respectfully borrow this symbol here not only as a tribute to African culture, but also because its meaning captures remarkably well the gist of Emanuel Adler's lifelong scholarship and service to the International Relations community.

1 Cognitive Evolution and World Ordering

Opening New Vistas

VINCENT POULIOT, MARKUS KORNPROBST
AND PIKI ISH-SHALOM

International Relations (IR) scholars have researched international orders for many decades. Every major school of thought produced frequently cited works on the topic, including Realism,[1] English School,[2] Liberalism,[3] Critical Approaches,[4] Feminism[5] and Constructivism.[6] Recently, interest in studying international orders has been surging to entirely new levels. In 2018, the journal *International Affairs* dedicated its annual special issue to the topic "Ordering the World? Liberal Internationalism in Theory and Practice." The *International Studies Review* followed suit with a special issue on changing international orders, featuring no less than nineteen articles. In 2021, *International Organization* celebrated its seventy-fifth anniversary with a special issue on "Challenges to the Liberal World Order." The latter title gives away what drives most of the surging scholarly interest: a hunch that the resilience of international ordering we have grown accustomed to remains no longer as unchallenged as it once may have been.

Emanuel Adler's recent *World Ordering: A Social Theory of Cognitive Evolution* is a highly welcome contribution to current debates. The book pushes us toward adapting our (meta-)theoretical toolboxes for studying processes of world ordering. Departures from the existing literature are rather pronounced. Most remarkably, Adler does not write about one single and static world order, but analyzes multiple and simultaneous processes of world ordering. These are underwritten by cognitive evolution, which describes changing landscapes of practices. About a decade ago, Adler likened cognitive evolution to "an evolutionary collective-learning process that explains how

---

[1] Waltz 1979; Gilpin 1981. [2] Bull 1977; Wight 1977.
[3] Keohane and Nye 1977; Krasner 1983b. [4] Wallerstein 1974; Cox 1981.
[5] Tickner 2001. [6] Ruggie 1993; Wendt 1999.

communities of practice establish themselves, how their background knowledge diffuses and becomes institutionalized, how their members' expectations and dispositions become preferentially selected, and how social structure spreads."[7] His 2019 book links cognitive evolution firmly to world ordering.

The purpose of this edited volume is to discuss how Adler's social theory of cognitive evolution helps us study international orders. This introduction provides an overview of his innovative ideas for researching world ordering, locates these in Adler's own "cognitive evolution" – so to say – as a scholar of world politics, and proposes vistas for doing research that extend his theory of world ordering. We proceed in four steps. First, we discuss the similarities and differences between Adler's thoughts on world ordering on the one hand and the existing literature on the other. Second, we unpack the building blocks of his theory of cognitive evolution. Third, we open up vistas for further research out of our critical discussion of Adler's (meta-)theoretical framework. Finally, we provide an overview of the chapters of this book, which follow-up on the vistas we sketch.

Theories of International Order

In this section, we seek to locate Adler's theory of world ordering in terms of its main alternatives on offer in IR. This exercise helps us identify a number of key innovations, as well as zoom in on areas of debate among scholars. Throughout, we use Ikenberry's seminal theory of international order[8] as our main foil, although we also touch on other IR works where relevant. The section is organized around five main questions, which overlap with the three interrogations that Adler mentions in opening his book:[9]

1) What is order?
2) How is order created?
3) How does order reproduce and change?
4) What is international order made of?
5) Where is the international order headed?

---

[7] Adler 2008, 202.   [8] Ikenberry 2001, 2011.
[9] The three questions that structure *World Ordering* are: (1) where do orders come from?; (2) why do they take the shape they do? and (3) how do they change? (p. 2).

Table 1.1 *Comparing theories of international orders*

	Ikenberry	Adler
What is order?	Settled rules (stable, unique)	Configurations of practices (in flux, multiple)
How is order created?	Material domination; rational bargain; functional institutions	Social emergence within communities of practice
How does order reproduce and change?	Rational interest, coercion and path dependence	Integrative effects of jointly enacted practices; practical reflexivity
What is the international order made of?	Open trade and rules to limit the exercise of power	Clashing communities of liberal and nationalist practices
Where is the international order headed?	Authority crisis under control due to low barriers to entry for challengers	Contingent balance of practices between liberal and nationalist modes of action

The first three questions deal with social ontology and are not limited to world politics; whereas the latter two concern the international realm specifically, including its contemporary evolution. Table 1.1 summarizes the main elements of our comparison.

1) What is Order?

In past decades IR scholars have espoused a variety of ontologies when it comes to theorizing order. The key issue here is to determine what social orders are *made of*. In IR, major alternatives include:

- order as a balance of power (in the form of a distribution of capabilities);[10]
- order as material hegemony;[11]
- order as a set of functional institutions and regimes;[12]
- order as a structure of norms, moral purposes and identities;[13]

[10] Waltz 1979.   [11] Modelski 1978; Gilpin 1981.
[12] Krasner 1983a; Keohane 1984.
[13] Hall 1999; Reus-Smit 1999; Wendt 1999.

- order as a combination of coercion and legitimacy;[14]
- order as a structure of institutional relationships;[15]
- order as a dominant economic and technological mode of production[16] and
- order as a settled pattern of action geared toward certain goals such as the preservation of sovereignty.[17]

Adler's social ontology departs from all these conceptions, as it conceives of order as based on the joint enactment of practices. Let us contrast his theory with that of Ikenberry, which is centered on rules and institutions. Similar to other internationalist writings, Ikenberry conceives of order as "settled rules and arrangements."[18] At any given point, one may identify a set of rules of the game that are relatively stable within a social configuration. Agents know these rules and, as will become clear later, generally feel an interest in upholding them.

Contrast this understanding of order with Adler's, which is premised on practice theory. For him, social orders are "configurations of practices that organize social life."[19] Social groupings coalesce around a set of ways of doing things, which stabilize expectations and relationships. As such, for Adler any social order may be located along a continuum between interconnectedness and dissociation. Indeed, the integrative effects of practices are never complete, not only because some practices are much more competitive than others, but also because communities of practice overlap with one another, generating friction and possibly conflict.

Two critical implications follow. First, contrary to Ikenberry and other conceptions prevalent in IR, Adler likens order to flux– not to stability. In Ikenberry, the rules of the game are "settled." More broadly, in the functionalist logic order is an equilibrium solution to collaboration problems. By contrast, for Adler "social orders are in a permanent state of nonequilibrium."[20] In the complexity ontology, order obtains "through fluctuations." We will return to the theme of change later, but for the time being, the second implication needs to be parsed out: if order is process, that is, if no social order is ever "congealed" or stable, then we need to open the door to the multiplicity of

---

[14] Phillips 2010.   [15] Nexon 2009.   [16] Wallerstein 1974; Cox 1986.
[17] Bull 1977.   [18] Ikenberry 2011, 12.
[19] Adler also speaks of "fields" and "landscapes" of practices (2019, 6).
[20] Ikenberry 2011, 32.

orders. In Ikenberry and others, the emphasis is generally on one dominant order, although some contestation is allowed around the edges.[21] Adler makes the opposite postulate: at any moment in time, there are several overlapping orders, some clashing and other mutually reinforcing. The multiple orders "constantly change"[22] and are never set for good – a point that begs the questions of creation, reproduction and change.

2) How is Order Created?

In IR, the dominant approach to the creation of international order is what Ikenberry calls the "political control model."[23] According to this view, rules and institutions are "tools" in the hands of states to achieve their objectives. We find this starting point in both realism (e.g., hegemonic stability theory)[24] and liberal internationalism.[25] In the former case, order is the creation of the powerful, and it serves to foster its dominant interests. In the latter case, order is designed by its participants to help resolve collective action problems. Interestingly, Ikenberry's own theory combines both insights. On the one hand, order is imposed by the strong, generally the winner(s) of a major war. This is the vertical or "hegemonic" aspect of order. Other participants buy into the imposed rules of the game in order to benefit from public goods, as well as to limit the use of arbitrary power by the hegemon. The latter amounts to the constitutional or horizontal dimension of order.[26] On the other hand, Ikenberry also acknowledges the functionalist logic, according to which rules serve to resolve collective action problems.[27]

The key point is that in IR order is generally thought of as volitional or intentional. Order is designed, by dominant countries or by the whole of participants, in order to effect some purposes. Adler considerably nuances this understanding, to emphasize the evolutionary dimension of social order. For him, social orders are primarily socially emergent; the result of the joint enactment of practices. That does not

---

[21] For example, Reus-Smit's "autarkic states" (1999). [22] Adler 2019, 1.
[23] Ikenberry 2011, 28. [24] Gilpin 1981. [25] Keohane 1984.
[26] This is an intriguing commonality between Ikenberry and Adler: both acknowledge the mixed nature of order (horizontal and vertical), although ultimately Adler is far more interested in the former than in the latter.
[27] Ikenberry 2011, 91.

preclude, however, a key role for reflexivity in the making of social orders: actors learn and seek to improve their conditions on that basis (more on this later). But it is a different kind of agency, flowing from the joint enactment of practices, as opposed to the expression of preferences. As Adler explains: "International social orders are neither purely spontaneous and detached from practitioners' dispositions and expectations nor the exclusive result of human design. They result from emergent processes *within* communities of practice."[28]

The key question thus becomes "why some international practices end up being adopted rather than others."[29] As for Ikenberry, Adler does introduce agency in the form of power. But he operates from a deeply different understanding than the ones usually on offer in IR, which center on material capabilities (primarily economic and military). Without denying the importance of such factors, Adler mainly focuses on the attachment of meaning, primarily in the form of deontic power, which is the glue that dynamically holds together the community of practice, but also performative power (which rests on the credible enactment of practice) and practical authority (which revolves around the struggle for competence, as well as epistemic knowledge, such as values and norms, making-up practices). Adler then adds a number of other social forces, ranging from dominant discourse to functionality through identity, in order to explain the particular shape that configurations of practice (orders) take at a particular point in space and time. Altogether, these factors drive what is arguably the most distinctive contribution of *World Ordering* to the question of order: explaining how practices spread within and across communities of practice.

3) How does Order Reproduce and Change?

We have already established that for Ikenberry, orders are created through coercion and rational interest or, to use his own words, "command" and "consent."[30] Actors comply because it is in their interest to do so, in order to control the hegemon (or, reversely, to enact domination), to benefit from global public goods, as well as to deal with institutional artifacts such as sunk costs and adaptation. As

---

[28] Adler 2019, 147.   [29] Ibid., 303.

[30] Ikenberry adds a third mechanism, balance, but it is not central to his theory.

equilibrium, order maintains itself so long as it resolves collective action problems. As a structure of power, alternatively, it reproduces to the extent that it reflects the distribution of material capabilities in the system. Thus, changes in the dominant actors, or in the nature of collaboration problems, are likely to lead to a new order, even though path dependence produces strong stabilizing effects (more on this later).

Adler gets to the problem of reproduction and change from the opposite angle. Remember that according to his theory, order is constantly in flux; it never stands still. Asking how order changes, then, is misplaced; the real question has to do with how practices are stable enough, locally, to (temporarily) fix a social order. Stability, here, is nothing but appearance; it rests on tons of political work and agency. The joint enactment of practices produces a number of integrative effects, in the form of mutual expectations, for instance. This is what explains continuity, according to Adler: "the intersubjective legitimacy of social orders is associated neither with utilitarian-functional considerations nor with the mere fact of their embeddedness in institutions. Foremost, it rests with practices' capacity to create interconnectedness and practitioners' mutual commitment to their practices."[31]

Here it is critical to confront the typical understanding of compliance in IR with Adler's. As he explains, whether one uses rational choice theory (logic of consequences) or normative constructivism (logic of appropriateness), ultimately the logic of compliance is one of rule-following. Order comes first (in the form of settled rules); then compliance follows (rule-following) and the order gets reproduced. By contrast, for Adler orders results from "enacting rules."[32] It is practice that comes first; order follows from joint performance, because of the socially integrative effects that it generates.[33] In a sense, we could say that, compared to the usual trio of explanations for compliance in IR (coercion; interest; legitimacy),[34] Adler suggests a fourth, complementary one, centered on the mutual accountability that practitioners party to a community of practice feel toward one another due to joint enactment and open social interaction.

In Adler's theory, then, a key engine of change comes from "liminars,"[35] that is, actors that are located on the periphery or at the

---

[31] Adler 2019, 148.   [32] Ibid., 40.   [33] See also Neumann 2007.
[34] Wendt 1999.   [35] Adler 2019, 3.

intersection of communities of practice. More broadly, because practice comes first, orders are always in the process of being made and remade. But this does not lead to instability – on the contrary. As Adler explains: "Fluctuations, such as practice learning, negotiation, and contestation, keep social orders in a metastable state."[36] This is where politics enter the picture the most clearly. Whereas conventional wisdom generally associates politics with change, Adler connects it to stability: "Politics," he writes, concerns how agents "strive either to keep social orders metastable or to bring about their evolution."[37]

Overall, then, evolutionary as Adler's theory of world ordering may be, he nonetheless gives pride of place to intentionality and value judgments as the bases for innovation or creative variation.[38] Agency connects to change in three main ways: (1) learning within communities of practice (negotiation and contestation of meanings); (2) competition between communities (with some having preferential growth over others) and (3) the invention of new actors. Ultimately, then, agency is central to the reproduction and transformation of social orders, but it is a form of agency that is based neither on instrumental calculation nor on deep internalization, but rather on practical reflexivity: "Practitioners make value judgments about their performance and its outcomes, and if disenchanted, intentionally act differently from before."[39] Social orders are always up for grabs at the individual level; but communities of practice tend to impose constraints on such volatility.

4) *What is the International Order Made of?*

We now switch gear and move from first-order to second-order issues, focusing on world politics per se. What do the different conceptions of order – including its creation, reproduction and change – have to say about the international realm? What, if anything, is particular to this level of analysis compared to other social spheres? A classic answer to this question comes from Bull, according to whom the preservation of sovereignty is the basic goal that all participants to the international order share. Fittingly, his definition of international order rests on this specificity – "a pattern of activity that sustains the elementary goals of the society of states."[40] The peculiar institutions of international

---

[36] Ibid., 3.   [37] Ibid., 21.   [38] Ibid., 30.   [39] Ibid., 30.   [40] Bull 1977, 8.

society, such as war, diplomacy, international law and the balance of power, are all geared toward the logic of state sovereignty. Note that there is nothing liberal about Bull's notion of the international order: in "the absence of social solidarity," he writes, only "common interests" can provide a stable foundation.

By contrast, Ikenberry explicitly qualifies the post-1945 international order as a liberal one. Like Bull (and contrary to Adler, see later), Ikenberry focuses on states and states alone. But the substance of the rules that comprise the international order is more specific than for Bull. Beyond the preservation of sovereignty, a liberal order is distinct in that it is "open" and "rules-based." Openness for Ikenberry primarily refers to "trade and exchange on the basis of mutual gain";[41] whereas a rules-based order is "at least partially autonomous from the exercise of state power."[42] Horizontal as both characteristics may be, liberal orders also admit variation along the vertical dimension. According to Ikenberry, for instance, the American-led international order is a hybrid form in which multilateralism combines with patron–client relationships, power balance and hierarchy. Put differently, there is one liberal order, structured around open rules, but it can accommodate hierarchical deviations.

Adler's notion of international order differs in significant ways, beginning with the fact that it admits a plurality of overlapping orders. His theory of world ordering also challenges state centrism, putting communities of practice (which may comprise not only powerful states but also any other kind of actor) in the driver's seat. What helps qualify the orders under study are the key practices around which communities converge. Adler suggests thinking of international orders as fluctuating along a continuum bordered by nationalism at one end and liberalism at the other. What he calls "global anchoring practices"[43] are dominant modes of action that help distinguish one order from the others (although they always overlap in some ways). Nationalistic practices, for instance, include mercantilism, power politics, populism and immigration controls. By contrast, liberal practices cover regional integration, free trade, multilateralism and international law. In our current era, Adler observes, liberal and nationalistic communities of practice clash through the enactment of these contending practices, generating fluctuations and contradictions.

---

[41] Ikenberry 2011, 18.   [42] Ibid., 18.   [43] Adler 2019, 153.

The fact that "[c]ognitive evolution theory suggests a concept of multiple international social orders"[44] significantly transforms our understanding of international orders, as well as their evolution. As Adler explains: "Existing and emerging international social orders can be superimposed for extended periods of time when the existing order has not yet evolved but the emerging order has still not taken hold."[45] In order to capture this flux, he coins the concept of "balance of practices," in which clashing modes of action coexist and often rub against one another. Adler gives the example of the European Union's response to the ongoing refugee crisis, in which liberal and nationalistic practices compete as part of the policymaking process. In addition, Adler's theory helps capture the infinite nature of international orders, which "have never covered the entire globe and have always been a matter of perspective and context."[46] Instead of unicity and homogeneity, then, we have an international realm characterized by multiplicity and heterogeneity at every step of the way.

5) *Where is International Order Headed?*

The final question that we address regards the current state and prospects of the international liberal order. Ikenberry's *Liberal Leviathan* makes a relatively sanguine appraisal here: the liberal international order is undergoing an "authority crisis," due to "shifts in power, contested norms of sovereignty, threats related to nonstate actors, and the scope of participating states."[47] That said, Ikenberry rushes to add, the resilience of the order remains unprecedented, primarily because of low barriers to entry, which facilitate the integration of challengers. In addition, the absence of a real contender to the liberal order helps maintain it even in the face of its authority crisis: "Appealing alternatives to an open and rule-based order simply have not crystallized."[48]

As we have already seen, Adler rejects such an assumption of unicity for the liberal international order: "Even at the height of American power after World War II, and after the fall of the Soviet empire in 1989," he writes, "international order consisted of a plurality of international social orders."[49] Put differently, the liberal order has never

---

[44] Ibid., 6.   [45] Ibid., 23.   [46] Ibid., 24.   [47] Ikenberry 2011, 46.   [48] Ibid.
[49] Adler 2019, 142.

been dominant to the point of displacing entirely its alternatives. That said, Adler and Ikenberry do agree that the liberal order is currently enduring a serious crisis. For the former, however, it is difficult to predict how competing communities of practice will feature in the making and remaking of international orders. Contrary to Ikenberry, then, it is not the substance of the liberal order, as much as the productive effect of practices and the competition between communities of practice, that are likely to determine the fate of multilateralism and open trade.

How can we conjecture about the future of the liberal order, then? While Adler provides analytically general mechanisms that operate in any social realm, Holsti suggests a series of requirements that are peculiar to the international realm of sovereign states.[50] On top of legitimacy, he argues that international order requires a system of governance, the possibility of assimilation, a deterrent system, conflict-resolving procedures, a consensus on war, procedures for peaceful change and some anticipation of future issues. These are, in fact, the conditions for stability in the international society. For Holsti, the post-World War II order suffers from insufficient mechanisms of deterrence, peaceful change and anticipation, a problem that has, and continues to, put its resilience to test. This argument, however, does not take into account the specificities of the current period, including the rise of nationalism across the globe.

Adler, for his part, understands the fate of the liberal order in terms of its main alternative, the nationalist one. His claim, which is partly indeterminate, is that "[f]luctuations of practices (particularly contestation of the present social order) may be approaching a sociocognitive threshold. If it gets crossed, Europe's social order could tip and evolve."[51] In order to tell where the liberal international order is headed, then, we need to study – empirically – the balance of practices that currently structure these two communities. Equipped with Adler's mechanisms of change, centered around performative power, learning and competition, we may not predict the future, but we can certainly better understand its making.

Adler does not stop with recognizing the contingency of world ordering, however. His theory is also explicitly normative. Practitioners have a responsibility in the evolution of international

---

[50] Holsti 1991.   [51] Adler 2019, 7.

orders: their practices are better, in the normative sense, when they are based on an acknowledgment of our common humanity. *A Theory of World Ordering*, then, not only puts forward a conceptual apparatus in which norms feature prominently, as in Reus-Smit or, to a lesser extent, Ikenberry. It also suggests that global practices can evolve toward the better – nondeterministic as these normative processes may be (more on this later).

The Building Blocks of Cognitive Evolution Theory

Now that we have located Adler's theory in the IR literature on international orders, we want to parse out the key components of his (meta-) theoretical framework. Adler's social theory of cognitive evolution is built on six core building blocks: (1) evolution and process; (2) social learning, agency and background knowledge; (3) practices and communities of practice; (4) creativity, reflexivity and deontic power; (5) social order and multiplicity and (6) bounded progress. This section discusses each of them in turn.

Evolution and Process

Adler's theory is based on evolutionary logic. Evolution describes the incremental process of social transformation. This is the key parallel between cognitive evolution and biological evolution. Notwithstanding their fundamental differences, the worlds that social scientists and natural scientists seek to understand do share a crucial feature: they are constantly changing. Beyond this similarity, there are also major differences between cognitive and biological evolution, starting with agency. Cognitive evolution is underpinned by agential processes. Political actors do certain things rather than others, and this makes the social world evolve in certain ways rather than others. Adler divides the process of cognitive evolution into three main phases: innovation, selection and diffusion.[52] Overall, the evolutionary metaphor is persuasive for two reasons: first, it shifts the analytical focus to the institutional environment, where the selection process takes place; and second, it points out that the process lacks a necessary direction. History and the evolution of ideas are not teleological processes guided by a supreme entity.

[52] Adler 1991, 55–58.

Adler's emphases on becoming and agency hang together. In the social world, the former cannot be explained without scrutinizing the latter. Equally important, Adler asserts that we cannot make sense of agency without taking a close look at the evolution of the social world. This kind of ontology requires not only an epistemology that helps make sense of change but also one that does not reduce the study of change to linear causal relationships. Adler, therefore, settles on what may be described as a pragmatist epistemology. Early American pragmatists, especially Peirce, James and Dewey feature prominently in his thinking, as do Mead, Toulmin and D. Campbell. Furthermore, Adler borrows from complexity theory and from Popper. The former is an important source of inspiration for him primarily because it is all about nonlinear relationships. For his part, Popper tried to grapple with something that makes Adler wonder too: there is not just a material world; there are also subjective and intersubjective worlds. It is Popper's epistemological ideas on these worlds that Adler is particularly interested in.

"Becoming" lies at the center of Adler's thinking about international politics and the social world. Taking his cue from Heraclitus, he starts from the premise that one can never cross the same river twice. For Adler "the idea of 'becoming' considers everything to be in flux, as a permanent process of change and evolution, even that which appears to be static."[53] This is a critical point for Adler, because in his view order happens through fluctuations (see earlier). Evolutionary logic is key because it paves the way to a thoroughly processual understanding of the social. The social world – interacting with the material world – is never carved into stone. It evolves.

In line with his ontology of becoming, Adler assumes that orders evolve. Not only do orders never stand still for portrait, but the kind of change to be understood is evolution rather than distribution (or redistribution), transformation or friction.[54] Material changes are connected to changes of order, for example, through external shocks. At the same time, order can also be meta-stable. But even meta-stability involves evolution, insofar as it is generated through expansion. Meta-stability, defined by Adler "as practices' continuity in a stable state of flow below a sociocognitive threshold,"[55] is akin to resilience.[56] Communities of practice (more on this later) expand to other

---

[53] Ibid., 43.   [54] Adler 2019, 156–64.   [55] Ibid., 3.   [56] Ibid., 18.

geographical and/or institutional environments. Echoing the literature on resilience,[57] this phenomenon is not about order staying exactly the same. It is about order being adapted over and over.

Social Learning, Agency and Background Knowledge

In Adler's theory, evolution is cognitive in the sense that it describes a process of social learning. Put differently, it is knowledge, especially background knowledge, which varies here. Accordingly, for Adler "learning means the evolution of background knowledge (intersubject-ive knowledge and discourse that adopt the form of human dispositions and practices)."[58] Here the connections to American pragmatism should be clear. Adler's understanding of pragmatism includes a careful theoretical engagement with constitutive and causal relation-ships. This sets him apart from epistemological postulates of "follow-ing the actors."[59] Adler vows not just to follow how actors cognitively cope with the world in a particular set of circumstances. He aims for uncovering generalizable processes through which agents figure out what to do, how this affects the social context that constitutes them, and vice versa.

Thus, learning describes the acquisition, transformation and inven-tion of knowledge. For Adler, learning occurs primarily – though not exclusively – via experience. Even more importantly, learning is social in that it occurs via joint participation in practice (more on this later). This is the agentic dimension of Adler's theory: people's ideas change because they do things together. He works from a socially thick notion of agency, which is very different from the focus on individual beliefs or perceptions that one often finds in social science. For Adler, agents "manage" selection according to their own agential plans, which are formed socially, intersubjectively and within an institutional structure. At least in that sense, learning and development are not purely arbi-trary, and furthermore the agents and structures are not separated.

How do orders evolve into certain directions rather than others? The short answer to this is: agency! Very few IR theorists have gone at such great length to address agency. Adler lists no less than seven attributes

---

[57] Young 1999, 133–62; Armitage 2008, 15; Schmidt 2016; Root 2017; Bourbeau 2018.
[58] Adler 2005, 20.   [59] Latour 2005, 12.

of the concept.[60] The most important one – something akin to his *Menschenbild* (image of human beings) – is creativity. This is an analytical clue he borrows from Joas.[61] In Adler's thought, context and creativity do not exclude one another. On the very contrary, context prompts agents to be creative.

Adler's understanding of cognitive evolution is informed by, but also goes beyond, what he labels Giddens' "social functionalism" as well as Elster's individualism and intentionalism. It is also quite removed from various established strands of institutionalism such as historical institutionalism and rational choice institutionalism. Adler elaborates much more on agency and change than Giddens does, and, in contrast to the British social theorist, he relies on the concept of practices in order to overcome the dualism of structure and agency.[62] Adler borrows considerably from the insightful questions that Elster asks about agency, but he rejects his eventual conclusion, that is, to settle for a focus on individual actors who act fully intentionally. Finally, while Adler is very interested in institutions, he criticizes historical institutionalism for reasons not all that dissimilar from his critique of Giddens. Relying too much on structural forces (path dependency), it is unclear where change should come from. His criticism against rational choice institutionalism echoes his remarks about Elster: Adler is skeptical about individualist and fully intentional accounts of agency.

For Adler, neither structure nor agency is ontologically prior. They affect one another in profound ways. While this is an argument about an *aurea mediocritas* (golden middle), it is important to underline that he puts more emphasis on agency than most IR theorists. This, of course, applies to systemic theories of IR, no matter whether they conceptualize structure in material[63] or ideational[64] terms. Yet it also applies to early studies on norms[65] in which norms were assumed to weigh heavily on political agency, poststructuralist work[66] and Gramsci-inspired research[67] in which intersubjectivities of domination leave little room for agency to overcome radical inequality, and even literature that draws on Bourdieu.[68] In Adler's work, the concept of practices features as prominently as in Bourdieu. He also draws from

---

[60] Adler 2019, 198–99.   [61] Joas 1996.   [62] Adler 2019, 39.
[63] Waltz 1979.   [64] Wendt 1999.   [65] Berger 1996.   [66] Walker 1993.
[67] Gill and Law 1989.   [68] Hopf 2010; Pouliot 2016.

Bourdieu's understandings of the field, doxa and habitus to a considerable extent. But he rejects Bourdieu's theory of agency as being too restrictive.

Practices and Communities of Practice

For Adler, the social gets manifested in practices, defined as "knowledge-constituted, meaningful patterns of socially recognized activity embedded in communities, routines and organizations that structure experience."[69] As he writes, "we know and understand through action and practice."[70] This is because practices "structure consciousness."[71] Their role is not causal but constitutive, by establishing a common platform for interaction: "rather than rules mechanistically 'telling' people what to practice, background knowledge works by enabling linguistic and perceptual interpretations, thus, by structuring consciousness." It is interesting to note how Adler's persistent interest in ideas fashioned his current understanding of practices. Unlike certain accounts of habitus, in Adler's hands practices bear the cognitive features of ideas, subject to learning, cognitive evolution and judgment. Those reflective cognitions mark humans as thinking agents, working relentlessly and consciously toward change and normative progress.

By analogy, think of a group of practitioners as being akin to a field of sunflowers. In general, the flowers look in the same direction – that of the sun, even though there always are a few plants defying the pattern for a variety of reasons. Human beings are similarly oriented by practice. Practices provide ready templates for action, which exert a centripetal force on practitioners. People need not use them all the time or always in the exact same way, but as a general rule, they will refer to them, if only because it makes social interaction possible in the first place. In the theory of cognitive evolution, then, collective-background knowledge creates the propensity for similar action.[72]

As such, practices are fundamentally social in nature. And because they produce "interconnectedness," practices lead to horizontal integration, which is – in contrast to vertical integration – conducive to learning.[73] For Adler, communities of practice are the agents of change. They play a crucial role in "meaning investment"[74] that can transform

---

[69] Adler 2008, 198.   [70] Ibid., 118.   [71] Ibid., 16.   [72] Ibid., 166–67.
[73] Ibid., 183.   [74] Ibid., 203.

even the most deeply held "background knowledge." Put differently, social learning – the essence of cognitive evolution – happens by way of communities of practice. Knowledge moves around and morphs via the joint participation in practices. This stands in opposition to what Adler calls the "'bucket' view of learning, in which people add knowledge and skills to the mind as if it were a bucket."[75]

The concept of communities of practice does a number of important things for Adler. Most centrally, it provides him with a vehicle for social learning. Social learning happens by way of communities of practice. Since these communities overlap, agents are never part of just one community. What Wenger refers to as boundary objects, that is, "artefacts, documents, terms, concepts, and other forms of reification,"[76] crisscross. This makes actors engage in brokering and translation. Brokering means that agents "introduce elements of one practice into another." Translation is "relating things that were previously different."[77] These overlaps also obtain at the global level: boundary regions, for instance, are productive spaces in terms of cognitive evolution.

Communities of practice are also important because, beyond being the crucible of learning, they also favor, to a variable extent, mobilization and collective action. For instance, a community's material and organizational capabilities help explain the differential rate of success that its practices enjoy, both within it and on its outside. As such, communities of practice "compete with other communities for the successful institutionalization of their practices."[78] A key part of the theory precisely seeks to explain the differential rate of success that various communities obtain.

Creativity, Reflexivity and Deontic Power

Joint participation is at the source of creativity, which Adler, taking his cue from Joas, conceives as a collective process. New knowledge is the product of interaction, which enables reflexivity and the problematization of existing background knowledge. Nothing comes out *de novo*.[79]

In line with his epistemology, Adler aims for a detailed theoretical specification of agential processes. He identifies four of them:

---

[75] Adler 2005, 18.   [76] Adler 2019, 226.   [77] Ibid., 226.
[78] Adler 2008, 201.   [79] Adler 1991, 56.

"practice-driven changes," "apprenticeship through learning," "agents' reflexivity and judgment" and "social power."[80] Through these processes, which are "inherently intertwined," actors come to learn together. Practice-driven changes naturalize new background knowledge "through self-fulfilling expectations." Apprenticeships change identities around. Judgment is of key importance. Actors denaturalize the old, for example, by delegitimizing it. This entails moving from habit to reflection. Change, according to Adler, involves reflective dimensions (alongside non-reflected ones).

How does new knowledge develop into a practice? Adler's answer to this question is selective retention. There are two kinds of selective retentions. Horizontal retention happens via expansion. Communities of practice expand further geographically or organizationally. Vertical retention is about inheritance. Actors pass on practices to one another. Thus, some may be new practitioners but they use (at least a considerable amount of) established practices. Selective retention is a particular kind of institutionalization. It is not the kind of institutional design that many scholars address, but rather the reification of social institutions as social practices. Adler again borrows from Wenger to argue that while designed institutions matter, ultimately it is practice that matters more.[81] This kind of institutionalization has, according to Adler, something to do with layering and conversion. The former is about grafting "new elements onto an otherwise stable institutional framework." The latter is more far-reaching. It is about the "adoption of new goals or the incorporations of new groups into the coalitions on which institutions are founded."[82] Adler hints here at something like rules of the game.

Agency naturally leads to the issue of power. As we have seen earlier, Adler conceives of power in two main ways: performative and deontic. To start with the former, he writes that "[p]erformative power is the capacity to present a dramatic and credible performance on the world stage."[83] In the dramaturgical tradition of Jeffrey Alexander, Adler is interested in the constitution of society via practice, that is, competent performance. In this scheme, "[p]erformative power means using the contingency of interpretations and performances."[84] When it comes to the deontic face of power, Adler builds on Searle and focuses on the

---

[80]   Adler 2019, 29–30.   [81]   Ibid., 252. See Wenger 1998.
[82]   Thelen quoted in Adler 2019, 258.   [83]   Ibid., 18–19.   [84]   Ibid., 112.

assignment of status and function to things, institutions and people. Deontic power is unequally distributed not only among practitioners but also between communities. This facilitates the diffusion of some background knowledge over other. As he explains, rights, duties, obligations, requirements, permissions, authorization and entitlements become stabilized by means of practice.[85]

This is where Adler's theory of cognitive evolution has a decidedly normative bent. In line with Rouse, mutual accountability is what allows practitioners to go on, to interact collaboratively or competitively around a variety of projects.[86] This deontic process explains how society comes together, including on the international stage. But the deontic power of practice also describes how normative change becomes possible, by allowing practitioners to reflect, critique and justify certain ways of doing things over others.

Social Order and Multiplicity

As discussed in the first section of this chapter, for Adler international order is not just one order but consists of a configuration of international social orders. In other words, social orders are multiple: coexisting, clashing or alternatively mutually reinforcing. In a coauthored 2009 article, Adler explored the overlap between distinct repertoires of security practices, for instance, security community and balance of power practices cohabiting in the very same regional space in the form of a "balance of practices." Emphasizing the heterogeneity of international order, Adler and Greve argued that different systems of governance coexist and overlap,[87] sometimes intentionally but often as historically contingent patterns. Later on, in 2010, Adler built on Eisenstadt's concept of "multiple modernities" as another instantiation of the fluidity and inchoateness of social orders as patterns of practices. Obama's nuclear disarmament agenda, which Adler discussed in a 2013 chapter, similarly combines realpolitik practices with the global governance repertoire. This is what social orders look like in practice.

Orders, which are akin to fields, are constituted by communities of practice. In Adler's process ontology of "order through fluctuations," "social orders originate and derive from, and are incessantly being constituted by, practices." Cognitive evolution happens through the

---

[85] Ibid., 130.   [86] Rouse 2007.   [87] Adler and Greve 2009, 80.

joining of, and competition between, communities of practice, which are the vehicles and sites of learning and innovation. Because cognition is social, based on interaction and engagement with practice, creativity is a socially emergent collective process. Here we see how the concept of practice provides Adler with an endogenous explanation for change and transformation. At the same time, resilience is also a product of contestation. This, of course, echoes complexity theory, from which Adler has taken inspiration for about half a century.

Thus, on top of agency and learning there are structural elements in the theory as well. By presuming the multiplicity of social orders, Adler locates a source of change in the inevitable friction between social configurations. Communities of practice bump into one another, and practitioners often participate in several of them at the same time. Reflexivity is made possible by such interference. And while "'friction' between orders promotes change," crises for their part act as "cognitive punches."[88] They form the structural context of creativity and reflexivity.

Multiplicity is important because for Adler changes emerge out of "liminar situations," which spark "cognitive thresholds." Of particular interest are the boundaries between these orders. Following Wenger, Adler directs our analytical gaze toward studying these boundaries.[89] To put this simply, actors are never just steeped in one context but always in several ones. Practices overlap. So do communities of practice and, thus, social orders. As Adler explains, "we should consider world order to be a constellation and landscape of practice fields and communities of practice, some of which overlap, others which complement and depend on each other, and still others which are in contestation ... Cutting across multiple international social orders, however, are *global anchoring practices* [which] straddle a spectrum between interconnectedness and disassociation."[90] For the former, Adler lists multilateral diplomacy and international contractual law; and national security, mercantilism and populist policy for the latter.

Better Practices and Bounded Progress

In 2005, Adler endorsed a communitarian multilateralism,[91] or cooperation of the like-minded, in effecting progress in world politics.

---

[88] Adler 2019, 162.   [89] Wenger 1998.   [90] Ibid., 153.   [91] Adler 2005.

His normative theory got even more explicit in his discussion of the European civilization and liberal practices.[92] In these works, Adler explicitly supports postmodern practices such as the elimination of borders and postnational citizenship, while also calling for more "relational practices" (e.g., self-restraint) to serve as "cultural roundabouts" for encountering the Other in world politics. As he concluded in 2010: "To my mind, practices of self-restraint and mutual tolerance are not only better practices than colonialism and imperialism – they also suggest the opportunity to establish civilizational encounters on mutual dignity and respect."[93] In this way, Adler comes full circle in his book. By emphasizing the deontic power of practice, he weaves together the analytical and the normative dimensions of world politics. Mutual accountability is what allows practitioners to go on, to interact collaboratively or competitively around a variety of projects. This deontic process explains how society comes together, including on the international stage. But the deontic power of practice also describes how normative change becomes possible, by allowing practitioners to reflect, critique and justify certain ways of doing things over others. This is, perhaps, the destination that Adler has pursued for his entire career – spanning the divide between explaining and effecting political change.

Coming full circle means that Adler revisits his former engagement with the notion of progress and also examines how progress conforms with cognitive evolution. As was analyzed earlier, for Adler the attractiveness of evolution as metaphor is, among other things, in its not being teleological. Evolution as we came to know it depends on contingencies, and it lacks any predestined direction. This is surely different from how we usually think of progress: as the opposite of random change, in being intended and directional. Thus, Adler has to come up with a theoretical framework combining the two distinct notions in relative comfort. He offers a fruitful middle ground that transcends what appears to be unbridgeable dichotomy between the analytical and the normative. Understanding "practices as the repositories of ethical collective knowledge,"[94] Adler goes on to develop a network of novel concepts that together help him overcome problematic dichotomies, such as positive approaches versus normative approaches, communitarianism versus cosmopolitanism, transcendental versus immanent

---

[92] Adler 2010, 2013. [93] Adler 2010, 91. [94] Adler 2019, 266.

values, the Enlightenment idea of progress versus normative relativism, practice versus discourse and interconnectedness versus disassociation.

The concepts that take center stage in Adler's normative/political theory are "better practices" and "bounded progress," along with "common humanity" and "realist humanism." In tune with his Dewey-inspired pragmatist ethics, he defines better practices as "those that carry in their background knowledge constitutive ethical values about common humanity's worth and are emergent in practice, namely practice (and practitioners) are creative of ethical values."[95] Pragmatism enables Adler to ground values in the practices and their communities, as well as in the background knowledge surrounding practices. It also allows him to avoid overly meta-ethical discussions: values and practices are united together and provide the justifications for each other. Values are endowed with quality, which in its turn means value. True, there is in here a bit of circularity, but from a pragmatist perspective this circularity means that ends are shaped in "processes of ends deliberation" and "in response to concrete dilemmas."[96] Circularity is resolved by theoretically turning to deliberation and thus practically to the intersubjective process of social construction. Moreover, the pragmatic moves allow Adler to conceive practices as endowed with deontic power, as the driving force of cognitive evolution directing common humanity in bounded progress. Progress can then conform with cognitive evolution because the above-mentioned conceptual schemata reconceptualizes it as bounded; that is, as "neither deterministic, unconditional, and teleological, a concept of progress usually associated with the Enlightenment idea of progress, nor relativist, as in anything goes, or as in 'good' is whatever I say it is."[97]

None of this means that progress is guaranteed. On the contrary, all we can say is that although "progress may not happen, it still can happen."[98] Bounded progress occurs in this torturous and nonlinear process, otherwise known as human history through which better practices carried in and by communities of practice "spread, both horizontally and vertically, perhaps even to the global level, they constitute propensities for individuals', peoples', and states' moving away from inequality, authoritarian rule, war, and human rights abuses." Those better practices are infused with collective knowledge of a common humanity and they place the quality of human life as

---

[95] Ibid., 270.   [96] Ibid., 272.   [97] Ibid., 267.   [98] Ibid., 279.

a primary entitlement to which we are all entitled, being members of common humanity. Those better practices, while not guaranteed, can still happen and evolve "away from international policies that cause war, poverty, and human rights violations" toward, that is, the "better angels" of "our social orders."[99]

Critical Questions and Extensions for Research

Innovative as it may be, Adler's social theory of cognitive evolution also raises a number of questions to be taken up by the community of IR scholars and beyond. One of the strengths of the book is that it succeeds in opening "new vistas" for studying world ordering. This section, engaging critically with Adler's descriptive, explanatory and normative theorizing, identifies seven key avenues for further research.

First, how exactly do social orders relate to one another? Adler seems to assume that they overlap and form horizontal relations. But we probably need more research into these relations. Some orders are related to one another while others are not. What is more, some orders that are related to one another may do so horizontally but others may do so vertically.[100] We may encounter subordinate and superordinate orders. Something like a diplomatic field may amount to a meta-order in this complex constellation. Related, how are orders constituted within? What about contestation and differentiation within an order, and, thus, within a community of practice? This is an important question because Adler pays close attention to boundaries. If there are important boundaries within a field, this should also prompt the creativity of agents and it should have repercussions for change. To put this differently, orders vary and some variations may make change more likely. This is a point that Krause makes convincingly for the study of fields.[101]

Second, how exactly does the material world shape cognitive evolution? Adler insists on the role of the physical world but he does not supply specific mechanisms. For example, Wendt argues that material conditions impact ideas at two main levels: they define the physical limits of possibility, and they help define the costs and benefits of alternative courses of action.[102] For his part, Adler refers to

---

[99] Ibid., 283. [100] Fligstein and McAdam 2015. [101] Krause 2017.
[102] Wendt 2000.

"assemblage" as "emergent unities of 'things' and 'sayings', which come together in a single context and respect the heterogeneity of their components"[103] – for example, the wasp and the orchid. But how do matter and knowledge come together in a social assemblage? What is more, what is the role of power and capacity here? Adler writes that "[p]ower is also associated with communities of practice's material and institutional resources, for instance, objects and technology that a community of practice shares."[104] By implication, power is not only performative and deontic, but also material, yet the connections between the three are in need of further clarification.

Third and related, why do some players have more deontic power than others? As Guzzini argues (this volume), the problem with any power argument is that it explains cause in terms of its effects: a powerful actor is one who exerts influence over others. But can we describe the power landscape otherwise than via its effects? If we are to avoid the *post hoc, ergo propter hoc* fallacy, this would seem to be an analytical requirement. Adler writes that "[t]he reason that practices and the background knowledge bound with them possess deontic power is easy to see: practicing or knowing in practice means to competently act on the basis of status-functions, which are collectively created, recognized, and legitimized by a community of practice."[105] Critics may find the argument a bit tautological.

Adler argues that a key to cognitive evolution is to explain "how communities of practice establish themselves preferentially." One way in which they do so is by wielding superior deontic power. But where do they get that power from? In other words, what are the sources of deontic power, other than successful performance, which it instantiates? How does one cultivate, or alternatively, lose such power? Is it possible for deontic power to be inefficient and if so why? And how can we operationalize deontic power? More broadly, in practice what is the difference between deontic power and what Adler calls epistemic practical authority? Last but not least, how do power and interests, as well as power and ideas, intersect and implicate each other?

Indeed, taking his cue from Wenger, Adler understands practice as the vehicle of horizontal social integration: shared patterns of doing things bring people together in the form of joint enactment. Correct as this insight may be, it is not entirely clear how it relates to another

---

[103] Adler 2019, 124–25.   [104] Ibid., 175.   [105] Ibid., 236.

aspect of practice, by which (in)competent performances foster vertical integration. Here practice pits people against one another, as part of an agonistic process of struggle over defining and molding the world and its unstable meanings. Of course, both views are probably correct, capturing complementary dimensions of social life. The challenge consists in understanding the competing effects of practice on social order and integration. For instance, while it is true that the mutual accountability upon which practice rests brings communities together, its mechanisms of reputation and peer recognition also generate friction and stratification dynamics. Can we square this circle, and if so, how?

Fourth, if reflectivity and creativity are the (agentic) engines of cognitive evolution, how can we determine the specific directions in which they move social orders? Put differently, what makes agents "tick"? This, of course, is one of the most difficult questions social scientists ask. Adler provides us with four different agential mechanisms and a number of related concepts, ranging from creativity to selective retention, from habit to reflection, from transaction to practices and so on. Different perspectives on cognitive evolution may rearrange these mechanisms and concepts somewhat differently. They may also part ways with some mechanisms and some concepts, moving, for example, away from reflexivity or even further toward it.

Adler argues that reflexivity emerges out of liminar situations; but aren't multiple orders always in tension? This is an important issue because liminar situations are arguably the norm rather than the exception. By implication, actors consistently find themselves in a potential cognitive crisis in which they need to resolve epistemic tensions. If that is the case, what explains that reflexivity is not more prevalent than it actually is in the world? Adler writes that "practices are also creative. Practitioners, through understanding, interpretation, imagination, and experimentation."[106] But then, what are the differences between reflexivity, creativity and judgment?

Furthermore, what can Adler's mechanism tell us about the substance of change, that is, the specific content of background knowledge that wins the day? Overall it seems fair to say that Adler specifies why actors are sometimes able to "think outside of the box"; yet he does not tell us what these outside-of-the-box ideas will be. For instance, he writes that "variation from a cognitive-evolutionary perspective is

---

[106] Ibid., 19.

always creative ... creative variation arises from the contingency of social life, rather than only from intentions and choices." The best we can say is that cognitive evolution is likely to point in the direction of those actors and communities that exert the most deontic power. But as we just explained, it is not clear that we can specify *ex ante* who these powerful players are; we often have to wait until change has occurred before we know.

Adler also suggests that "change is nonlinear and dynamic: social orders evolve pushed by past practices and pulled by future practices."[107] But what does it mean, exactly, to say that future practices pull current ones? Here the critical link is provided by the notion of expectations, which Adler theorizes as a key component of human dispositions. Human beings formulate plans; these plans are informed by the past, concern the future and are acted upon here and now: "Action is 'pushed' by the past from background knowledge dispositions, but is also 'pulled' toward the future with foresight, anticipation, and expectations."[108]

Fifth, what role does communication play in cognitive evolution? If learning takes place via joint participation, then chances are that the participants will communicate, tacitly and/or explicitly, with each other along the way. Instead of a broader concept or set of concepts addressing communication, Adler relies on a narrow one, that is, performances. While discussing performances, however, the authors he cites firmly link performances to other aspects of communication. For all the differences in the arguments they put forward, this similarity applies to Dewey, Alexander as well as Boltanski and Thévenot.[109] While picking a certain aspect of communication at the expense of others is fully in line with current IR theorizing,[110] we are not sure whether it is entirely in sync with a social theory of cognitive evolution.

Authors taking the multiple aspects of communication seriously have long pointed out the importance of liminal spaces. This applies especially to Bakhtin.[111] His work provides important clues for how

[107] Adler and Greve 2009, 83.
[108] Adler 2019, 212. Note that even the label "social theory of cognitive evolution" suggests bridging the gap between cognitive psychology ("cognitive evolution") and constructivism ("social theory"). Recent works trying to do so include Lebow (2008), Hymans (2010) and Kornprobst (2019).
[109] Dewey 1925; Alexander 2004; Boltanski and Thévenot 2006.
[110] For a critique, see Kornprobst and Senn 2016.   [111] Bakhtin 1986.

communication and liminal spaces hang together. Indeed, another promising starting point for developing a fuller understanding of communication is Adler's own previous work, for instance, when he engages with Deutsch and his transactionalist understanding of communication,[112] writes about narratives[113] and does empirical work on seminar diplomacy.[114]

Sixth, more work remains to be done about what triggers the seven mechanisms of cognitive evolution that Adler theorizes. Following Elster, mechanisms are conceived of as propensities and potentials, which need to be sparked in order to produce their effects. In Adler's theory, it is not always clear what exactly these triggers are. We know that crises give "cognitive punches," but we do not know how to specify crises *ex ante*, that is to say, prior to becoming an opening for change. For example, there are four agentic mechanisms of cognitive evolution: (1) practice-driven changes in dispositions and expectations; (2) transactions, negotiation and contestation processes; (3) socially generated reflection and judgment and (4) practitioners' usage of material and sociocultural environments (deontic power). The connections and overlap between these agentic processes are not always easy to pin down, especially when it comes to empirical operationalization.

The same goes, although perhaps to a lesser extent, for the "three sociocultural mechanisms" of cognitive evolution: (1) endogenous collective learning within communities of practice; (2) competition among them and (3) innovation of communities ("invention of new actors"). How do these structural, macro forces interact with the processes of agency? More to the point, how do they connect to what Adler calls the mechanisms of socio-cognitive evolution – epistemic practical authority of communities of practice and meaning fixation by practices? In this overabundance of social mechanisms, the empirical researcher is a bit at loss in order to trace changes in international orders.

Seventh, there are normative issues awaiting further reflection. Throughout his writings Adler explored the power of ideas in their various facets and mechanisms. As a constructivist, he is keenly aware of the relationships between ideas and power, so much so that he develops the notion of epistemic security, "the validity of what we can collectively consider as knowledge." Yet Adler spends less time pondering the complementary critical sensitivity of the obverse

---

[112] Adler 1992.   [113] Adler 2010, 204–05.   [114] Adler 1997a, 268–71.

relations: that between power and ideas. For instance, how do hegemonic actors influence the working of epistemic communities, and even
more deeply the constitution of ideas, intersubjective knowledge, background knowledge and knowledge as being manifested in practices and
in communities of practice? It is not that Adler is oblivious to the
possibility that ideas create wrong and even evil. He knows history
well enough to be aware of this possibility (and this is another source
for his attempt to weave together normative and explanatory theories).
But the development of ideas and the selection process – that is, cognitive evolution – at points glosses over the many ways in which power
and interest meddle in the life of ideas.

From a more critical perspective, a perspective committed to the
emancipatory potential of ideas, ideas need not be some neutral apparatus, fitting and serving a universal purpose. Interestingly enough,
Adler argues with Bernstein that authority is involved in the constitution of epistemes.[115] Add this to his correct observation that constructivism lacks a theory of politics,[116] and what we get is a major gap to be
filled. One way would be to embrace the full potential of critical theory
and explore in depth the constitutive relations of ideas and power,
which are reciprocal and mutual. Theorizing these relations would
open the door to a fruitful constructivist theory of politics and to
a fuller understanding of the relations between multiple potential pro-
gresses and cognitive evolution.

Chapter Overview

The contributors to this book explore different vistas for researching
world ordering by engaging with Adler's work at the meta-theoretical,
conceptual and/or analytical-normative level(s). In Chapter 2, Stefano
Guzzini zooms in on power, observing some inconsistencies in the way
that Adler borrows from John Searle's and Jeffrey Alexander's respect-
ive social theories. Because he equates power with agency rather than
with structural domination, argues Guzzini, Adler ends up overbur-
dening what the concept of power can deliver, especially in light of his
communitarian political theory and process ontology. In Chapter 3,
Alena Drieschova looks into the nexus between the material and the
ideational. Linking New Materialism to cognitive evolution, she seeks

---

[115] Adler and Bernstein 2005, 297–98.   [116] Adler 2005, 5.

to move beyond the New Materialism's fixation on macro-historical theorization of changes of international order on the one hand, and the social theory of cognitive evolution's heavy reliance on ideas and practices on the other. Drieschova's chapter elaborates on how functionality and aesthetics can operate as material criteria for selective retention, and highlights the relevance of network memory for the kinds of information that are stored and, therefore, retained.

In Chapter 4, Simon Frankel Pratt criticizes Adler's social theory of cognitive evolution for the lack of an explicit phenomenology. Pratt addresses this lacuna by drawing on the philosophy of John Dewey and Maurice Merleau-Ponty, thus moving Adler's theory from strict pragmatism to one more informed by phenomenology. Pratt's reasoning is that a phenomenological elaboration of cognitive evolution makes significant contributions to several debates in the field of IR, including those on micro-foundations, ontological security and materiality. Chapter 5, by Maïka Sondarjee, looks for clues about discourses in Adler's theoretical framework. Fully agreeing with Adler's meta-theoretical focus on evolution, Sondarjee criticizes the theory for side-lining the meaning-making repercussions of discourse. In order to make a case for the salience of narratives, she develops an argument for how narratives could be included in the social theory of cognitive evolution, using the World Bank and participatory development practices as a case study. In Chapter 6, then, Peter M. Haas starts by asking the question of where the agents are in Adler's theory. His vehicle for answering this question is comparing the social theory of cognitive evolution with their past collaborative work on epistemic communities. Haas, empirically focusing on global environmental governance, concludes that cognitive evolution is heavily shaped by epistemic communities.

In the final two substantive chapters, Beverly Crawford Ames and Christian Reus-Smit engage with an analytical-normative theme that has always been crucial for the discipline of IR in general and Adler's work in particular, that is, progress. Is progress possible in international politics? If so, how? Crawford's chapter focuses on the evolution of the refugee regime. Applying the theory of cognitive evolution, she contends that there has been, despite some setbacks, an overall pattern of progress for much of the twentieth century. At the same time, however, she cautions that post-truth undermines what Adler refers to as "epistemological security" and identifies as a driving force for progress. Reus-Smit also engages with the issue of progress but his means for doing so are different. Looking back to Adler's often-cited 1997 article "Seizing the Middle Ground: Constructivism in World Politics,"[117] he asks whether Adler succeeds in holding the middle ground that he advocates. Applying English School theorizing on interpreting the middle ground, Reus-Smit contends that there are notable tensions between how Adler used to pursue the middle ground in his past work and how he does so in the social theory of cognitive evolution. Reus-Smit also contends that both avenues struggle to arrive at a sound normative account.

The book concludes with a commentary by Emanuel Adler, which engages with the vistas for studying world ordering that are explored in this book, as well as with the criticisms raised by contributors. In a new and exclusive extension of his thinking, Adler then develops a rough sketch of what a theory of politics looks like, from a cognitive evolution perspective, using the concept of practical democracy as an anchor, and the case of artificial intelligence as an illustration.

References

Adler, Emanuel. 1991. Cognitive Evolution: A Dynamic Approach for the Study of International Relations and their Progress. In *Progress in Postwar International Relations*, edited by Emanuel Adler and Beverly Crawford, 43–88. New York: Columbia University Press.

Adler, Emanuel. 1992. Europe's New Security Order: A Pluralistic Security Community. In *The Future of European Security*, edited by Beverly Crawford, 287–326. Berkeley: University of California Press.

Adler, Emanuel. 1997a. Imagined (Security) Communities: Cognitive Regions in International Relations. *Millennium: Journal of International Studies* 26(2): 249–77.

Adler, Emanuel. 1997b. Seizing the Middle Ground: Constructivism in World Politics. *European Journal of International Relations* 3(3): 319–63.

Adler, Emanuel. 2005. *Communitarian International Relations: The Epistemic Foundations of International Relations*. London and New York: Routledge.

Adler, Emanuel. 2008. The Spread of Security Communities: Communities of Practice, Self-Restraint, and NATO's Post-Cold War Transformation. *European Journal of International Relations* 14(2): 195–230.

---

[117] Adler 1997b.

Adler, Emanuel. 2010. Damned If You Do, Damned If You Don't: Performative Power and the Strategy of Conventional and Nuclear Defusing. *Security Studies* 19(2): 199–229.

Adler, Emanuel. 2013. Resilient Liberal International Practices. In *Liberal World Orders*, edited by Tim Dunne and Trine Flockhart, 53–68. Oxford: Oxford University Press.

Adler, Emanuel. 2019. *World Ordering: A Social Theory of Cognitive Evolution*. Cambridge: Cambridge University Press.

Adler, Emanuel and Steven Bernstein. 2005. Knowledge in Power: The Epistemic Construction of Global Governance. In *Power and Global Governance*, edited by Michael Barnett and Raymond Duvall, 294–318. Cambridge: Cambridge University Press.

Adler, Emanuel and Beverly Crawford. 2006. Normative Power: The European Practice of Region-Building and the Case of the Euro-Mediterranean Partnership. In *The Convergence of Civilizations: Constructing a Mediterranean Region*, edited by Emanuel Adler, Federica Bicchi, Beverly Crawford and Raffaella Del Sarto, 3–47. Toronto: University of Toronto Press.

Adler, Emanuel and Patricia Greve. 2009. When Security Community Meets Balance of Power: Overlapping Regional Mechanisms of Security Governance. *Review of International Studies* 35(S1): 59–84.

Alexander, Jeffrey C. 2004. Cultural Pragmatics: Social Performance between Ritual and Strategy. *Sociological Theory* 22(4): 527–73.

Armitage, Derek. 2008. Governance and the Commons in a Multi-level World. *International Journal of the Commons* 2(1): 7–32.

Bakhtin, Mikhail. 1986. *Speech Genres and Other Late Essays*, translated by V. W. McGee. Austin: University of Texas Press.

Berger, T. 1996. Norms, Identity, and National Security in Germany and Japan. In *The Culture of National Security: Norms and Identity in World Politics*, edited by Peter J. Katzenstein, 317–56. New York: Columbia University Press.

Bernstein, Richard. 1991. *The New Constellation: The Ethical-Political Horizons of Modernity/Postmodernity*. Cambridge: Polity.

Boltanski, Luc and Laurent Thévenot. 2006. *On Justification: Economies of Worth*. Princeton: Princeton University Press.

Bourbeau, Philippe. 2018. *On Resilience: Genealogy, Logics, and World Politics*. New York: Cambridge University Press.

Bull, Hedley. 1977. *The Anarchical Society: A Study of World Politics*. New York: Colombia University Press.

Cox, Robert W. 1981. Social Forces, States and World Orders: Beyond International Relations Theory. *Millennium: Journal of International Studies* 10(2): 126–55.

Cox, Robert. 1986. States, Social Forces and World Orders: Beyond International Relations Theory. In *Neorealism and Its Critics*, edited by Robert Keohane, 204–54. New York: Columbia University Press.

Dewey, John. 1925. *Experience and Nature*. Chicago: Open Court.

Dewey, John. 1934. *A Common Faith*. New Haven: Yale University Press.

Fligstein, Neil and Doug McAdam. 2015. *A Theory of Fields*. Oxford: Oxford University Press.

Gadamer, Hans-Georg. 1972. *Wahrheit und Methode*. Tübingen: J. C. B. Mohr.

Gill, Stephen R. and David Law. 1989. Global Hegemony and the Structural Power of Capital. *International Studies Quarterly* 33(4): 475–99.

Gilpin, Robert. 1981. *War and Change in World Politics*. Cambridge: Cambridge University Press.

Hall, Rodney Bruce. 1999. *National Collective Identity: Social Constructs and International Systems*. New York: Columbia University Press.

Holsti, Kalevi J. 1991. *Peace and War: Armed Conflicts and International Order, 1648–1989*. Cambridge: Cambridge University Press.

Hopf, Ted. 2010. The Logic of Habit in International Relations. *European Journal of International Relations* 16(4): 539–61.

Hymans, Jacques E. C. 2010. The Arrival of Psychological Constructivism. *International Theory* 2(3): 461–67.

Ikenberry, G. John. 2001. *After Victory: Institutions, Strategic Restraint, and the Rebuilding of Order after Major Wars*. Princeton: Princeton University Press.

Ikenberry, G. John. 2011. *Liberal Leviathan: The Origins, Crisis, and Transformation of the American World Order*. Princeton: Princeton University Press.

Joas, Hans. 1996. *Die Kreativität des Handelns*. Frankfurt am Main: Suhrkamp.

Keohane, Robert O. 1984. *After Hegemony: Cooperation and Discord in the World Political Economy*. Princeton: Princeton University Press.

Keohane, Robert O. and Joseph S. Nye. 1977. *Power and Interdependence*. Boston: Little, Brown.

Kornprobst, Markus. 2019. *Co-managing International Crises: Judgements and Justifications*. Cambridge: Cambridge University Press.

Kornprobst, Markus and Martin Senn. 2016. A Rhetorical Field Theory: Background, Communication, and Change. *British Journal of Politics and International Relations* 18(2): 300–17.

Krasner, Stephen D. 1983a. *International Regimes*. Ithaca: Cornell University Press.

Krasner, Stephen D. 1983b. Structural Causes and Regime Consequences: Regimes as Intervening Variables. In *International Regimes*, edited by Stephen D. Krasner, 195–232. Ithaca: Cornell University Press.

Krause, Monika. 2017. How Fields Vary. *British Journal of Sociology* 69(1): 3–22.

Latour, Bruno. 2005. *Reassembling the Social: An Introduction to Actor-Network-Theory*. Oxford: Oxford University Press.

Lebow, Richard Ned. 2008. *A Cultural Theory of International Relations*. Cambridge: Cambridge University Press.

Modelski, George. 1978. The Long Cycle of Global Politics and the Nation-State. *Comparative Studies in Society and History* 20(2): 214–35.

Neumann, Iver B. 2007. "A Speech That the Entire Ministry May Stand For," Or: Why Diplomats Never Produce Anything New. *International Political Sociology* 1(2): 183–200.

Nexon, Daniel H. 2009. *The Struggle for Power in Early Modern Europe: Religious Conflict, Dynastic Empires, and International Change*. Princeton: Princeton University Press.

Paul, T. V. 2017. Recasting Statecraft: International Relations and Strategies of Peaceful Change. *International Studies Quarterly* 61(1): 1–13.

Phillips, Andrew. 2010. *War, Religion and Empire: The Transformation of International Orders*. Cambridge: Cambridge University Press.

Pouliot, Vincent. 2016. *International Pecking Orders: The Politics and Practice of Multilateral Diplomacy*. Cambridge: Cambridge University Press.

Reus-Smit, Christian. 1999. *The Moral Purpose of the State: Culture, Social Identity, and Institutional Rationality in International Relations*. Princeton: Princeton University Press.

Root, Hilton L. 2017. Network Assemblage of Regime Stability and Resilience: Comparing Europe and China. *Journal of Institutional Economics* 13(3): 523–48.

Rouse, Joseph. 2007. Social Practices and Normativity. *Philosophy of the Social Sciences* 37(1): 46–56.

Ruggie, John Gerard. 1993. Territoriality and Beyond: Problematizing Modernity in International Relations. *International Organization* 47(1): 139–74.

Schmidt, Vivien A. 2016. The Roots of Neo-liberal Resilience: Explaining Continuity and Change in Background Ideas in Europe's Political Economy. *British Journal of Politics and International Relations* 18(2): 318–34.

Tickner, Ann J. 2001. *Gendering World Politics: Issues and Approaches in the Post-Cold War World*. New York: Columbia University Press.

Walker, Rob B. J. 1993. *Inside/Outside: International Relations as Political Theory*. Cambridge: Cambridge University Press.

Wallerstein, Immanuel. 1974. The Rise and Future Demise of the World Capitalist System: Concepts for Comparative Analysis. *Comparative Studies in Society and History* 16(4): 387–415.

Waltz, Kenneth. 1979. *Theory of International Relations*. Reading: Addison-Wesley.

Wendt, Alexander. 1999. *Social Theory of International Politics*. Cambridge: Cambridge University Press.

Wendt, Alexander. 2000. On the Via Media: A Response to the Critics. *Review of International Studies* 26(1): 165–80.

Wenger, Etienne. 1998. *Communities of Practice: Learning, Meaning, and Identity*. Cambridge: Cambridge University Press.

Wight, Martin. 1977. *Systems of States*. Leicester: Leicester University Press.

Young, Oran R. 1999. *The Effectiveness of International Environmental Regimes: Causal Connections and Behavioral Mechanisms*. Cambridge, MA: MIT Press.

2 Power in Communitarian Evolution

STEFANO GUZZINI

World Ordering[1] ties several modes of theorizing together. It is about an intersubjective, relational and processual ontology that gives rise to a social world in flux, indeed as flux, in what Adler calls "evolution." It anchors such evolution in a theory of action where the driving forces of change, communities of practice, are socially embedded in, perhaps constituted by, background dispositions. This, in turn, informs a theory of history in that social evolution is understood in terms of learning that works both as a normatively open analytical concept (learning is learning) and, eventually, also as a normative yardstick (not all learning is true or good learning). And it combines this cognitive evolution with a political theory that envisages anew the perennial quest for the understanding of (more or less communitarian) order, that is, the central because unreachable core of the study of politics.

Needless to say, such an enterprise cannot be a final word and should not be understood in terms of it. Its ambition is twofold. It is a plea for this particular vision of world ordering and also an invitation to follow this strategy of parallel theorizing. Just as much as it aims to make a point of how to think *order*, it makes a point on *how to think* order. The many threads and levels of theorizing are hence not meant to impress the reader with a long and varied bibliography; they require each other. Whether or not Adler envisaged to do them all from the start is a moot question; he certainly became convinced that he needed to do them for reaching the ambition of the book. The more the research advanced, the heavier it became. If he had lost the momentum, the weight could have become overpowering.

My intervention is an attempt to see how power travels with Adler on these multiple journeys. This does not mean that power is the most important concept in the book, but it is sufficiently central to use it as way to approach Adler's theorizing. For power has itself been used in

---

[1] Adler 2019.

all these different types of theorizing and can therefore serve as a privileged entrance point to see how the different types of theories meet. In the realm of ontology, power has often been likened to, and sometimes even used interchangeably with, agency and cause. To be considered agential, a capacity to "change" something in the social world (= power) is often considered a constitutive feature. And since it involves an effect, power has been likened to cause.[2] For this reason, both agency and power often appear in frameworks that work on change and its causes.

In a theory of action, this ontological closeness of power to agency and cause has turned power into a central explanatory variable, whenever the underlying political theory ties action to struggle or competition. This is obviously the case for political realism, where power is not only the means but also always the immediate aim of international actors, whatever other aims the actor may have.[3] In other social theories, power is, however, not the explanans but the explanandum. Rather than explaining action or behavior, power is likened to government or social–political order that needs to be itself explained. When power features prominently in such conceptions of order, theories of action turn into theories of domination. Power is linked to the logic of a political order as a structured configuration that is asymmetrical and/or hierarchical. This again mobilizes a certain set of political theories that not only systematically link all power to order but, more contentiously, also all order to power. Yet even if power systematically refers to order, order does not need to be defined through power.

Power has also been used prominently in some theories of history. It is fundamental for Social Darwinism, that is, the idea that human evolution is about the "survival of the fittest," connected to the struggle with and for power. Such theories reach IR usually via the backdoor of geopolitical writings that implicitly or explicitly rely on environmental (i.e., natural) determinacy. They are often part of the realist family of theories. Yet also other theories than realism have mobilized it,[4] and not all realists would subscribe to it.[5]

In the following, I will discuss Adler's use of deontic and performative power within his vision of social orders before turning to the usage

---

[2] Famously in Dahl 1968; for a critique and discussion, see Morriss 1987; Guzzini 2017.

[3] See, for example, the verbatim passages in Morgenthau 1945, 14; 1946, 195.

[4] See the discussion in Hobson 2012.   [5] See the discussion in Guzzini 2012c.

of "epistemic practical authority" as an explanatory factor. In the first context, I will argue that his conceptual decisions are driven by a certain understanding of politics. It is this vision of politics that informs many of the choices not only how to use and define power but also his general theory of cognitive evolution. In the end, it is a certain commitment to communitarianism[6] that provides coherence to his theoretical and conceptual choices. In the second context, Adler uses epistemic practical authority as a cause for explaining the evolution of social orders. In doing so, I claim, he overburdens what such a power concept can deliver when a process-oriented and contingent meta-theory would allow for explanations only at a lower level of abstraction.

Power: Deontic and Performative

Adler locates the analysis of power mainly in his theory of action, which is a theory of practices. He uses two concepts of power that are important for two different moments in the understanding of action, namely *deontic power*, which he takes from John Searle's[7] revised constructivist social theory and *performative power*, which Adler borrows from Jeffrey Alexander's cultural pragmatics.[8] Whereas Searle's concept provides him with the socially or intersubjectively dispositions, which can empower actors (here: communities of practice), Alexander's concept allows him to include an improvisational moment of performance into the analysis in which such dispositions may, but also may not, be realized and potentially changed. Audiences are the silent but consequential backdrop against which deontic power can arise and the visible sphere where performances can affect them, but also where the credibility of these performances is negotiated. As this section will argue, Adler's particular reconceptualization of these two concepts and his concomitant downgrading of understandings of power in terms of domination are not preordained by his underlying social theory; they are prompted by a certain political theory, based on communitarian agency.

Searle's status functions carry "'deontic powers'. That is, they carry rights, duties, obligations, requirements, permissions, authorizations,

---

[6] As he had earlier called it in Adler 2005.   [7] Searle 2010.
[8] Alexander 2011.

entitlements, and so on."[9] It fits the meta-theoretical setup in that it includes an idea of performativity. Searle thinks of it as constituting (sic) social ontologies; consequently, it connects well to the construct-ivist and process ontology of Adler's theory where all entities are continuously "in the making" and where their "being" is in the "becoming."

"Performative power means using the contingency of interpretations and performances, the figures and forms of script to impose their meaning onto" an audience.[10] It responds to the relational demands of the ontology in that it connects power to an audience, or, put differently, establishes the origins of authority in a certain type of symbolically shared action where power originates from the audience. Although often connected to the idea of "performativity" in the text, it is merely about the power of or through performance. It fits a stronger concept of performativity much less than deontic power, since it does not stand for an interactive ontological process.

Adler rearranges slightly those two concepts which, although com-binable, do not stem from the same tradition. When Adler uses "deontic power," he shifts the focus to the agency of the community of practice rather than to the conditions for the possibility of that very agency. Therefore, deontic power sometimes reads more like the effect of power relations than their very condition. He writes that:

From an agential perspective, power [SG: here not specified] enters practi-tioners' competence and performative capacity to transform their communi-ties of practice endogenously, as well as to affect the boundaries of their communities of practice, and endow material and social processes with collective meaning, particularly functions and status, thus creating entitle-ments (deontic power).[11]

The causal "power" at the start of the sentence will interest us in the second section. For the purpose of the argument here, suffice it to know that deontic power is the effect of practices or the agency of the community of practices (contextualized through background know-ledge), since it "rests on the collective creation and recognition of, and confidence in, these institutions' statuses and functions over time."[12]

This is different from Searle. For Searle, deontic powers (sic, in plural) come in a chain of social ontologies, but not at the start. For him,

---

[9] Searle 2010, 8–9.   [10] Adler 2019, 112.   [11] Ibid., 176.   [12] Ibid., 67.

collective intentionality creates institutional facts like status functions which carry[13] deontic powers which, in turn, provide desire-independent reasons for action.[14] Status functions can "carry" negative deontic powers (e.g., obligations) or positive ones (e.g., rights). Obviously, such deontic powers "exist only to the extent that they are recognized and accepted as existing."[15] But it is those status functions that endow agents with their deontic powers: agents are, to use another language, dis/empowered by them.

These can be seen as two sides of the same coin. Searle's concept of deontic powers concentrates on the processes that dis/empower actors, whereas Adler focuses on the recognition within social environments, the communities of practices, which are necessary for their creation and ongoing existence. Yet it is consequential, if one concentrates only on one of the two sides in that it downgrades the way that "background power" (Searle) conditions our dispositions.

Indeed, Searle uses his theory as a way to connect the discussion of power to the analysis of political order and individual freedom, to political theory. Deontic powers are both the cement of society, and part of his approach to understand the idea of free will. When this is translated into a social theory, Searle refers to (and borrows the idea from) Bourdieu. But Adler does explicitly not want to follow him there (to this, later).

Adler's second component of power is Jeffrey Alexander's performative power. It is also embedded in a political theory that cannot be really divided from its use in a social theory. Alexander opposes a vertical, materialist and coercive vision of the (democratic) order.[16] Instead, he develops a historical discussion in which classical *Gemeinschaft* and the taken-for-granted rituals that performatively constitute communities have to be replaced by performances that unite the different spheres of society. Hence, such power, and the order it constitutes, is not automatic or guaranteed; it is in a constant re-fashion and process, dependent on the way audiences accept the symbolic proposals of their elite. In other words, his theory of domination is not primarily inspired by a social theory of process, but by a political theory of possible democratic government. Alexander's main aim is to show that such vertical order is shot through with the ordering

---

[13] Or: create, see Searle 2010, 24.   [14] Searle 2010, 23.   [15] Ibid., 88.
[16] Alexander 2011, chapter 2.

role of rituals or performances. As a result, his opposition to a materialist and coercive version of rule does not exclude, indeed relies upon, an understanding of informal rule that make successful performances possible. Coercion and domination have been disentangled. There are noncoercive versions of domination. Again, also the second concept of power seems almost to invite for an analysis, which looks at processes of domination that are not necessarily agential, but of informal rule, of dis/empowering and where the social conditioning of dispositions is significant. But Adler chooses not to go this way. For him, power will not be particularly connected to domination but to agency and change.

A comparison with the social theory of Pierre Bourdieu – sometimes inspiration, sometimes whipping boy in Adler's book – may help to clarify this take. The two approaches are very similar. In Bourdieu, fields, habitus and practices are co-constituted in a relational manner. Adler is using a very similar setup with background knowledge as Searle's usage of Bourdieu's habitus.[17] Such knowledge informs practices in both approaches. But then there is one difference. As Adler says, he substitutes Bourdieu's concept of habitus with the concept of practice.[18] This sounds odd since habitus clearly corresponds to background knowledge, and practice appears as a concept in both approaches. But the sentence may become clearer once we look at the conceptualization of agency in both approaches. In Bourdieu, fields have to be seen individually, and in their combination, to figure out the existence of social groups, in his case: classes. Critical of a certain Marxist take to reduce the genesis of collective actors to purely materialistically established classes, his analysis of multiple fields is exactly meant to show the fluidity of the boundaries of social groups and their multiple constitutive components (and capitals), as well as the diversity of practices and hence political action which can ensue. In the end, although there is lots of agency within the field, Bourdieu's interest in agents is usually tied to the way their positioning co-constitutes an order.

Adler includes the concept of field in his "communities of practice," which are "simultaneously, (a) social and spatial structural sites where the emergence and selective retention of practice takes place and (b) collective agents whose actions matter for social order's meta-stability

---

[17] Searle 1995, 132.   [18] Adler 2019, 18.

or, alternatively, its evolution."[19] This is curious, since it mixes a site and agency. Also, it does not reflect on the *"sens pratique,"* which provides the logic (and interpretive background) for the field, reduced to a topography of collective action (but then, "social orders" are also fields for Adler[20]). In doing so, Adler really wishes to foreground agency. The driving forces here are communities of practice, who, like classes, are the bearer of historical evolution.

In this context, Adler considers power as domination a hindrance to his approach. He tries to stay clear from what he would see as too vertical and too materialist conceptualizations of power, for which he criticizes Bourdieu's field theory.[21] Indeed, at times, it reads as if for Adler, theories of domination are necessarily linked to vertical analyses of power and to structuralism and materialism. But they are not. Foucault-inspired analysis or different versions of intersectional analysis, none of which treated in the book, are all about more horizontal understandings of how domination works. But for Adler, domination is too much about positions, about hierarchies, and most centrally, about stasis, while the book tries to understand change. For him, Bourdieu's "interest in explaining power stratification [?] and social domination led him to highlight how things are more than how they become."[22] But it simply is not true that a theory of domination, be it Bourdieu's or others, can in principle not account for change or cannot rely on a process ontology in which the constitution of units is endogenized in the analysis. In fact, despite the usual reduction of such

---

[19] Ibid., 123.   [20] Ibid., 21.

[21] This is probably not the place to discuss the reception of Bourdieu more generally. Suffice it to say that the US context has tended to read anything which is not as individualist as its more common theories of action in a structuralist vein, as done to Bourdieu, and as Rogers Brubaker (1985) bemoaned from early on and set out to rectify. In IR, in particular, the discussion on Bourdieu's general approach shows his attempt to deny either structuralism and individualism (through the habitus) or materialism and idealism (Guzzini 2000; Leander 2008, 2010). Bourdieu's concept of capital, which encompasses many nonmaterial ones, and of misrecognition, which sees domination in a relational manner (Guzzini 2013b), as well as his take on change and reflexivity (Leander 2002) have been used within a constructivist IR setting perfectly compatible with Adler's approach, and arguably necessary to it. Indeed, the very metaphor of "stage," so important for Alexander's "power in performance," has been thoroughly applied in a congenial and consistent reading of Bourdieu's theory of action (Leander 2011). For a related take on Bourdieu's analysis of power, see Bigo 2011.

[22] Adler 2019, 57

theories to mere reproduction, the whole idea of field theory includes also change, from within the field and through transfers across fields.[23] It is a theory of change without telos and without efficient causation – but so is Adler's. It also includes performativity in the stronger sense, in which our ideas of the world interact with it and where the origins of the social positions, what Bourdieu calls the "social magic."[24] Indeed, the repeated historicization of structures, institutions and agent's dispositions, as well as the disclosure of the ritualized mobilizations of bias ... all refer to "becoming." It is, however, the becoming that goes into being, not the being that is part of a project of becoming. Put differently, when Adler stresses the difference to Bourdieu, it is less about processes of constitution, the becoming that made the present, as it were, but about the becoming of the political future.

Hence, perhaps the issue is not about power in a social theory setting at all. Adler's repeated distancing from Bourdieu, despite the obvious similarities, may have to do with his underlying political theory, more particularly with the very definition of politics, which has Arendtian undertones when Adler sees social order constituted by what actors "do together, the quality of human interactions, and their social and normative achievements."[25] As mentioned earlier, power has a central place in Western understandings of politics. Adler writes:

Social orders are profoundly associated with politics. Politics is a constellation of practices through which agents govern societies; manage and resolve conflict, organize, guide and control interconnectedness and dissociation processes; and strive either to keep social orders metastable or to bring about their evolution.[26]

This is again a fairly agential understanding of politics that is not self-evident from the process ontology espoused in the book. For if all is in the becoming, then so are agents, as Adler writes elsewhere, yet without carrying this insight to its conclusion.[27] Making them the solid starting point of a vision of politics as a more or less intentional steering capacity through a constellation of practices is surely possible but his agential focus is a choice, not a necessity, for a processual and relational ontology.

---

[23] Bourdieu 1980, chapter 3.   [24] For example, Bourdieu 2001, 286ff.
[25] Adler 2019, 125. See also the explicit reference to Arendt's view on power on p. 174.
[26] Ibid., 21.   [27] Ibid., 61, 73.

All this goes simply to underline why the book insists so heavily on these communities of practice. They are not just a set of agents with shared background knowledge. Whenever such communities of practice form, that very formation affects politics. In the overall theory, they are the central proxy for understanding the dynamics of history, since they are the agents of change. They are also a proxy for the state of politics and the polity, since their composition and background knowledge indicate the state and stage of evolution itself ("social order"), whether characterized by interconnectedness or disassociation, that is a world with communities that link up to each other or not. Adler's communitarian assumption shows when he automatically connects such interconnectedness with more informal forms of rule and "epistemic practical authority" (see later) and disassociation with vertical hierarchies that dominate politics.[28] Communities of practice are best when they "horizontalize" politics, when they hold world society together.[29]

When all this is said and done, the analysis of these power travails ends with the diagnosis that the co-constitutive relation between communities of practice and social order narrows the role of power in the analysis of order; more precisely, it sidelines the role of domination in the establishment of such communities of practice and in their effects. If power is also outside communities of practice and vertically there,[30] how does this outside relate to the inside? How can we neglect that it is the very positioning that is responsible for the ways such communities develop as sites and actors? The theory of action may be consistent with a theory of social order,[31] but for a book that is about world ordering, these power processes that are outside the site and agency of communities of practice remain unreflected. When Adler says that "social orders are therefore what communities of practice have learned to become,"[32] and when the latter are defined as both a site and horizontal collective agency, then the idea of order is substantially narrowed to its agential part, even if that is clearly socially embedded.

Sure, no concept of social order is truly comprehensive and hence the issue here is not that some conceptual choice has been done. Such choice is necessary. My aim was simply to use the analysis of power in its conceptual connection to "politics" and to theories of domination and order to shed light on Adler's theory of *world ordering*. And here

---

[28] Ibid., 22.   [29] Ibid., 191.   [30] Ibid., 114.   [31] Ibid., 117.   [32] Ibid., 123.

the finding is a certain mismatch. Neither the inspirations for his usage
of the concept of power, nor Adler's ontology and social theory require
the specific cut he proposes. It seems to be his theory of politics, in his
agential take on governance, the role of collective and prospective
agency (communities of practice) and the normative role of such communities, which lead him to this circumscribed vision of order. Put
differently, whereas his social theory would rather prompt him to also
think of horizontal relations of domination within and across fields, his
take on evolutionary social change and his communitarian political
theory led him to think power in the constitution of polities and the
propensity for historical change. His theory of order provides only
a part of the understanding of order that his own ontology and social
theory would allow. By emphasizing agency, the book can hence not
sufficiently reflect on the wide variety of more structural processes of
domination (capitalism?) that go into constituting world order.

Power in the Explanation of Evolution

Power plays not only a role in the very understanding of practices and
social order; it is also used as an explanatory factor in the analysis. In
this context, it has often been used as a form of cause. And just as the
first section used power as a way to unpack his conceptualization of
order in cognitive evolution, the present section will use power to probe
into the explanatory setup used in Adler's theory of cognitive evolution. For Adler not only posits ontological links between his central
concepts; he also wishes to use them for explanatory purposes.

Applying power to explanatory contexts can be a lure, as Peter
Morriss argued a long time ago. When conceived of in causal terms,
power often ends up being used in circular manner, since it is inferred
from the effects it then no longer can be used to explain. When framed
in less demanding dispositional, not causal, terms, as Adler seems to do,
power stands for an ability or capacity. But in either case, power
statements "*summarize* explanations; they do not *explain* them."[33]
Originally targeting behavioralist power analysis, Morriss' dictum is
also applicable to other power analyses, however. Whereas in the
previous section the ontological and political primacy given to communities of practice and the role of agency in evolution may have pushed

---

[33] Morriss 1987, 44. Original emphasis.

him to downgrade aspects of domination in the analysis of power, his ambition to combine a framework of analysis with an explanatory theory may have misconceived and overburdened power (here: epistemic practical authority) as a causal variable.

One of the book's ambitions is explicitly explanatory. In a critique of Bhaskar and Archer's approach, Adler mentions their inability to "explain how and why certain practices survive rather than others, and why social orders evolve." Instead, his theory of

social mechanisms and processes explain both the differential, albeit variable, replication of the practices of the communities of practice and of their background knowledge, their selective retention in space and time, as well as social order evolution.[34]

In a similar vein, "assemblage theory" is very quickly dismissed for, among other things, missing an answer to "why do assemblages acquire one form rather than another?," and, more generally, being "hard to generalize, which makes it unsuitable for the social sciences, including post-positivist social science ... "[35]

In this explanatory endeavor, power plays a central role. It comes in the form of "epistemic practical authority," which is nothing less than the "master mechanism for understanding cognitive evolution, and particularly selective retention processes."[36] Epistemic practical authority is a composite concept made out of deontic and performative power. It is defined as "the legitimate power to rule on the adoption of practices and their meanings."[37] More precisely, it is "the capacity for practical meaning fixation or the structural and agential authoritative ascription of practical meaning to material and social reality to 'stick', or to be authoritatively selected and retained."[38] It is "not located only in people's bodies and minds ... [i]nstead, epistemic practical authority is intersubjectively located in communities of practice."[39] As such it is closely connected to deontic power, providing a potential whose realization is contingent on being competently performed.[40] This competent performance is, as seen earlier, dependent on the audience to which it is directed, and which is the origin of the legitimate claim to define

---

[34] All quotes from Adler 2019, 217. [35] All quotes ibid., 125. [36] Ibid., 3.
[37] Ibid., 4. [38] Ibid., 236; see also p. 27. [39] Ibid.
[40] This is quite close to Bourdieu's understanding of the field of politics organized around the monopoly of legitimate symbolic violence and its role in defining the "vision and division of the world." See, for example, Bourdieu 2001, 239.

practical meanings. "The continuous selective retention of practices and their background knowledge depends on whether a sufficiently large number of members of a community of practice continue to recognize and accept the shared meanings on which such practices rely."[41] "From this perspective, social order is not a goal pursued but an effect that occurs and field of practices that continually becomes."[42] In a nutshell: "epistemic practical authority is the combined result of both types of social power and itself is a cause of practices' selection and social orders' evolution."[43]

How does epistemic practical authority exactly explain selection and evolution? The two are closely connected. It is the variance in the creation, and then selection and retention of communities of practices and their background knowledge that defines the (cognitive) evolution of social orders. Social orders are understood as "fields, configurations, or 'landscapes' of practices and communities of practice, whose *epistemic practical authority* assigns functions and status thus organizing, stabilizing, and managing social life."[44] Put differently, communities of practice and social order are co-constitutive and since epistemic practical authority is what keeps communities of practice together, any change in that authority affects communities and hence the order. Anything that explains the change of this authority explains, by implication, the evolution of social orders. Since epistemic practical authority is but the combination/sequence of deontic and performative power, any change in those social powers is ultimately a cause for social evolution, as for example, when Adler writes that "if deontic power diminishes . . ., practices lose their epistemic practical authority and social order evolves: the configuration of practices that constitute it are replaced."[45] The change of epistemic practical authority can also be the effect of changing bearers of those powers, "[b]ecause new polities and organizations often mean new bases of epistemic practical authority."[46]

Hence, the causal path goes further back from epistemic practical authority to its constituents: what changes deontic and performative power? Well, many things can. Basically, any process that undermines the recognition and legitimacy of communities of practice, whether in their background knowledge or the competent enactment of practices,

---

[41] Searle 1995, 117.   [42] Adler 2019, 237.   [43] Ibid., 27.
[44] Ibid., 21, 122. Original emphasis, references omitted.   [45] Ibid., 237.
[46] Ibid., 190.

undermines *ipso facto* this power and hence affect epistemic practical authority, since one is defined or constituted by the other. Consequently, the evolution of epistemic practical authority in social orders is ultimately indeterminate and contingent.

> Whether social order's resilience or demise take place is indeterminate. The propensity for one or the other outcome will depend on context and on how particular situations processually unfold .... the outcome will also largely depend on the differential purchase of epistemic practical authority. The pattern, in turn, will depend on resourcefulness and innovation in creative variation processes, as well as on learning, contestation and negotiation processes within, and deontic and performative power of, communities of practice in selective-retention processes, particularly when approaching intersubjective threshold.[47]

It is in this context that Adler's remark makes sense that "power refers not to a determinant 'variable' but to processes and relations characterized by propensity and contingency."[48]

But how can we combine this idea of power in terms of a contingent and indeterminate process with the claims earlier mentioned in which epistemic practical authority is the master mechanism that causes, nothing less, practices' selection, retention and social orders' evolution? Something will have to give; and it is "cause." From his repeated distance to other post-positivist theories, as mentioned earlier, it is clear that Adler wishes to retain a stronger concept of cause to allow for generalizations. If so, then it makes little sense to use open-ended relational and process ontologies. If however he uses the latter, then cause is redefined in a way that makes his approach no different from the ones he criticizes.

I think the latter is the more consistent approach, since Adler cannot really cut out the theory's process ontology without losing its very foundation. For the first to work, the analysis of the causal paths needs factors independent of each other. Yet, besides the contingency of the processes, the relationship between the main concepts is constitutive, not causal. This applies for practices, background knowledge and epistemic practical authority that constitute communities of practice, and then epistemic practical authority constituted by deontic power and performative power, which in turn are constituted by/ enabled (empowered) by the members of communities of practice.

[47] Ibid., 189.   [48] Ibid., 23.

Hence, whereas Adler claims that the stretching out of the causal links in a process allows him to avoid circularity,[49] this is already achieved by the constitutive nature of his conceptual framework.

Shedding the generalizable and causal language does not mean that one sheds explanation and transferable knowledge, as Adler seems to imply in his criticism of post-positivist theories. To the contrary, the latter offer ways forward in this regard. As a first step, the relationship between grand theory and actual explanation needs to be rethought. Whereas Adler tries to combine the two, it makes more sense to distinguish between the abstract framework of analysis and a more empirical level at which explanations are handled. Rather than having general processual social mechanisms, as Adler proposes, the analysis would handle explanation at a significantly lower level of abstraction. Here, it can establish contingent causal paths, as done in process-tracing, and particular mechanisms within it. So has Ish-Shalom developed an approach to discourse-tracing, yet embedded in a Gramscian environment that endogenizes material factors.[50] He identifies hermeneutical mechanisms that he retraces in a process that translates theoretical constructs into public conventions (understood as background knowledge) and finally political convictions.[51] Whether called interpretivist process-tracing[52] or practice-tracing,[53] the idea is the same, namely, to establish a causal path within an open process ontology on the basis of a previously abstracted framework of analysis. This path includes social mechanisms, established by observers, which are transferable to, yet significantly affected by, other contexts.[54]

In this reconstruction, Adler's theory is unpacked so that the relationship between empirics and theory is not thought in terms of generalizations which are then put to a test. Indeed, when the book ends with the invitation to develop "case studies [that] will help test the arguments and the concepts I raised here, for example, deontic power, epistemic practical authority, common humanity, epistemological security, practical democracy, and many more,"[55] it misconstrues the theoretical movement as one of empirical generalization and general testing, when it is based on *abstraction and translation*.[56] Theorizing-as-abstraction happens when observers impose concepts that organize

---

[49] Ibid., 189.   [50] Ish-Shalom 2006.
[51] See also the congenial analysis of causal mechanisms in Jackson 2006, chapter 2.
[52] Guzzini 2012a.   [53] Pouliot 2015.   [54] Guzzini 2011, 2012b; Pouliot 2015.
[55] Adler 2019, 301.   [56] Guzzini 2013a.

our way of distinguishing the significant from the insignificant in our analysis, as in Weber's ideal types.[57] Theorizing-as-translation happens when mechanisms or other patterns are moved, and thereby adapted, from one context to another.[58] Both make knowledge transferable, indeed, in a hermeneutic circle, they make knowledge possible in the first place.

Consequently, epistemic practical authority cannot be a master mechanism for explaining evolution, if this is to retain any classical causal meaning. It is pitched at the wrong (because too high) level of theoretical abstraction for explanation when couched in an open process ontology. When Adler puts one central power claim as

[t]he more a claim in the name of a valuable practice, which is grounded on collective intentionality, is endowed with deontic and performative power, thus with epistemic practical authority, the more the propensity for the horizontal spread of practices and background knowledge to take place,[59]

it looks like a causal, if probabilistic claim; yet it cannot deliver on these terms. Since deontic and performative power is constituted by its acceptance within communities of practice, and since the processes of this acceptance are contingent and open, as Adler shows at other places (cited earlier), all the sentence can say, avoiding tautology, is that it makes sense to abstractly understand the role of power in social evolution in this way. Power does not explain here, it stands in for explanations which, contingent and contextual, will have to be found on another level and in another manner.

Conclusion

World Ordering is a synthesis and development of Adler's thought that aims to make constructivist macro-level analyses of order more dynamic. The book clearly avoids any functionalist or teleological trap often connected to evolutionary theories by placing the theory on a processual and relational ontology. It centrally conceptualizes change but in an open manner. This does not exclude, indeed logically includes, a normative analysis of the most valued type of cognitive

---

[57] For a recent assessment of Weber's ideal types, see Jackson 2017.
[58] For an argument defending the combination of the two as "logical generality," see Jackson 2011, 153, 199.
[59] Adler 2019, 244. Original emphasis.

evolution or social learning constituting the preferred social order. But although the cognitive interest in such normative aim is clear, it does not provide a necessary endpoint of the analysis of evolution.

The present chapter used his analysis of power to unpack his political and explanatory theory. It claims that by making the theory more dynamic, Adler tends to accentuate the agentic components of power – and hence order – that is, the communities of practice, their deontic and performative power and their propensity to affect future change. This choice was informed more by his communitarian political theory than by his social theory. Moreover, tying his conceptual framework to an explanatory theory, the concept of epistemic practical authority, based on deontic and performative power, becomes crucial as cause for understanding the evolution of social orders – while assuming evolution to be constituted by contingent and contextual processes that remain indeterminate. In short, the chapter argues that when it comes to the analysis of power, Adler's political theory downgrades the role of domination in social order, whereas the explanatory ambition overburdens epistemic practical authority as cause.

Managing all these different levels and types of theorizing at the same time is a formidable challenge that Adler went explicitly out to face in a book that anticipates and engages counterarguments at every twist and turn. Whether or not there is true learning in the cognitive evolution of the social order, there is in any of his readers.

References

Adler, Emanuel. 2005. *Communitarian International Relations: The Epistemic Foundations of International Relations*. London: Routledge.
Adler, Emanuel. 2019. *World Ordering: A Social Theory of Cognitive Evolution*. Cambridge: Cambridge University Press.
Alexander, Jeffrey C. 2011. *Performance and Power*. Cambridge: Polity Press.
Bigo, Didier. 2011. Pierre Bourdieu and International Relations: Power of Practices, Practices of Power. *International Political Sociology* 5(3): 225–58.
Bourdieu, Pierre. 1980. *Le sens pratique*. Paris: Les Éditions de Minuit.
Bourdieu, Pierre. 2001. *Language et Pouvoir symbolique*. Paris: Seuil.
Brubaker, Rogers. 1985. Rethinking Classical Theory: The Sociological Vision of Pierre Bourdieu. *Theory and Society* 14(6): 745–75.
Dahl, Robert A. 1968. Power. In *International Encyclopedia of the Social Sciences*, vol. 12, edited by David L. Sills, 405–15. New York: Free Press.

Guzzini, Stefano. 2000. A Reconstruction of Constructivism in International Relations. *European Journal of International Relations* 6(2): 147–82.

Guzzini, Stefano. 2011. Securitization as a Causal Mechanism. *Security Dialogue* 42(4–5): 329–41.

Guzzini, Stefano. 2012a. The Framework of Analysis: Geopolitics Meets Foreign Policy Identity Crises. In *The Return of Geopolitics in Europe? Social Mechanisms and Foreign Policy Identity Crises*, edited by Stefano Guzzini, 45–74. Cambridge: Cambridge University Press.

Guzzini, Stefano. 2012b. Social Mechanisms as Micro-Dynamics in Constructivist Analysis. In *The Return of Geopolitics in Europe? Social Mechanisms and Foreign Policy Identity Crises*, edited by Stefano Guzzini, 251–77. Cambridge: Cambridge University Press.

Guzzini, Stefano. 2012c. Which Geopolitics?. In *The Return of Geopolitics in Europe? Social Mechanisms and Foreign Policy Identity Crises*, edited by Stefano Guzzini, 18–44. Cambridge: Cambridge University Press.

Guzzini, Stefano. 2013a. The Ends of International Relations Theory: Stages of Reflexivity and Modes of Theorizing. *European Journal of International Relations* 19(3): 521–41.

Guzzini, Stefano. 2013b. Power: Bourdieu's Field Analysis of Relational Capital, Misrecognition and Domination. In *Bourdieu in International Relations: Rethinking Key Concepts*, edited by Rebecca Adler-Nissen, 79–91. Abingdon: Routledge.

Guzzini, Stefano. 2017. Power and Cause. *Journal of International Relations and Development* 20(4): 737–59.

Hobson, John M. 2012. *The Eurocentric Conception of World Politics*. Cambridge: Cambridge University Press.

Ish-Shalom, Piki. 2006. Theory as a Hermeneutical Mechanism: The Democratic Peace and the Politics of Democratization. *European Journal of International Relations* 12(4): 565–98.

Jackson, Patrick Thaddeus. 2006. *Civilizing the Enemy: German Reconstruction and the Invention of the West*. Ann Arbor: University of Michigan Press.

Jackson, Patrick Thaddeus. 2011. *The Conduct of Inquiry in International Relations: Philosophy of Science and Its Implications for the Study of World Politics*. Abingdon: Routledge.

Jackson, Patrick Thaddeus. 2017. The Production of Facts: Ideal-Typification and the Preservation of Politics. In *Max Weber and International Relations*, edited by Richard Ned Lebow, 79–96. Cambridge: Cambridge University Press.

Leander, Anna. 2002. Do We Really Need Reflexivity in IPE? Bourdieu's Two Reasons for Answering Affirmatively. *Review of International Political Economy* 9(4): 601–09.

Leander, Anna. 2008. Thinking Tools: Analyzing Symbolic Power and Violence. In *Qualitative Methods in International Relations: A Pluralist Guide*, edited by Audie Klotz and Deepa Prakash, 11–27. London: Palgrave Macmillan.

Leander, Anna. 2010. Habitus and Field. In *Blackwell: International Studies Compendium Project/Oxford Research Encyclopedia of International Studies*, edited by Robert A. Denemark, 3255–70. Oxford: Wiley-Blackwell.

Leander, Anna. 2011. The Promises, Problems, and Potentials of a Bourdieu-Inspired Staging of International Relations. *International Political Sociology* 5(3): 294–313.

Morgenthau, Hans J. 1945. The Evil of Politics and the Ethics of Evil. *Ethics* 56(1): 1–18.

Morgenthau, Hans J. 1946. *Scientific Man vs. Power Politics*. Chicago: University of Chicago Press.

Morriss, Peter. 1987. *Power: A Philosophical Analysis*. Manchester: Manchester University Press.

Pouliot, Vincent. 2015. Practice Tracing. In *Process Tracing: From Metaphor to Analytical Tool*, edited by Andrew Bennett and Jeffrey Checkel, 237–59. Cambridge: Cambridge University Press.

Searle, John R. 1995. *The Construction of Social Reality*. New York: Free Press.

Searle, John R. 2010. *Making the Social World: The Structure of Human Civilization*. Oxford: Oxford University Press.

3 | In Consideration of Evolving Matters

A New Materialist Addition to Emanuel Adler's Cognitive Evolution

ALENA DRIESCHOVA

Early on in his book *World Ordering: A Social Theory of Cognitive Evolution*, Emanuel Adler introduces the example of the Heiki people and Samurai crabs to illustrate the mechanisms of cognitive evolution: The Heiki people had an emperor who drowned in the ocean, and several centuries later, when the Heiki were fishing they discovered a certain type of crab, which they "imagined to resemble the drowned emperor."[1] Following this imagination, they threw the crab back into the sea; they developed a practice of throwing the crab back into the sea based on an established myth. The practice reinforced the myth and it had the material impact of promulgating the spread of Samurai crabs. In his account, Adler focuses on how the Heiki attached symbolic meaning to the crab, how ideas help to interpret material reality. He explains the survival of the crab as an unintended material effect of Heiki people's background knowledge (the drowned emperor), which prompted the emergence of a practice, namely, throwing the crab back into the sea. Admittedly, the crab's markings on the back permit the retention of the myth, because they permit the retention of the practice to throw the crab back into the sea. "Without the crab's markings on its back there would be no myth."[2] Yet, Adler does not consider the possibility that the characteristic features of the crab imposed a certain kind of meaning on the Heiki people and thus might have led the Heiki to invent their myth in the first place. After all the exoskeleton of the crab has indentations that make it resemble the face of a Samurai. If the crab did not look the way it does, myth nor practice might have emerged in the first place, or myth and practice could have looked very differently. Rather than being a symbol, the

[1] Adler 2019, 17. [2] Ibid., 18.

crab is an icon, it bears a certain resemblance,[3] and the crab's aesthetics are consequential for the emergence of a specific kind of practice.

The story of the Samurai crab and the Heiki people illustrates nicely how material features are intricately intertwined with the mechanics of cognitive evolution. We can easily introduce New Materialist features into cognitive evolution, and thus develop mechanisms for how material features enter into cognitive evolution as per the editors' call in the Introduction to this volume.[4] Simultaneously, this provides New Materialism with a cognitive evolutionary account of changes of social orders.

In his book, Adler attributes a supporting role to materiality in the processes of cognitive evolution, and acknowledges that technology can exogenously shape cognitive evolution,[5] but he does not develop any mechanisms for how material characteristics can be right at the heart of cognitive evolution, and contribute significantly toward driving changes of international orders. For Adler the main driving forces of social order change are of an ideational type. The present chapter thus adds to Adler's monograph.

A New Materialist account of materiality can provide an avenue for understanding long-term social order change. Of notable interest is the attention New Materialist scholarship gives to the ways in which technology and artifacts and practices co-emerge together. The concept of affordances allows us to understand that technology and artifacts provide opportunities for use, which only gain meaning when they are recognized as such within communities of practice. At the same time, technology and artifacts hold epistemic credit. Background knowledge not only leads to the production of technology and artifacts, but technology and artifacts also contribute to the production of background knowledge. With this richer theoretical understanding of materiality, the chapter will demonstrate that materiality shapes in a myriad of meaningful ways not just the consequences of practices, but also practices' initiation, emergence and selective retention.

For cognitive evolution two mechanisms are central: creative variation and selective retention. In the realm of creative variation, the material environment can produce an impetus for the emergence of creative thought. It also shapes which creative ideas can be represented

---

[3] Drieschova 2017.   [4] Pouliot, Kornprobst and Ish-Shalom, this volume.
[5] Adler 2019, 7.

and how they can be represented. In other words, technology and artifacts define the parameters of thought. A key mechanism of creative variation is "forbidden fruit blending," which entails combining two material elements together that do not typically belong together, to create something new. Innovations in technology and artifacts can inspire the emergence of new practices as well. In the realm of selective retention, the material environment influences the criteria of selective retention. Beyond such criteria as legitimacy and normative considerations, whether something works and the aesthetic appeal of practices and artifacts can be the key for their retention. Another element for selective retention is network memory, which goes beyond individual people's memory and plays an important role for learning and dissemination, particularly in large communities of practice. The characteristics of network memory determine what can be remembered and how it can be remembered.

The chapter first characterizes the specific account of materiality, which informs the mechanisms of long-term social order change developed here, and that hinges on New Materialism. I then analyze Adler's treatment of materiality in cognitive evolution and claim that he provides a merely supporting role for material factors in the mechanisms of cognitive evolution. I argue that we can nonetheless adapt cognitive evolution's mechanisms of creative variation and selective retention and add a New Materialist dimension to them. In the last section, the chapter illustrates how New Materialist mechanisms of cognitive evolution can be useful to understand long-term social order change on the example of the evolution of the Internet.

A New Materialist Conception of Materiality

International Relations (IRs) scholars have directed attention to material features to explain international orders for a very long time. Realist scholars focus on the distribution of capabilities (such as weapons and Gross Domestic Product) to explain international order in the form of a balance of power or hegemony,[6] and some predict the stability of the order on the basis of prevalent weapon technology.[7] Liberally inclined scholars study communication and transportation technologies, for example, to explain globalization and more peaceful forms of

---

[6] Waltz 1979; Wohlforth 1999.   [7] Jervis 1978; Craig 2019.

international ordering.[8] A wave of constructivist approaches critiqued these forms of "old materialism" for being too functionalist and therefore unable to account for qualitative change.[9] Instead they put the roles of ideas, identities and norms at the center of their studies. Their argument was that material factors need to be interpreted to obtain societal relevance and define social orders.

New Materialists argue that constructivists threw the baby out with the bathwater. They agree with the constructivist critique that material features do not follow a purely functional logic, and that it is therefore impossible to predict which effects technological change will have, for example. Simultaneously though they do attribute a certain role to matter. New Materialists differ on the extent of that role, with some going as far as seeing a life force in matter,[10] but most focus on the entanglements between people and matter. Neither does the material world determine how people will act, nor do people impose meanings on things, but rather societies and their material surroundings and toolboxes co-evolve together in profoundly interpenetrated ways. For New Materialists material objects influence social relations, but not in a deterministic way. Matter rather plays a role in interaction with humans, their practices and discourses. Scholars from different strands within New Materialism have developed conceptual tools and conducted empirical research that underlines the complexity of materiality and the ways in which it shapes social relations.

Actor-network theorists focus on the role of actants[11] to "highlight the quasi-agential properties of matter."[12] Material objects are actants to the extent that they are a part of networks or assemblages, in which actions are "the emergent product of myriad interacting forces and bodies that collide, respond, react, and counteract one another."[13] The "intra-active entanglements"[14] between technologies and practices play a key role in these assemblages.

The notion of affordances sheds light on how exactly practices and technology and artifacts are entangled.[15] Affordances are the opportunities for use specific to our body and perceptions, that artifacts and technology provide us with.[16] While artifacts and technology do have

---

[8] Deutsch 1953; Keohane and Nye 1977.   [9] Ruggie 1983; Kratochwil 1993.
[10] Alexander Wendt (2015) is not typically considered a New Materialist, but in his Quantum Mind and Social Science he argues that matter has consciousness.
[11] Latour 2005.   [12] Mitchell 2014, 12.   [13] Ibid.   [14] Aradau 2010, 498.
[15] Adler-Nissen and Drieschova 2019.   [16] Gibson 1979; Gibbs 2005.

a specific materiality that inscribes itself on users, it is necessary to analyze that materiality in conjunction with practices of usage.[17] Communities of practice can imprint their own usages on those devices. The "uses may not be those intended by their inventors or makers, but they must potentially exist, must be immanent, as affordances of those artefacts."[18] A typical example of these unanticipated effects of affordances is the popularity of email, as one of the key usages of the Internet. Initially, when Roberts designed it, he thought email was "not an important motivation for a network of scientific computers."[19] The initial goal of the network was to interconnect computing power – software and hardware – not people. The network did have the inherent affordance to become a communication network, though, and that was how people started using it.

Beyond directly shaping practices, technology, artifacts and other elements in the material environment can also shape our thoughts, cognition or background knowledge directly. Clark and Chalmers refer to "active externalism" to highlight the "active role of the environment in driving cognitive processes."[20] Because of active externalism we should attribute "epistemic credit" not just to humans, but also to objects.[21] For example, our writing process is tightly connected to moving chunks of text around on a computer screen. If we were to write with a typewriter our practices of writing would be quite different, and perhaps even the text that results from those practices. This perspective connects well with phenomenology, which Frankel Pratt proposes as a microfoundation for cognitive evolution, notably with the notion that habit (as a category of action that is very similar to practices) is "knowledge in the hands."[22] To some extent it also goes against the notion that "discourse is necessary for *all* practices to be meaningful [emphasis in the original],"[23] a perspective which gives preference to a representational logic stored in the mind, as opposed to acknowledging also the meaningfulness of unconscious, unarticulated and embodied dimensions of practices.

It is not necessarily the case that the background knowledge, which went into the production of material objects is the same background knowledge that people will perceive when they experience the finished

---

[17] Orlikowski et al. 1995.   [18] Graves-Brown 2000, 6.
[19] Roberts 1967, 1, in: Abbate 2000, 108.   [20] Clark and Chalmers 1998, 7.
[21] Ibid., 8.   [22] Merleau-Ponty 2002 [1945], 166 in Pratt, this volume.
[23] Sondarjee this issue, 130.

product. For example, Branch has shown how changes in the production of maps led unintentionally and for nonpolitical reasons to the conception of the territorial state.[24] It was the materiality of the finished product, which created the relevant background knowledge so to speak (the existence of territorial states), while the background knowledge that went into the production of the object (Cartesian mapping) was an entirely different one.

In sum, New Materialist scholarship highlights via the concept of affordances that material objects and technology co-emerge with practices, and via the concept of epistemic credit that background knowledge not only leads to the production of technology and artifacts, but that technology and artifacts can also produce an entirely new and different background knowledge. In this sense, a New Materialist understanding of matter provides an important addition to Adler's cognitive evolution.

At the same time, the chapter introduces cognitive evolution to New Materialist scholarship. New Materialists have exposed a certain disdain for grand theorizing. Instead they often focus on the temporal emergence, contingency and volatility of assemblages, which hold structures momentarily stable, but can be disrupted at any moment. Ad hoc disruptions, for example, of critical infrastructure, illustrate the independent force of matter particularly well.[25] Another feature of New Materialist scholarship links to one of Nexon's and Pouliot's concerns about Actor Network Theory (as a popular sub-branch of New Materialism), namely, that it tends to focus on micro-processes, which does not sit very easily with IR's focus on macro-processes and the analysis of order, stability and change.[26]

While random events, coincidental temporal emergences and the volatility of structures certainly deserve analytical and empirical attention, there is no inherent reason why some of the significant insights of New Materialism could not also contribute to analyzing longer-term and larger-scale processes of social order emergence and change. The micro-level processes that New Materialists focus on can very well have impacts on macro-level social aggregates, but scholars have to direct their attention to both of these levels simultaneously. A marriage of New Materialist insights with Adler's rendition of cognitive evolution

---

[24] Branch 2012.   [25] Aradau 2010; Lundborg and Vaughan-Williams 2011.
[26] Nexon and Pouliot 2013.

provides a promising avenue to theorize hitherto unexplored elements of changes in social orders.

Adler's Conception of Materiality in Cognitive Evolution

Adler's cognitive evolution focuses on the evolution of practices, their background knowledge and communities of practice. Communities of practice are the main vehicle through which practices spread and are instantiated. Although this theoretical focus allows materiality to be a part of the framework and a key driving force of changes of social order, the role of materiality remains underspecified in Adler's account. Matter is to be acted upon and shaped, rather than being a shaping force in its own right. In those passages in which Adler acknowledges that materiality could influence the development of social orders, he does not provide precise mechanisms of how that could take place.

Adler defines "cognitive evolution theory [as] a learning theory, whose socio-structural manifestation is the socio-cognitive selection of collective consciousness and meanings, which become institutionalized in human practices, and held subjectively as dispositions and expectations."[27] The quote makes it clear that the main focus is on the meanings that are integral to practices, while material resources serve to execute practices, which have been endowed with meaning ex ante. Yet, technology and artifacts are arguably just as important as background knowledge to sustain practices. One would, for example, be hard-pressed to explain how the practice of nuclear deterrence could continue without nuclear weapons, even if the relevant background knowledge remained in place.

Several passages in which Adler considers the role of materiality in international order sustenance and change are scattered throughout the volume. First, he acknowledges the typical realist and liberal notion of materiality as material resources that help execute tasks and accumulate power. To maintain their stability communities of practice require material resources, and in their competition with other communities of practice material resources can provide communities of practice with the necessary cutting edge to win the race. "However, without social purpose (Ruggie 1982, 1983) and social power, particularly deontic

---

[27] Adler 2019, 54.

power (Searle 2010), and performative power (Alexander 2011), material power is neutral and aimless."[28]

Second, Adler considers the classical constructivist notion that materiality exists, but humans endow that materiality with meaning. Artifacts become placeholders; they do not contain any meaning of their own. People rather impose meanings on them by using them in certain ways or by seeing and reflecting upon them in socially recognized modes. With this understanding of materiality we can lose its material features, the practical, nonrepresentational effects it can have, and the embodied and experiential effects it can provoke.

Third, Adler attributes an important role to material processes, rather than substances. Practices are the primary processes which gather his attention, and they are material (as well as ideational), because they are embodied "doings enacted in and on the world."[29] In other words, they are the material version of norms, materially enacted, and therefore observable social understandings with direct material impact. Adler does not deny the existence of material substances, but he proposes that they are better subsumed under processes, as "instantiations of processes."[30] He provides money as an example. While the example of money works well given that its physicality is minimal, it might be more difficult to subsume more substantial substances, say nuclear weapons, computers, and so on, under processes. These substances might enforce their physical presence much more vehemently than pieces of paper.

Finally, Adler considers materiality in the sense that practices are doings in and on the world, and as such they have real material consequences; they change the world we live in.

In sum, for Adler materiality plays only a marginal role in shaping social outcomes. He acknowledges that technology can externally influence social orders and cognitive evolution, but he does not theorize how that could take place.

An Ideational Bias in Cognitive Evolution's Mechanisms of Change

"Cognitive evolution refers to an evolutionary collective-learning process."[31] Creative variation and selective retention are cognitive

---

[28] Ibid., 194.   [29] Ibid., 148.   [30] Ibid., 59.   [31] Ibid., 34.

evolution's vocabulary to define change. In Adler's rendition creative variation and selective retention rely primarily on ideational factors, and this comes to the detriment of material components, which can play an equally important role in animating change.

For Adler creative variation emerges from "nascent forms of awareness,"[32] and the "irreversible unfolding of collective consciousness and knowledge."[33] Environmental changes can occasionally provoke experimentation, but they do not determine practices. "Because environmental events can have a measurable influence only as interpreted by practitioners, and as based on their dispositions and expectations, practitioners may respond to social and physical environmental challenges differently."[34] The key driving force of creative variation that shapes its directionality then lies in the ideational realm; in the emergence of new thoughts in people's minds, even if those new thoughts can lead to new practices and activities in the world, which will change people's material surroundings.

Selective retention are the processes of horizontal replication, when communities of practice dissipate into new geographical areas or new domains of applicability; and vertical retention, when new practitioners, the next generation, enter established communities of practice. The survival of some communities of practice and their practices, and the demise of others, is according to Adler "primarily a function of practices' and practitioners' capacity to endow material (also digital) and social objects and rules with practical meanings and deontic power which, because they have normative power that rests on communities' recognition, are seen as self-evident."[35] This is the constructivist claim that material objects are always interpreted, even as material resources can play a role in the selection of communities of practice. Social order then changes, because "communities of practice are 'dissipative structures'[36] that 'dissipate' to the environment meanings and practices considered to be destabilizing to the social order they sustain,"[37] which leads to the establishment of a new social order.

In sum, the main driving forces of cognitive evolution are ideational, while material factors play a supporting role. Yet, we do not have to adopt materialist determinism to attribute a larger role to material forces in cognitive evolution. In the following I develop mechanisms

---

[32] Ibid., 307.   [33] Ibid., 308.   [34] Ibid., 318.   [35] Ibid., 334.
[36] Prigogine 1980.   [37] Adler 2019, 337.

of creative variation and selective retention that hinge on a New
Materialist conception of materiality.

Evolving Matters

Based on the previous discussion of materiality, and its connections to
practices, communities of practice and cognition, this section provides
mechanisms through which materiality shapes processes of cognitive
evolution. Technology and artifacts influence the creative variation and
selective retention of practices. When new practices, technologies and
artifacts, and background knowledge emerge, they provoke the emergence of a new social order. Leaning on Adler's definition of international social orders I define an international social order as
a configuration of practices, background knowledge and practitioners,
which "organize, stabilize, and manage international social life"[38] in
a particular domain of activity.

Creative Variation

Beyond the mechanisms of creative variation Adler developed in cognitive evolution, the material environment can provide impeti for creativity. People's material surroundings can serve as the starting point
for their creative endeavors. Turner identified, for instance, a technique
that he terms "forbidden fruit blending" as one of the key engines of
human creativity.[39] It entails blending together things that exist in the
real world and which do not typically belong together in order to
obtain a new phenomenon. The building blocks for forbidden fruit
blending come from people's perceptions of the material features that
exist in the world. For example, techno music developed in Bell Labs
out of the use of digital technology and electron tubes.[40] Interestingly
the same Labs also developed the programming languages C, C++ and
the UNIX operating system.

  Beyond providing the building blocks for creativity, the material
environment, and technology and artifacts in particular, affect which
creative ideas can be represented, and how they can be represented,
thereby not just shaping the form of the idea, but also its very content
and essence. Artifacts and technology have epistemic credit. Changes in

---

[38] Ibid., 128.   [39] Turner 2006, 111.   [40] Parikka and Ernst 2012, 171–72.

available technologies and artifacts (admittedly themselves based on processes of creative variation and selective retention), or merely the introduction of specific technologies and artifacts into existing communities of practice thus influence the background knowledge that can emerge, and thereby the practices, which have a specific background knowledge at their foundation.

The invention of new artifacts and technologies (or the introduction of existing artifacts and technologies into new social contexts, i.e., new communities of practice) can lead to a change in practices more directly, because the affordances inherent in those technologies and artifacts change. Thus, Crawford Ames makes the case that smart phones have changed both practices of surveillance to detect refugees, as well as refugees' and their allies' practices to escape prosecution through encrypted mobile communication.[41] The introduction of nuclear weapons technology shaped the practices of nuclear deterrence that emerged, and which fundamentally influenced the Cold War order. Conversely, even after an artifact or a technology has been developed, practices of usage and maintenance practices can inspire changes in the design of technologies and artifacts.[42] Apple introduces regularly new devices on the market, not all of which are a success or retained, but the ones that are retained are gradually updated.

One of the most striking examples of how technology shapes the creative variation of practices and background knowledge is perhaps the case of coding. In the 1940s there was no such thing as software. The ENIAC, the first digital computer, had to be rewired for every single problem set. At the time "programming" was a woman's job. Men used to give their female subordinates instructions how to rewire the computer. Only with the emergence of switches was it possible to develop specific instructions, which formed the embryo of programming as we know it.[43] The switches became translated into a binary code of 0s and 1s, no charge and charge. All higher-level computer languages have to be translated into this basic code of 0s and 1s, which has led Kittler to argue (perhaps slightly on the extreme) that there is no software.[44] We should not dismiss the intellectual capital that went into the development of ever higher-level programming languages, so that millions of people know how to program today. Simultaneously,

---

[41] Crawford, this volume.   [42] Langins 2004, 406.
[43] Hui Kyong Chun 2004.   [44] Kittler 1995.

though, it is worth bearing in mind that hardware confines how programming operates. "Algorithms are step-by-step procedures for calculations that consist of instructions and follow a finite set of rules to carry out a computation."[45] The finite set of rules is not as much given by social conventions, but established by the hardware, the need to translate everything into a code of 0s and 1s, which symbolize charge and no charge. The practices of programming have evolved historically with the technology, and so has the background knowledge.

Selective Retention

A focus on materiality in processes of selective retention draws our attention to two main features: first, the criteria based on which practices, background knowledge, technologies and artifacts get selectively retained when we take materiality into account; and second, the material features and technologies that make the retention of some practices, and background knowledge possible in specific forms, while others might not possibly be retained.

   First, if we take materiality seriously we should also pay attention to the different principles and criteria based on which practices and technology and artifacts are selectively retained. Beyond such ideational elements as legitimacy or ethical considerations, sensitivity to materiality requires also attributing a certain role to "whether things work," that is, there is a need for a functional dimension. Technologies and artifacts are objects-for-use, which can be selectively retained if they serve particular purposes well, and if other objects appear that make those usages easier they might replace existing technologies and artifacts in the way in which the computer replaced the typewriter. A similar logic can then apply to practices as well, given that they are doings on the world. How well people can do things with certain practices can influence their selective retention.

   We should further consider an aesthetic dimension against which practices and artifacts can be selectively retained. Materiality also means appearance and perception, and appearance can be aesthetically pleasing or unpleasing. Practices and artifacts can have an inherent appeal, a certain "mystery" that resides in them, as Brunnée and Toope have remarked with regard to legal practices.[46] This aesthetic

---

[45] Bunz 2014, 6.   [46] Brunnée and Toope 2011, 352.

dimension can be most closely linked to Jeffrey Alexander's notion of performative power, which is one of the two forms of power Adler discusses in cognitive evolution. Performative power depends on whether or not audiences recognize it,[47] and aesthetic factors can play a role in this recognition. A growing literature directs attention to affects, emotions, aesthetics and phenomenology to highlight that the form an appearance takes can have political effects.[48] The role of the aesthetic dimension is quite obvious for communities of practice coalescing in the arts, such as dance, or music, but it might also play an important role in unanticipated realms such as the military. One can think, for example, of military parades: the North Korean military parade made headlines in the spring of 2017 in a signaling game between the United States and North Korea that left the world wondering whether a war between the two nuclear powers was imminent. The aesthetics of the parade was a key signaling device from the North Korean regime to the world to express the country's sophistication and development.

Beyond the criteria of selective retention, it also matters what can be selectively retained. For practices to be selectively retained, they have to be remembered. Whenever we are dealing with a large group of individuals, as is the case with communities of practice, the "network memory,"[49] or the communitarian memory, becomes a lot more important than each individual's memory. This network memory is significantly shaped by "technology [rather] than by the properties of biologically defined memory in the individual."[50] Whether practices are remembered by writing them down in books, or by filming them, makes a qualitative difference for which features will be retained and in which form they will be remembered; it possibly even influences what kinds of practices can be retained. Technology also matters for how that memory can be retrieved, and how accessible it is. Technology thus shapes both horizontal and vertical selective retention, but not necessarily both in the same way. For example, digitization has enhanced horizontal selectivity of digitized practices, because significantly more people have access to online material.[51] With social media people can even easily become the spreaders of (fake) news items. As Crawford Ames highlights, the new horizontal selectivity has, for example,

---

[47] See Guzzini, this volume.   [48] Bleiker 2012; Austin 2016; Drieschova 2017.
[49] Donald 2006, 7.   [50] Ibid.   [51] Bunz 2014.

impacted the dissemination of fake news items about refugees, and is shaping the contemporary refugee regime.[52] At the same time, digitization might actually decrease vertical selectivity given the fleeting and ever changing nature of cyberspace, which is based on "volatile electric charges as carriers of signals," that can be continuously reprogrammed.[53] Digital images and video can always be manipulated and adapted, which potentially complicates the transmission of practices to future generations. In fact, a computer file's shelf life is five years. We celebrate digital archiving not because it lasts, but because it significantly increases the accessibility of the stored material.[54]

Considering Evolving Matters in the Emergence of the Internet

This section illustrates through the example of the evolution of the Internet how a stronger focus on materiality in cognitive evolution provides an enhanced understanding of the emergence of international social orders. Not many scholars think of the Internet as an international social order. It is rather common to refer to internet governance, and analyze a set number of formal institutional bodies who seek to regulate the Internet.[55] Yet, thinking of the Internet as a specific social order permits scholars to notice that it is not simply governed by formal standard setting and regulatory organizations, but involves many decentralized activities by individual users.[56] Instead of centralizing decision-making authority into a small managerial body, the Internet permits any user with the necessary skills to create new features. Thus, users have the ability to design the network in a way that meets their needs. "Low formalization, heterogeneous organizational forms, large numbers of actors and massively distributed decision-making power"[57] characterize the cyber order. Its success arguably depends on these features. Understanding how these characteristics have come to define the cyber order and lead to its evolution might be just as important as the analysis of formal institutions, if not more so.[58] The empirical analysis focuses on how the Internet has evolved, and how this order is characterized by specific features that have emerged in

---

[52] Crawford, this volume.   [53] Parikka and Ernst 2012, 95.
[54] Hui Kyong Chun 2011, 138.
[55] See, for example, Bygrave and Bing 2009; DeNardis 2009; Carr 2015.
[56] Abbate 2000, 4.   [57] van Eeten and Mueller 2012, 731.   [58] Ibid.

the absence of formalized regimes, but that continue to define this large decentralized networked system.

The hacker community of practice has historically significantly shaped the internet order. Practices of open-source programming define the hacker community. By now that community is global in reach, and it is largely virtual, although occasional physical encounters at conferences, fairs and parties take place. Perhaps because the members of this community know each other largely by their internet names, and from behind their computer screens, a high degree of informality characterizes the community.[59] "The hacker culture is, in its essence, a culture of convergence between humans and their machines in a process of unfettered interaction. It is a culture of technological creativity based on freedom, cooperation, reciprocity, and informality."[60]

This background knowledge shapes the practices of the community, but so do the material features of the Internet and its evolution. In the following, I will focus on digitization, packet switching technology, protocols to interconnect networks, the LINUX operating system and the World Wide Web to highlight the interconnections between materiality and practices, and how these have affected the internet's evolution (Table 3.1). Many of these technologies found their inspiration in

Table 3.1 *The materialist effects in the evolution of the internet*

Internet's technological features	Creative variation	Selective retention
Digitization	Epistemic credit and affordances	Functional, network memory
Packet switching	Forbidden fruit blending and affordances	Functional, network memory
Internet protocols	Affordances and epistemic credit	Functional, network memory
LINUX	Affordances and epistemic credit	Functional, network memory
World Wide Web	Forbidden fruit blending and affordances	Aesthetic and functional, network memory

[59] Russell 2014.   [60] Castells 2002, 50.

forbidden fruit blending, and they were typically retained for their functional and/or aesthetic superiority. These technologies made practices of open-source coding possible, while those practices also shaped the technologies. The technologies and practices are inherently intertwined:

> The material substrate of code, which must always exist as an amalgam of electrical signals and logical operations in silicon, however large or small, demonstrates that code exists first and foremost as commands issued to a machine. Code essentially has no other reason for being than instructing some machine in how to act. One cannot say the same for the natural languages.[61]

The Internet's material features cardinally shaped its social order.

The digital revolution is one of the main industrial revolutions. It centers on the ways in which data are stored and retrieved. Digital data are stored in a digital format, which means that they need to be stored in a binary code, as per convention composed of 0s and 1s, which represent the equivalent of charge and no charge. Their material equivalents are circuit switches. The opposite of digital data storage is analog data storage, which stores data as waves. The overwhelming majority of contemporary practices of coding, programming and computing were developed for digital data storage, and would look entirely differently if data were stored in an analog format. Digital data thus hold epistemic credit by structuring the thought processes that go into coding (just as any kind of language structures thought processes). They simultaneously hold affordances, because it is on the basis of these data that practices of coding and computation proceed in an interaction between humans and machines.

The primary technological invention that made the Internet possible was packet switching technology, which made it significantly faster and cheaper to transport data.[62] Packet switching technology divides data up into smaller chunks and allows them to travel through whatever channels are available in a cable network to reach their destination, whereas circuit switching reserves a time in one particular channel to transmit all the relevant data at once. Packet switching technology fundamentally depends on digital data storage, as it would be

[61] Galloway in Hui Kyong Chun 2011, 22.
[62] Kleinrock 2010; Cohen-Almagor 2011; Campbell-Kelly and Garcia-Schwartz 2013.

impossible to divide analog data based on waves into smaller chunks to transport them to their destination.

The key mathematical background for packet switching technology is queuing theory, which Kleinrock conceptualized, one of the early contributors to the development and operationalization of the Advanced Research Projects Agency Net (ARPANET).[63] Kleinrock applied forbidden fruit blending when establishing the basis of packet switching. In his own words, the concept of resource sharing that is at the origin of packet switching technology "was emerging at that time in a totally different context: that of timesharing of computer power."[64] Given that computers were very rare (as are some super computers today), to avoid wastage several people were sharing a single computer, and it was more efficient to develop adequate mechanisms to allocate time on a computer. "The principles and advantages of timesharing were key to [Kleinrock's] realization that resource sharing of communication links in networks could provide for efficient data communications, much like the resource sharing of processors in timeshared systems was accomplishing."[65] And so data are packaged into smaller chunks, which wait in a queue and get transported through whatever channel happens to be free to reach their final destination, at whose port the different data chunks get reassembled before they reach their end user.

Paul Baran at Rand Corporation in the United States and Donald Davies at National Physical Laboratory in England then developed the actual packet switching technology independently from each other. Both had entirely different perspectives about the purpose of packet switching, but they still invented the same technology. While for Baran packet switching technology allowed for a more robust network that permitted to maintain communications even under severe stress, such as from a nuclear attack, for Davies it was primarily a more efficient and cheaper communication technology.[66] The differences highlight how the same technology can have entirely distinct affordances, which permit for different purposes and usages.

The ARPANET was the first large-scale network that used packet switching. Lawrence Roberts was the lead computer scientist to build the ARPA network, but initially he did not know how to do it. He

---

[63] Abbate 2000, 64.   [64] Kleinrock 2010, 27.   [65] Ibid.
[66] Russell 2014, 167.

thought about using ordinary phone calls to establish connections between computers, which would have been prohibitively expensive. Packet switching technology was thus instrumental for the emergence of the network. Interestingly, Bolt, Beranek and Newman (BBN), a Boston engineering acoustics firm, was responsible for implementing the design of ARPANET,[67] and we can speculate that some further forbidden fruit blending might have occurred when engineering acoustics met applied computer science.

Once ARPANET with its packet switching technology was up and running, its director wanted to privatize the system and make it available for commercial use. He offered it to the telephony company AT&T. AT&T declined the offer, because it was too dependent on analog telephony. As late as the 1990s telephone companies refused to participate in the development of the Internet because of their dependence on analog data.[68] Analog technologies engineers hesitated to take on digital packet switching, as they lacked the relevant expertise, and also did not fully understand the advantages of packet switching.[69] Furthermore, telephone companies had analog infrastructure in place, and thus high sunk costs. Yet, ultimately the packet switching technology with digital data usage was retained over analog data not because the communities of practice who promoted it were more powerful (they were not), but for its higher efficiency, speed and lower costs in data transmission. The functional characteristics of the technology led to its retention.

Next to packet switching technology the advent and rapid spread of PCs was the second key material development based on which the Internet could evolve.[70] These two technologies provided the necessary conditions for the spread of a whole series of different computer networks, of which ARPANET was one among many. Increasingly actors sought to interconnect these different networks. In 1977 a few British computer scientists envisaged to develop "network standards needed for open working." At the root here was an ideal of openness that was in opposition to closed systems, such as IBM's or telephony. Yet, the ways in which that ideal was implemented and retained was subject to functional constrains, which further affected the internet's trajectory.

---

[67] Castells 2002.   [68] Ibid.   [69] Abbate 2001.
[70] Campbell-Kelly and Garcia-Schwartz 2013.

To establish open systems, it was necessary to develop a common standard, but disagreements prevailed between various actors. On the one hand, there were commercial private actors such as IBM with its proprietary System Network Architecture whose goal was to control the market and establish network standards that were exclusively compatible with its products with the motive to increase commercial profits.[71] In response Canada, Britain and France initiated the X.25 protocol "as a public standard freely available to all private firms."[72] The X.25 established the same protocol across all networks.[73] By contrast, the ARPANET had its TCP/IP protocol, which aimed to establish connections between different networks, each of which could retain its own protocol.[74] The goal was thus to ensure interoperability between all standards. The TCP/IP protocol as well as any other protocol had to be developed on the basis of what the digital data format and network properties afforded. Simultaneously, these provided the epistemic credit on the basis of which the protocols could be developed.

Next to the TCP/IP protocol, the rival goal of the International Organization for Standardization (ISO), a formalized intergovernmental organization, was to develop an Open Systems Interconnection model (OSI), which would be an internationally sanctioned protocol to interconnect all networks. Developing OSI was a very cumbersome effort, which ultimately failed because it never became fully functional. According to Lyman Chapin, one of the few engineers who participated in OSI, as well as the development of TCP/IP protocols "it didn't take long to recognize the basic irony of OSI standards development: there we were, solemnly anointing international standards for networking, and every time we needed to send electronic mail or exchange files, we were using the TCP/IP-based Internet!"[75] The ARPANET/Internet protocols won out not because the communities promoting them were more powerful. Quite to the contrary, "even IBM felt pressure from its customers to offer OSI products,"[76] yet those products simply did not work.

The ARPANET community, the hacker community of practice, won out in the standards fight, and its normative principles contributed to shape the internet order. Massachusetts Institute of Technology

---

[71] Drezner 2004.   [72] Ibid., 492.   [73] Abbate 2000, 162.   [74] Ibid., 161.
[75] Cited in Russell 2014, 246.   [76] Abbate 2000, 172.

computer scientist David D. Clark coined the motto that underlies the hacker community of practice: "We reject: kings, presidents and voting. We believe in: rough consensus and running code."[77] Yet, this is not just a normative statement, but also an inherently practical one: the code needs to work. This functional dimension played a key role in the success of the hacker community of practice, in opposition to the OSI process, which was highly democratic, political and state-led, but also very cumbersome, and ultimately impracticable.

The technological and functional features of the Internet and the normative values embedded in it, the high speed and cheapness of data transmission and the openness of the network, provided the material conditions based on which the internet culture of freedom, meritocracy, communitarian proprietary relations and an absence of regulation and state intervention could flourish. These cultural features manifested themselves in the practices of open-source programming that in turn contributed to the unprecedented growth of the Internet.[78] Learning from the use of technology, and then contributing to the technology's further improvement has historically not been an uncommon practice, but in the case of the Internet

new uses of the technology, as well as the actual modifications introduced in the technology, are communicated back to the whole world, in real time. Thus, the timespan between the processes of learning by using and producing by using is extraordinarily shortened, with the result that we engage in a process of learning by producing, in a virtuous feedback between the diffusion of technology and its enhancement. This is why the Internet grew, and keeps growing, at unprecedented speed.[79]

The internet's technical features, such as high speed and cheapness of data transmission serve as affordances that make the practices of open-source coding possible. The digital data format provides the epistemic credit on the basis of which the coding practices proceed. The prototypical example of open-source software is LINUX. The twenty-two-year old Linus Torvalis made the source code of Linux available online, and asked others to improve it, and make their improvements of the code publicly available "to the point that Linux is now widely considered one of the most advanced operating systems in the world, particularly for Internet-based computing."[80]

---

[77] Cited in Russell 2014, 24.   [78] Cohen-Almagor 2011.
[79] Castells 2002, 28.   [80] Ibid., 14.

The Internet and the widespread use of PCs then also supplied the technological infrastructure based on which the World Wide Web could emerge, spread and gain unprecedented popularity. The World Wide Web provided an application of the Internet that attracted millions of users on the net, and transformed the Internet into a mass public phenomenon:[81] a technology that is key for spreading network memory and therefore fundamental for the horizontal selective retention of the cyber order. Ideas about a global hypertext that would link the world's information through an interconnected computer system had already existed since the end of the second world war, but the advantage of Tim Berners-Lee, the inventor of the World Wide Web, "was that the Internet already existed, and he could find support on the Internet and rely on decentralized computer power via workstations."[82] These provided the affordances for the emergence of the World Wide Web.

Tim Berners-Lee was an employee at CERN, the European Organization for Nuclear Physics. His major creative innovation that led to the design of the web was in the realm of forbidden fruit blending: he made use of hypertext, which was a technology at the time used on educational CDs and encyclopedias to cross reference texts, and linked it up with the Internet. "He later described the web as a 'marriage of hypertext and the Internet'."[83]

Next to the web other systems of navigation emerged, such as gopher and Wide Area Information System (WAIS), both of which even preceded the web. Yet, the web was selectively retained against these alternative options primarily for two reasons. First, the web was aesthetically more appealing than its alternatives. It provided "a user friendly, visually compelling, content rich experience to which ordinary users could relate."[84] Gopher had only plain text documents, whereas the web could distribute a large variety of font sizes, graphic designs and images. The web's aesthetic appeal lay in that. Second, different from gopher and WAIS, the web did not depend on a central directory, and so anyone could post things on the web, without any restrictions or having to wait for someone to add a document to the directory.[85] Once the World Wide Web existed,

---

[81]   Abbate 2000, 213.   [82]   Castells 2002, 16.
[83]   Berners-Lee 1999, 28 in Campbell-Kelly and Garcia-Schwartz 2013, 30.
[84]   Campbell-Kelly and Garcia-Schwartz 2013, 19; see also Abbate 1999; Adler 2019.
[85]   Campbell-Kelly and Garcia-Schwartz 2013, 31.

search engines such as Yahoo! and Lycos emerged, which helped to catalogue the net, because otherwise it would be very difficult to find anything online.

Even as it appears that the cyber realm is not physical or material, there are cables, packet switching technologies, charges and no charges that are material. Indeed, they have shaped the ways in which the Internet has developed. In 1994 "the US Court of Appeals Federal Circuit held in re Alappat (1994) that all software was inherently machinic, since it changed the material nature of a computer."[86] Practices of open-source programming, the background knowledge and norms of transparency, open access, participation and entrepreneurialism, the hacker community of practice, and the material features of digital data storage and packet switching technology are all mutually entangled and reinforce each other; they define the internet order.[87] That order is based on a huge open network that connects many minds at a high speed. The creative flows that emerge from it have led and will likely continue to lead to large-scale innovations, which are typically unanticipated, sometimes disruptive, sometimes positive, sometimes negative and often times all at once.[88] Many of the Internet's initial designers made assumptions of usage that did not prove accurate. That the Internet thrived nonetheless highlights the key role of technological affordances in its evolution.

According to Adler and Deibert the global cyber order of freedom is threatened by a new community of practice, which considers "cyberspace as a national domain that should be at the service of state security."[89] When studying the emergence of this new community it would be good to focus not just on the practices and background knowledge that sustain and define it, but also on the material and technological developments that make the censorship and filtering practices of the cyber securitization community feasible and support them. Not too long ago, filtering practices were in fact thought impracticable, and they have become possible thanks to the proliferation of filtering technologies and specific commercial products such as Smartfilter, or Websense.[90] At the same time cyberspace has material characteristics that elude state control to some extent.[91] "Once

---

[86] Hui Kyong Chun 2011, 4.   [87] Russell 2014, 2.   [88] Naughton 2012.
[89] Deibert 2013; Adler 2019, 265.   [90] Deibert and Crete-Nishihata 2012.
[91] Deibert and Rohozinski 2010.

released into cyberspace, the distributed properties of the network help ideas and information circulate, duplicate and proliferate."[92] Not acknowledging that technology poses limits to what is possible can result in a dangerous notion of uninhibited technological progress. Technological trends might in fact even play a key role in determining which of these two communities will ultimately win in their contestation over the cyber order, and whose practices will get to define the new order.

Conclusion

This chapter provides a New Materialist approach to changes of social order by adapting Emanuel Adler's theory of cognitive evolution to New Materialism. In line with Adler I define social orders as configurations of practices, background knowledge and practitioners. Technologies, artifacts and material objects are intimately interrelated with practices and background knowledge, so that changes in technologies, artifacts and material objects can lead to changes of social orders. The process of change focuses on creative variation, where forbidden fruit blending is an engine of creativity. People mix together objects and practices from realms that do not typically belong together to create something new. Furthermore, technology, artifacts and material objects have epistemic credit and thereby constitutive effects on the ideas that can emerge. Technologies and artifacts also interrelate with practices, because of their affordances. Thus, creative variation in technologies and artifacts can lead to creative variation in practices through mutually reinforcing loophole effects. Most creative variations do not get retained. In the process of selective retention, beyond paying attention to a fit with the normative environment, it is also important to focus on whether things and practices work, and on their aesthetic appeal. Technologies of memory retention have a direct effect on selective retention, because they shape network memory, the ways in which societies collectively store information. Only what can be remembered has the potential to be selectively retained.

I applied these mechanisms to understand the emergence and evolution of the Internet. Key technologies without which the Internet could not have emerged in its current form, such as packet switching and the

---

[92] Ibid., 16.

World Wide Web were the product of forbidden fruit blending. Functional and aesthetic features played an important role in the selective retention of some technologies over others, notably the retention of packet switching and digital data over analog data and circuit switching, and the retention of the web over gopher and WAIS. Finally, defining practices, such as open-source coding co-emerged with the technological features of the Internet and background knowledge based on freedom, informality and communitarian property rights. The resulting internet order is characterized by a low degree of formalism, highly decentralized action conducted by many actors, practices of open-source coding, and high-speed interactions. Competing communities of practice are currently challenging this order, and they are also using new technological innovations to further a different set of practices.

   A consideration of evolving matters could similarly enhance our understanding of the evolution of other social orders, such as the European Union or the corporate business order. For example, a New Materialist approach to cognitive evolution could look at how technological developments have supported the evolution of negotiating practices that have defined the development of the European order. Along these lines, Adler-Nissen and Drieschova have looked at the development of Information and Communication Technologies such as the Word program, the use of mobile devices and email and demonstrated how these technologies made complex high-speed negotiations between a large number of geographically dispersed actors possible.[93] The evolution of the corporate business order, in turn, was shaped not just by various economic theories, norms and ethics of interaction, but also by accounting practices, software programs for the calculation of profits and tools that help conduct market analyses. Big data analyses have, for example, entirely changed the business model of companies such as Amazon, Uber and Airbnb compared to the production model of the Fordist assembly line. Studying the effects of technology, artifacts and material objects not in a deterministic way, but in interaction with norms, practices and communities of practitioners can massively improve our understanding of the longer-term evolution of social orders.

[93] Adler-Nissen and Drieschova 2019.

References

Abbate, Janet. 1999. Cold War and White Heat: The Origins and Meanings of Packet Switching. In *the Social Shaping of Technology*, edited by Donald MacKenzie and Judy Wajcman, 351–71. New York: Open University Press.

Abbate, Janet. 2000. *Inventing the Internet*. London: MIT Press.

Abbate, Janet. 2001. Government, Business, and the Making of the Internet. *The Business History Review* 75(1): 147–76.

Adler, Emanuel. 2019. *World Ordering: A Social Theory of Cognitive Evolution*. Cambridge: Cambridge University Press.

Adler-Nissen, Rebecca and Alena Drieschova. 2019. Track-Change Diplomacy: Technology, Affordances, and The Practice of International Negotiations. *International Studies Quarterly* 63(3): 531–45.

Alexander, Jeffrey C. 2011. *Performance and Power*. Cambridge: Polity.

Aradau, Claudia. 2010. Security That Matters: Critical Infrastructure and Objects of Protection. *Security Dialogue* 41(5): 491–514.

Austin, Jonathan Luke. 2016. Torture and the Material-Semiotic Networks of Violence Across Borders. *International Political Sociology* 10(1): 3–21.

Berners-Lee, Tim. 1999. *Weaving the Web: The Past, Present and Future of the World Wide Web by Its Inventor*. London: Herper Paperbacks.

Bleiker, Roland. 2012. *Aesthetics and World Politics*. London: Palgrave Macmillan.

Branch, Jordan. 2012. "Colonial Reflection" and Territoriality: The Peripheral Origins of Sovereign Statehood. *European Journal of International Relations* 18(2): 277–97.

Brandt, Per Aage. 2006. Form and Meaning in Art. In *The Artful Mind: Cognitive Science and the Riddle of Human Creativity*, edited by Mark Turner, 171–88. Oxford: Oxford University Press.

Brunnée, Jutta and Stephen Toope. 2011. History, Mystery, and Mastery. *International Theory* 3(2): 348–54.

Bunz, Mercedes. 2014. *The Silent Revolution: How Digitalization Transforms Knowledge, Work, Journalism and Politics Without Making Too Much Noise*. London: Palgrave Macmillan.

Bygrave, Lee and Jon Bing. 2009. *Internet Governance: Infrastructure and Institutions*. Oxford: Oxford University Press.

Campbell-Kelly, Martin and Daniel Garcia-Schwartz. 2013. The History of the Internet: The Missing Narratives. *Journal of Information Technology* 28(1): 18–33.

Carr, Madeline. 2015. Power Plays in Global Internet Governance. *Millennium: Journal of International Relations* 43(2): 640–59.

Castells, Manuel. 2002. *Internet Galaxy: Reflections on the Internet, Business, and Society*. Oxford: Oxford University Press.

Clark, Andy and David Chalmers. 1998. The Extended Mind. *Analysis 58* (1): 7–19.

Cohen-Almagor, Raphael. 2011. Internet History. *International Journal of Technoethics* 2(2): 45–64.

Craig, Campbell. 2019. Solving the Nuclear Dilemma. Is a World State Necessary? *Journal of International Political Theory* 15(3): 349–66.

Deibert, Ronald. 2013. *Black Code: Inside the Battle for Cyberspace*. Toronto: Signal.

Deibert, Ronald and Masashi Crete-Nishihata. 2012. Global Governance and the Spread of Cyberspace Controls. *Global Governance* 18(3): 339–61.

Deibert, Ronald and Rafal Rohozinski. 2010. Risking Security: Policies and Paradoxes of Cyberspace Security. *International Political Sociology* 4(1): 15–32.

DeNardis, Laura. 2009. *Protocol Politics: The Globalization of Internet Governance*. Cambridge, MA: MIT Press.

Deutsch, Karl. 1953. *Nationalism and Social Communication*. Cambridge, MA: MIT Press.

Donald, Merlin. 2006. Art and Cognitive Evolution. In *The Artful Mind: Cognitive Science and the Riddle of Human Creativity*, edited by Mark Turner, 3–20. Oxford: Oxford University Press.

Drezner, Daniel. 2004. The Global Governance of the Internet: Bringing the State Back In. *Political Science Quarterly* 119(3): 477–98.

Drieschova, Alena. 2017. Peirce's Semeiotics: A Methodology Bridging the Material-Ideational Divide in IR Scholarship. *International Theory* 9(1): 33–66.

Gangopadhyay, Nivedita, Michael Madary and Finn Spicer. 2010. Perception, Action, and Consciousness. In *Perception, Action, Consciousness: Sensorimotor Dynamics and Two Visual Systems*, edited by Nivedita Gangopadhyay, Michael Madary and Finn Spicer, 1–18. Oxford: Oxford University Press.

Gibbs, Raymond. 2005. *Embodiment and Cognitive Science*. Cambridge: Cambridge University Press.

Gibson, James. 1979. *The Ecological Approach to Visual Perception*. Boston: Houghton Mifflin.

Grahame, Peter. 1994. Objects, Texts, and Practices: The Refrigerator in Consumer Discourses between the Wars. In *The Socialness of Things: Essays on the Socio-Semiotics of Objects*, edited by Stephen Harold Riggins, 285–307. Berlin: Mouton de Gruyter.

Graves-Brown, Paul. 2000. Introduction. In *Matter, Materiality and Modern Culture*, edited by Paul Graves-Brown, 1–9. London: Routledge.

Hui Kyong Chun, Wendy. 2004. On Software or the Persistence of Visual Knowledge. *The Grey Room* 18(Winter 2005): 26–51.

Hui Kyong Chun, Wendy. 2011. *Programmed Visions: Software and Memory*. Cambridge, MA: MIT Press.

Jervis, Robert. 1978. Cooperation under the Security Dilemma. *World Politics* 30(2): 167–214.

Keohane, Robert and Joseph Nye. 1977. *Power and Interdependence*. Boston: Longham.

Kittler, Friedrich. 1995. There Is No Software. *C-Theory: Theory, Technology, Culture* 32(October 18, 1995): 10–18. www.ctheory.com/a rticle/a032.html.

Kleinrock, Leonard. 2010. History of Communications. *IEEE Communications Magazine* 48(8): 26–36.

Kratochwil, Friedrich. 1993. The Embarrassment of Changes: Neo-Realism as the Science of Realpolitik without Politics. *Review of International Studies* 19(1): 63–80.

Langins, Janis. 2004. *Conserving the Enlightenment: French Military Engineering from Vauban to the Revolution*. Cambridge, MA: MIT Press.

Latour, Bruno. 2005. *Reassembling the Social: An Introduction to Actor-Network-Theory*. Oxford: Oxford University Press.

Lundborg, Tom and Nick Vaughan-Williams. 2011. Resilience, Critical Infrastructure, and Molecular Security: The Excess of "Life" in Biopolitics. *International Political Sociology* 5(4): 367–83.

Merleau-Ponty, Maurice. 2002. *Phenomenology of Perception*. New York: Routledge Classics.

Mitchell, Audra. 2014. Only Human? A Worldly Approach to Security. *Security Dialogue* 45(1): 5–21.

Naughton, John. 2012. *What You Really Need to Know about the Internet: From Gutenberg to Zuckerberg*. London: Quercus.

Nexon, Daniel and Vincent Pouliot. 2013. "Things of Networks": Situating ANT in International Relations. *International Political Sociology* 7(3): 342–45.

Norman, Donald. 1988. *The Psychology of Everyday Things*. New York: Basic Books.

Orlikowski, Wanda J., JoAnne Yates, Kazou Okamura and Masayo Fujimoto. 1995. Shaping Electronic Communication: The Metastructuring of Technology in the Context of Use. *Organization Science* 6(4): 423–44.

Parikka, Jussi and Wolfgang Ernst. 2012. *Electronic Mediations: Digital Memory and the Archive*. Minnesota: University of Minnesota Press.

Prigogine, Ilya. 1980. *From Being to Becoming: Time and Complexity in the Physical Sciences*. San Francisco: W. H. Freeman.

Roberts, Lawrence G. 1967. "Multiple Computer Networks and Intercomputer Communication." ARPA document, spring 1967. National Archives Branch Depository, Suitland, Maryland, RG 330-78-0085, box 2, folder "Networking 1968–1972."

Ruggie, John Gerard. 1982. International Regimes, Transactions, and Change: Embedded Liberalism in the Postwar Economic Order. *International Organization* 36(2): 379–415.

Ruggie, John Gerard. 1983. Continuity and Transformation in the World Polity: Toward a Neorealist Synthesis. *World Politics* 35(2): 261–85.

Russell, Andrew. 2014. *Open Standards and the Digital Age: History, Ideology, and Networks*. Cambridge: Cambridge University Press.

Searle, John R. 2010. *Making the Social World: The Structure of Human Civilization*. New York: Oxford University Press.

Turner, Mark. 2006. The Art of Compression. In *The Artful Mind: Cognitive Science and the Riddle of Human Creativity*, edited by Mark Turner, 93–113. Oxford: Oxford University Press.

Van Eeten, Michel and Milton Mueller. 2012. Where Is the Governance in Internet Governance? *New Media & Society* 15(5): 720–36.

Waltz, Kenneth. 1979. *Theory of International Politics*. Reading: Addison-Wesley.

Wendt, Alexander. 2015. *Quantum Mind and Social Science: Unifying Physical and Social Ontology*. Cambridge: Cambridge University Press.

Wohlforth, William. 1999. The Stability of a Unipolar World. *International Security* 24(1): 5–41.

4 | *The Phenomenology of Cognitive Evolution*

SIMON FRANKEL PRATT

International Relations (IRs), as a discipline, have had little to say about phenomenology. While a small set of IR scholars have averred the value of phenomenology,[1] most in the field rarely provide an account of the basic processes and kinds of perception and sensation that condition the human *experience* of politics, perhaps on the grounds that it does not matter. A growing and productive body of IR scholarship does address emotions, and branching off from the "emotional" turn are also projects that focus more specifically on sensations, affect and embodiment.[2] Yet this work does not, for the most part, elaborate a systematic account of experience and action,[3] instead studying the situational dynamics of feelings and bodily or somatic[4] states, often through psychoanalytic and psychological frameworks of analysis. The process of cognitive evolution as Adler theorizes it is also silent on the experience of that evolution from the perspective of those undergoing it, immersed in it and engaged in it. This is no criticism; to quote Kenneth Waltz, "Any theory covers some matters and leaves other matters aside."[5] However, I think Adler's approach is highly suggestive of particular understandings of experience and sensation, and cognitive evolution as a framework has phenomenological implications worth exploring. Elaborating this phenomenology would not only add to Adler's own account, but clarify themes that link cognitive evolution to current work on emotions in IR. In this chapter I will try to do this, and provide an account

---

[1] See, for example, Higate 2012; Weinert 2018; Drieschova 2019.
[2] For some excellent overviews of this literature, see Åhäll and Gregory 2015; Sucharov and Van Rythoven 2019. See also Mercer 2006; Ross 2006; Reus-Smit 2014; Koschut 2017.
[3] With the odd notable exception, such as Ross's (2019) discussion of emotion and experience through the pragmatist phenomenologies of John Dewey and William James.
[4] McDermott 2014.
[5] See, for instance, Solomon 2014; Hutchison 2016; Dittmer 2017; Åhäll 2019.

of what it means to experience "becoming" in the relational settings that characterize international politics.

The phenomenology of cognitive evolution extends from the pragmatist social theory undergirding the approach. By pragmatism I mean an action-centric, relational, and processual view of the social world. It is action centric because the ontological focus is on practice rather than on practitioners, agents or actors – a move that, as Haas also discusses in this volume, allows for agency to vary, be discovered or generated and emerge. It is relational because practices emerge out of configurations of interactions between people and their environments, such that any account of them must include both. It is processual because the social world is defined as an unfolding "becoming" rather than a stable arrangement of things. Adler's book builds on these philosophical commitments in ways that have phenomenological implications, suggesting definitions and roles for experience and sensation as part of action. By following these implications, I hope to expand the explicit scope of cognitive evolution in ways that will appeal to a broader section of the discipline.

Specifically, I begin with the insights of John Dewey to argue that cognitive evolution is phenomenologically driven by the frustration and anxiety of action inhibited, and by the satisfaction of action made effective. I then introduce the work of Maurice Merleau-Ponty to Dewey's perspective, to better trace how the process of cognitive evolution is experienced as the expansion of mind across its environment. Together these two philosophers are especially helpful for understanding how the cognitive differentiation of mind and world is episodically (and perhaps only partially) interrupted to expose, emotionally and representationally, how they are ontologically continuous. Merleau-Ponty, more so than his German phenomenologist forbearers and his French existentialist cousins, is heavily preoccupied with the body, environment and habit, and thus already may be understood as a kind of pragmatist in the same vein as Dewey.[6] Both advance a view of the mind as embodied within a moving tapestry of habits, pressures and sensations, as the constituents of the world. If read as theorists of cognitive evolution, they show our place within a co-evolving *ecology of all*.

---

[6] I recognize that labeling Merleau-Ponty a pragmatist runs the risk of antagonizing some of those reading him. I am not categorically positioning him within the pragmatist project, nor ignoring that other elements or preoccupations of his work differ from those of the American pragmatists.

The philosophical reexamination I conduct here has several implications. It shows that collective intentionality, like everything affective, is embodied and nonrepresentational, consisting in joint and entangled collective projection toward shared ends. This implication goes beyond the claims of IR literature on embodiment, which focuses on the bodily, carnal or physiological as a site and instrument of politics. It is a thesis on the fundamental nature of being: that it has direction, or at least directionality. In other words, I advance a view of embodiment that focuses on the experience of growth and change as a physical and social process. It also shows that ontological security – or more accurately, ontological insecurity – is a core meta-mechanism, or causal condition of possibility, underlying all other mechanisms of cognitive evolution, even if it need not be explicitly referenced in many explanations for actual events. Finally, it shows that cognitive evolution is ontologically flat, which implies that any differentiation of structural and agentic mechanisms is merely heuristic, and clarifies when or how they might be helpful as such.

These implications in turn help cognitive evolution speak to three ongoing discussions in the field. First, phenomenology gives an account of both the *triggers* and *ends* of the mechanisms of cognitive evolution. It explains how experience and sensation provide the impetus for action and the point where satisfaction is realized, resulting in the termination of a process of change or the stabilization of a practice undergoing revision. Second, phenomenology links cognitive evolution to ontological security – the latter being a burgeoning research program – by providing a meta-theoretical basis for sociologizing anxiety and emotion, and by providing novel mechanisms by which these things have institutional effects. Third, phenomenology adds momentum to the ways cognitive evolution can advance constructivism, first by giving it a clear material basis – the body and its projection within its environment[7] – and second, by connecting it to some existing conversations not typically preoccupied with institutional transformation.

I make my argument in three sections. First, I briefly outline where in Adler's approach to cognitive evolution the role of experience and sensation should lie, and what its links are to his causal mechanisms. Second, I connect his ontological premises to the phenomenology of Dewey and Merleau-Ponty, approaching them as two pragmatist

---

[7] Drieschova, in this volume and in 2017, further elaborates the processual and experiential ways new materialism approaches cognitive evolution.

philosophers – explicitly in the case of Dewey and implicitly in the case of Merleau-Ponty – whose perspectives are consistent with Adler's own. I explain how these insights inform discussions on causal mechanisms and microfoundations,[8] ontological security[9] and materiality.[10] Third, I offer some remarks on how phenomenology facilitates and complements Adler's normative project by grounding the possibility of humanist progress in shared human experience. I then conclude with some speculative remarks on how the phenomenology of cognitive evolution can help clarify "post truth" as a moment of epistemic crisis in political discourse, as an illustrative example.

The Absence of, and Place for, Phenomenology in *Cognitive Evolution*

Adler's book offers a seminal approach to cognitive evolution as a process of significance in international politics, focusing on relational and structural evolution in communities of practice. While Adler devotes significant time to process ontology and evolutionary epistemology, the actual mechanisms of his theories refer to things the agent can do within the world, and the processes the agent can undergo while doing them. The closest this comes to an account of the experience of undergoing cognitive evolution is in his first mechanism, of practice-driven changes in disposition and expectations.[11] Yet dispositions and expectations, while they imply orientations toward and away from things, are not themselves feelings or experiences. Explaining the evolution of order and practice at the institutional or collective level may not need a phenomenological account, but the possibility of providing one opens up greater scope for empirical input and theoretical synthesis.

One area where phenomenology clearly contributes to cognitive evolution theory would be to explore the triggers of Adler's seven mechanisms.[12] Fundamentally, cognitive evolution is a theory of situated, collective learning. Once learning starts, we can use agential mechanisms to trace how individuals revise their practices, and how broader social forces condition individuals as they do so, but it is in perceptions and emotions of human beings that the learning process is

---

[8] Sil and Katzenstein 2010; Bennett 2013; see also Kurki 2008; Guzzini 2011.
[9] Kinnvall 2004; Mitzen 2006; Steele 2008; see also Pratt 2017.
[10] Dittmer 2017; Drieschova 2017; Mac Ginty 2017.   [11] Adler 2019, 198.
[12] These mechanisms are covered at length in chapters 6 and 7 of his book.

initiated, and where its outcomes are found – are *felt* – to be adequate or wanting. In phenomenology we can find clues as to what kinds of situations generate cognitive evolution, and thus, in theoretical and empirical terms, what would impel it. Put differently, phenomenology offers us a way to grapple with the causal foundations of human action without being individualistically micro-foundational.

The other significant contribution phenomenology may offer here is to clarify the ontological status of individuals and collectives when approached through cognitive evolution theory, both in terms of the nature of intersubjectivity and in the knitting together of "agential" and "socio-cultural" mechanisms, rendering both into a single field of action. Regardless of the level of aggregation or locus of causal action, these mechanisms all impose themselves upon human experience, unfolding for us in felt, bodily ways. Phenomenology, in other words, is not only the beginning of cognitive evolution but its end: the point-space whereby it crystalizes into transactions of organism and environment, and where the subjective and objective meet.

For both contributions, I draw on the phenomenology of Dewey and Merleau-Ponty, whom I group together on the basis of their complementary accounts of action and experience. Adler himself draws heavily on Dewey's writings in his book, both directly and through his a contemporary interlocutor, Hans Joas, while a number of other IR scholars have also found Dewey's work to be especially helpful for conceptualizing institutional change.[13] Merleau-Ponty, however, is an unknown figure in IR scholarship, though this is perhaps unsurprising given that the similarities of his views to pragmatism are underappreciated in general.[14] In the next section, I survey these two philosophers as they pertain to the experience of learning.

Dewey and Merleau-Ponty as Phenomenologists of Learning

Learning processes are of interest to many scholars of IR, and not only those interested in cognitive evolution.[15] While Dewey is primarily

---

[13] Schmidt 2014; Pratt 2020.
[14] One acquaintance of mine described this as a similarity that many have remarked upon but not yet done the labor of elaborating. This is not strictly true, however, as some scholars have done some of the work (Kestenbaum 1977; see also Standal and Aggerholm 2016).
[15] Levy 1994; Stein 1994; Knopf 2003; Harnisch 2012.

read in IR as a theorist of habit and practice,[16] learning is a central preoccupation throughout his life's work. His model of the learning process, very generally, is connected to his more general theory of action. Actors encounter problematic situations – those in which our streams of habituated, situated ways of interacting with the world around us are interrupted. When habit is interrupted or inhibited, the organism must select and synthesize from a wide range of mutually exclusive responses. The way by which it does so is through reflective self-awareness, from the consideration and selection of alternatives[17]. Thus, people's minds are extended throughout the various activities they engage in, and those minds transform, or learn, when ongoing activities become impeded. Learning consists in finding ways to overcome such impediments. This model appears in basic form, and then receives further articulation, across most of Dewey's most prominent works – *Democracy and Education,*[18] *Experience and Nature,*[19] *Logic,*[20] *Art as Experience.*[21]

As important as the concept of situated habit is to Dewey, equally key to his understanding of learning is the concept of experience, where perception is ordered by action, into an "organized context of meanings and activities."[22] For Dewey, experience is a sort of existential unity in which action, emotion and being are knit together, and wherein judgments about objects and events are formed in a "contextual whole."[23] Habit and inquiry unfold in a "universe of experience,"[24] in which problems must be "felt, before [they] can be stated," and are "unique and inexpressible in words," at least in their first and primary sense.[25] While he employs multiple, not entirely consistent definitions of the term, the mature articulation of his thought on experience is clearest in the chapter of *Art and Experience* titled "Having an Experience."[26] To quote from its opening paragraphs:

Experience occurs continuously, because the interaction of live creature and environing conditions is involved in the very process of living. Under

---

[16] Hopf 2010; Pratt 2016.   [17] Hildebrand 2008, 28–30.   [18] Dewey 1916.
[19] Dewey 1929.   [20] Dewey 1939b.   [21] Dewey 1939a.
[22] Alexander 1987, 133. Yet Dewey establishes communicative meanings as a second-order manipulation of experience: "Where communication exists, things in acquiring meaning, thereby acquire representatives, surrogates, signs and implicates, which are infinitely more amenable to management, more permanent and more accommodating, than events in their first estate" (1929, 167).
[23] Dewey 1939b, 66.   [24] Ibid., 68.   [25] Ibid., 70.   [26] Dewey 1939a.

conditions of resistance and conflict, aspects and elements of the self and the world that are implicated in this interaction qualify experience with emotions and ideas so that conscious intent emerges. Oftentimes, however, the experience had is inchoate. Things are experienced but not in such a way that they are composed into an experience. There is distraction and dispersion; what we observe and what we think, what we desire and what we get, are at odds with each other ... In contrast with such experience, we have *an* experience [emphasis original] when the material experienced runs its course to fulfillment. Then and then only is it integrated within and demarcated in the general stream of experience from other experiences.

Later in the chapter, Dewey is more explicit about the perceptual quality of experience, and on what delimits and establishes, cognitively and emotionally, *an* experience as a discrete thing: "The action and its consequence must be joined in perception ... .No one ever arrives at such maturity that he perceives all the connections that are involved."[27] Experience is thus where actors confront problematic situations, in which their activities are inhibited, and is where "reflective thinking transforms confusion, ambiguity, and discrepancy into illumination, definiteness, and consistency."[28] In short, experience is sensate, directed, holistic and the locus of learning and reflection.

A phenomenological reading of the foregoing should revolve around three things, as it applies to the issue of learning and cognitive evolution. First, experience is not merely temporally prior to learning, it is *ontologically* prior, and indeed transcendental – that is, a condition of possibility. The formation of concepts, the apprehension, exchange and transmission of ideas through social intercourse, the rendering of action as an object of reflection, all happen because learners exist in a field of feelings and perceived pressures, apprehended in ambiguous ways. For Dewey, life and the mind do not merely start and end in experience, but are *of it*.

Second, cognition is oriented around situations, as concrete arrangements of not-always-clear entities and events, into which we are always already thrust, and an already ongoing stream of situation-navigation. That is, situated habits undergoing revision might be made objects of reflection, but they are not initiated by conscious decisions. Rather, they are ongoing, and consciousness rides atop them, occasionally steers them, and is ultimately itself a situated habit. Put differently,

[27] Ibid.   [28] Dewey 1929, 67.

the action process in its entirety is existential – it is *in the world*. This view of action is, in IR, a central precept for many scholars in the practice turn, and Dewey can broadly be categorized as a practice theorist.[29]

Third and finally, the character of *an* experience is the product of second-order apportioning of experience into discrete units, with apprehensible temporal, teleological and symbolic properties. It is conditioned by our unique individual (and social) perceptual trajectories, and to ascribe meaning to an experience, to revise our actions as a conscious result of it, and to render it as part of our personal histories, is a cognitive maneuver intervening on experience in its first-order character.

This directly speaks to a number of the mechanisms Adler describes in his theory of cognitive evolution. Not only does it shed light on practice-driven changes in dispositions and expectations, but also socially generated reflection and judgment – albeit on a particular view of those two things. More broadly, it should speak to all of his mechanisms, as Dewey's views of action and experience comprise a holistic theory of learning. It does not, however, offer an especially operationalizable set of categories, meaning that while it may provide a sense of what kinds of things in principle trigger cognitive evolution, it does not make it easy to specify them in actual cases. To develop a more concrete set of definitions, Merleau-Ponty's own phenomenology is helpful.

Merleau-Ponty is not primarily a philosopher of learning, but his phenomenology – developed as a response to empiricist and idealist views of judgment and the mind – develops a corporealized view of perception and judgment sympathetic to Dewey's own perspective.[30] This is most clearly articulated in his earlier work *Phenomenology of Perception*.[31] He too positions us in a holistic tapestry of experience: "Consciousness is no less intimately linked with objects of which it is unheeding than with those which interest it, and the additional clearness brought by the act of attention does not herald any new relationship."[32] Then later: "experience is [that to which] the perceived object and the perceiving subject owe their thickness. It is the

[29] Büger and Gadinger 2014.
[30] Both, for example, offered more or less identical criticisms of the reflex-arc model of psychology (Carmen 2008, 86–87).
[31] Merleau-Ponty 2002 [1945].   [32] Ibid., 32.

intentional tissue which the effort to know will try to take apart."[33] He is more explicit than Dewey in presenting experience as a condition of possibility:

[P]henomenology, alone of all philosophies, talks about a transcendental field. This word indicates that reflection never holds, arrayed and objectified before its gaze, the whole world and the plurality of monads, and that its view is never other than partial and of limited power. It is also why phenomenology is phenomenology, that is, a study of the advent of being to consciousness, instead of presuming its possibility as given in advance.[34]

He and Dewey are of a kind, however, in describing habit and action as the subjects of learning and as having an embodied, world-distributed nature:

It is quite true that what brings together, in habit, component actions, reactions and "stimuli" is not some external process of association ... the learning process is systematic; the subject does not weld together individual movements and individual stimuli but acquires the power to respond with a certain type of solution to situations of a certain general form.[35]

Or, more succinctly: "habit is neither a form of knowledge nor an involuntary action ... It is knowledge in the hands, which is forthcoming only when bodily effort is made, and cannot be formulated in detachment from that effort."[36]

Finally, Merleau-Ponty shares with Dewey the premise that understanding is a matter of effectuality in the world rather than the systematic representation of information: "[I]t is the body which 'understands' in the acquisition of habit....To understand is to experience the harmony between what we aim at and what is given, between the intention and the performance – and the body is our anchorage in a world."[37] Having established that understanding has an embodied basis, Merleau-Ponty clarifies how intentionality is not about how we project the world to ourselves, but how we project ourselves *to the world*:

The body's motion can play a part in the perception of the world only if it is itself an original intentionality, a manner of relating itself to the distinct object of knowledge. The world around us must be, not a system of objects

---

[33] Ibid., 62.   [34] Ibid., 71.   [35] Ibid., 164.   [36] Ibid., 166.   [37] Ibid., 167.

which we synthesize, but a totality of things, open to us, towards which we project ourselves.[38]

This culminates in assigning intentionality the role of orienting us in relation to the ends of our actions, and in relation to the processes through which those ends are realized:

> [M]y world is carried forward by lines of intentionality which trace out in advance at least the style of what is to come (although we are always on the watch, perhaps to the day of our death, for the appearance of something else). The present itself, in the narrow sense, is not posited. [Its objects] are there for me, but I do not explicitly perceive them. I do not so much perceive objects as reckon with an environment; I seek support in my tools, and am at my task rather than confronting it.[39]

Merleau-Ponty is to a large degree responding to a different philosophical context than is Dewey, but the above summary of his views establishes numerous points of intersection and elaboration.

Merleau-Ponty's phenomenology extends Dewey's own insights in two key ways. First, he more clearly states the ways in which life – in the "transcendental field" – comprises a holistic range of potential connections between the sensing subject and its objects of perception. More so than Dewey, he thus establishes experience not just as formation of transactions between organism and environment, but a horizon of intentional possibilities. As such, we can conceive of perception as a space of action, and define learning not just as the revision of habit but the (re)direction of the body – something that can be concretely mapped.[40]

Second, he develops intentionality, typically understood in representational terms,[41] in an explicitly nonrepresentational, bodily and enacted direction. While Dewey argues that mind lies in action, Merleau-Ponty elaborates how it does, in finer-grained philosophical terms. By connecting the ends and means of action and habit to intentionality, and by defining the latter as movement toward the objects of the world, he offers a conception of mind *as practice*. For this reason, it

---

[38] Ibid., 450.   [39] Ibid., 483.

[40] In other words, Merleau-Ponty shares Dewey's essential insights into habit and experience, but offers some conceptual levers for field-mapping as a methodological move for studying specific cases of learning.

[41] Perhaps most famously by Searle, on whose social ontology Adler draws.

is surprising that his work has not made a significant appearance in the practice turn in the field, as nonrepresentationalist and embodied view of intentionality offers a way for practices to be traced, placed within context and interpreted without needing to make assumptions about actors' beliefs. In other words, Merleau-Ponty's intentionality is methodologically well-suited for operationalizing the mechanisms of cognitive evolution.

The Phenomenology of Cognitive Evolution and IR Theory

The phenomenology of cognitive evolution, if it follows Dewey and Merleau-Ponty, can be summarized into several basic properties. First, it is experiential, meaning it is embedded in the sensory and perceptual process of subject engagement with the world; it cannot refer to change in logical relations empty of content. Second, it is bodily, meaning that it happens in the way the body works on, with, and through the world; it cannot be some kind of purely internal or intellectual process of rethinking ideal categories. Third, it is habitual, meaning it consists in the evolution or revision of acquired modes of bodily action and reaction; it cannot be the outcome of a process that begins in the will of the subject absent both existing habit and will already being and being conditioned. Fourth, it is motile, meaning that it involves the processual movement of the body through space; it cannot involve a change without movement because all change involves a movement of the body into a new place, with concurrent changes in the particular conditions and impositions of the world at hand.

This yields a number of critical insights into cognitive evolution. Perhaps the most significant concerns intentionality. Adler frequently references and draws upon Searle's[42] representationalist approach to collective intentionality, assigning it to communities of practice as a property.[43] Nor is he the only constructivist in IR to rely heavily on Searle in this way.[44] Yet – and as Adler himself seems to acknowledge at points – this approach coexists uneasily with the "exosomatic"[45] and practical components of intentionality emphasized by cognitive evolution. By approaching the issue of collective intentionality through a phenomenological perspective, Searle's approach is shown to be

---

[42] Searle 1995.   [43] Adler 2019, 20, 73, 132, 210.
[44] See, for example, Evers 2020.   [45] Adler 2019, 71 (note 19) and 111.

incompatible with cognitive evolution. That is, Searle cannot be correct in defining intersubjectivity and collective intentionality as "we" representations of the relationship between mind and world, because this understanding of intentionality is at odds with an embodied, motile view of mind.

However, if we understand intentionality in embodied and motile terms, in line with Merleau-Ponty's explicit definition and Dewey's implicit one, it is easier to grant it to collectives like communities of practice. Simply put, a group of people bound together by participation in collectively implicating habits share "lines of intentionality" as they move together through a shared perceptual space and project themselves toward shared ends. On this view, "background" cannot be pre-intentional because nothing is pre-intentional, and the philosophical difficulties of parsing group minds is sidelined, because mind is, per Dewey, a verb – mind lies in practice, and a practice (and therefore a mind) is a social and collective endeavor.

This is not merely commentary on Adler's pathbreaking book; a phenomenology of cognitive evolution also offers a number of insights relevant to the work of others in the field. Namely, it contributes to work on micro-foundations, ontological security and materialism. In the next section I discuss each in turn.

Microfoundations and the Phenomenology of Cognitive Evolution

The search for microfoundations preoccupies many corners of the social sciences, and the field of international relations is no exception. Predominant suggestions include rational choice theory[46], psychology[47], emotions and habit or practice[48]. However, to sidestep the ontological debates that separate and place into conflict these options, a number of prominent scholars have instead suggested a methodological alternative: microfoundations are just causal mechanisms.[49] Their argument is that regardless of the ontological basis on which the social world rests, the epistemic basis on which

---

[46] See, for example, Levy 1997.
[47] See, for example, McDermott 2004; Hopf 2010. Note that I include Hopf (2010) in this category as despite claiming "habit" as an alternative, Hopf explicitly reduces habit to "cognitive neuropsychology."
[48] See Adler and Pouliot 2011.   [49] Sil and Katzenstein 2010; Bennett 2013.

theories rest is some specification of a causal link or process by which the object of investigation is generated. Rather than take a position on this debate, I instead suggest that there is value in making clear the relationship between ontological microfoundations and the definition of a mechanism, because this clarifies just what, conceptually, a mechanism is and does.

The microfoundations of cognitive evolution lie in practice and habit, and the discussion of Dewey and Merleau-Ponty I provide here contributes to this position. However, I also argue that phenomenology clarifies two things: what triggers a mechanism and what the relationship is between structural and agentic mechanisms.

Emotion – as discussed in the introduction to this chapter – is a trigger for mechanisms of cognitive evolution.[50] For Dewey, emotion is a key response to inhibited habit; it is not just part of *an* experience, as previously discussed, but a form of anxiety that indicates and induces a revision in habit.[51] For Merleau-Ponty, emotion is another kind of embodied sensory awareness, akin to memory or proprioception,[52] and thus part of the apparatus of intentionality. Emotion, in other words, is not just an outcome of habits, actions, practices and the like, but a driving force for them. An implication of this view is that cognitive evolution can be a process of re-feeling emotions, of changes in the way emotion is experienced and expressed.

Emotion thus performs two roles for theorizing a causal mechanism of cognitive evolution. First, why a mechanism begins to operate – meaning how a particular case of cognitive evolution begins – is a function of the anxieties and affective perturbations experienced by human beings in a given situation. This carries a methodological implication: the start of a case study, at least as an account of cause and effect, is the point at which key actors involved feel dissatisfied enough to start doing things differently. It is an emotional threshold, beyond which actors take novel risks and expend greater creative efforts to find new avenues of action. Second, the time and place at which a mechanism ceases to operate, or at least a helpful endpoint in an

---

[50] A role that deviates from many more conventional assumptions of constructivist theories of international relations, which are ontologically ill-suited to accounting for emotion as a causal force (Ross 2006).
[51] For this reason, emotion is assigned a roll as causal trigger in Gross's (2009) pragmatist view of social mechanisms.
[52] Carmen 2008, 102.

account of its operation, is the point at which anxiety settles, and a situation of "adequacy" has been reached, where the risks and efforts of creative revision of habit appeal less than the *status quo*, and where the "lines of projection" of intentionality seem clear and unimpeded. This too carries the implication of an empirical investigation of what people perceive and feel, as a way to know when a process of change stabilizes.

Another micro-foundational insight offered by phenomenology concerns the distinction between "agentic" and "socio-structural" mechanisms, which Adler draws and which, arguably, track with long-standing ontological commitments within the field of IR to the differentiation of structure and agency.[53] For Adler, cognitive evolution is ontologically flat, meaning it does not propose a stratified world of layered and supervening structures. In his approach this distinction is a valuable device for clarifying and organizing the relationship between processes occurring at different scales of time or community involvement. Phenomenology can disclose the shape of the flat ontological space these two categories of mechanisms share, describing how all mechanisms of cognitive evolution proceed through organisms and their environments. If we understand intentionality, whether individual or collective, as embodied and motile, then we can also understand the intentional trajectories of large groups of people as an arrangement of physical conditions with effects upon the potentialities and contents of our perceptual fields.

In other words, if socio-structural mechanisms involve the movement of intentional organisms through the world, their impact upon practice resolves in the same basic encounters as those produced by agentic mechanisms. It is not that phenomenology *solves* the "problem" of structure and agency; rather, this problem is not a first-order ontological problem *for* phenomenology. Beginning with phenomenology makes it easier to see that the language of description and explanation can focus on individual agency or on larger-scale structural dynamics, but this is a matter of methodological convenience in mapping out what happens in the same kind of environment – much as the language of ecology and zoology both refer to the study of animals (albeit not exclusively, for the former).

[53] Wendt 1987; Wight 2006.

Ontological Security and the Phenomenology of Cognitive Evolution

As noted earlier, the phenomenology of cognitive evolution also bears on the problems, themes and theoretical commitments associated with IR research into ontological security. In particular, it offers a key link between ontological security research as it currently stands, and the practice turn. The concept of ontological security – meaning security of the self – originally derives from psychoanalytic accounts of self, with IR scholars[54] importing the concept over from psychiatry[55] and sociology,[56] but it has since expanded to include a range of emotion-management investigations.[57] Attempts to reformulate ontological security away from psychological and into practice-theoretical terms have proceeded largely by diminishing the role of emotion in an account of how actors pursue ontological security or respond to onto-logical insecurity.[58] Yet the phenomenology of cognitive evolution shows that this is not necessary; or, at least, it clarifies the connection between the psychical/affective and the practical or institutional.

As I have argued, ontological insecurity – the feelings of existential anxiety brought on by experiences of alienation from sources of self-stability – plays a key causal role in all mechanisms of cognitive evolu-tion. Ontological insecurity, when understood broadly, may encom-pass a wide range of experienced interruptions in the projection of one's body through the world – that is, in intentionality – and cognitive evolution, whether at the level of personal dispositions or socio-structural arrangements, is the process by which practice is revised until the anxiety of ontological insecurity wanes. This links the causal mechanisms of cognitive evolution to ontological security by way of the anxiety as a trigger for action. As a result, the theory of cognitive evolution has built *via media* between ontological and epistemological approaches that otherwise have a gulf between them – this being the first of Adler's two *vias medias* Reus-Smit refers to elsewhere in this volume (the second being normative). Because of their different com-mitments, scholars studying institutions, even from a constructivist standpoint, have little to say to scholars in the psychoanalytic or psychological tradition prevalent in most ontological security scholar-ship. The phenomenology of cognitive evolution locates a point at

---

[54] Kinnval 2004; Mitzen 2006; Steele 2008.   [55] Laing 1969.
[56] Giddens 1979.   [57] See, for example, Solomon 2014.   [58] Pratt 2017.

which these approaches meet – where the genesis of institutional change arises out of the impetus to resolve anxiety and maintain composure of the self.

Materiality and the Phenomenology of Cognitive Evolution

The final contribution of the phenomenology of cognitive evolution lies in how it speaks to debates in the field on materiality.[59] These debates actually range several distinct questions. One concerns the relationship between "social" and "material" reality, with one position holding that these are distinct things,[60] and another holding that the social is also material.[61] Another concerns the nature of power, which Guzzini explores in greater detail elsewhere in this volume; namely, whether something exists that can be called "material power" and whether it is distinct from other kinds of power. On the one hand, material power is a distinct concept in extensive use in the field, but on the other hand, it does not seem to coherently fit within the constellation of social meta-theories of power underlying more specific conceptions[62]. Finally, there is a debate on the role of cognitive and emotional factors on institutional outcomes – these things being physiological, and therefore material, but also manifestly influential in socially meaningful behavior. Arguments for foregrounding these factors range from psychology[63] to affect,[64] while skeptical positions may be found especially in either rationalist[65] or relational[66] theorizing – and for that matter in practice theory, where cognition is not defined in psycho-affective terms.

The phenomenology of cognitive evolution can resolve some of these debates. First and foremost, it clarifies that the social is thoroughly material, as Drieschova also points out in this volume, and that meaning arises out of bodily engagements between organism and environment. This does not imply crude biological determinism, but it does suggest that the distinction some scholars have drawn between a social world and a material one is ontologically incoherent. Phenomenology offers a well-developed critical alternative to the Cartesian dualism that under-lies the social/material dichotomy. It does so without closely binding

---

[59] Dittmer 2017; Drieschova 2017; Mac Ginty 2017.   [60] Wendt 1999.
[61] Deudney 2000; Acuto and Curtis 2014.   [62] Barnett and Duvall 2005.
[63] Stein 2002; McDermott 2004; Hopf 2010.
[64] Hall and Ross 2015; Hutchison 2016.   [65] Kahler 1998.   [66] Jackson 2004.

social formations to environmental constraints, however; rather, it projects the social into the environment by way of intentionality.

The second is that psychology is a legitimate part of social explanation, at least insofar as it considers the conditions of embodied perception and interaction, while models of action that leave it out are lacking. Yet there is also an implied limit to psychology here, as while the physiology of sensation matters, action nevertheless has a broader horizon of possibility than is captured by investigations of cognitive biases or behavioral tendencies.

Third and finally, phenomenology shows "material power" to be no different from any other kind of power, and in its simplest terms is a misleading Cartesian formulation. This goes some of the way toward acknowledging the roles of domination and coercion – roles which, as Guzzini argues elsewhere in this volume, are underplayed in Adler's book. However, an interest the *materiality* of power is especially significant to the phenomenology of cognitive evolution, because it foregrounds bodily responses to external impositions. This may be a helpful corrective for sociological accounts of power that ignore the ways some means of coercion acutely and overwhelmingly manipulate the senses, especially or primarily by inducing pain and terror.

Cognitive Evolution, Phenomenology, and Normative Theory

Can cognitive evolution offer a basis for normative political theorizing? For Adler, cognitive evolution implies a horizon of bounded progress, in which practices might evolve to become universally held as an empirical fact, constituting advancement without requiring an *a priori* definition of the good against which progress must be measured. He begins with a communitarian moral ontology, but advances the emergence and growth of "common humanity" as an idea with universalizable potential, as an empathetic acknowledgment (open-ended in form, *contra* recognition as a more determined good) that can proliferate across and throughout distinct communities of practice.

Phenomenology adds to this project in two ways. First, it offers depth to the establishment of a humanist "middle ground" between descriptive and normative theory, which Reus-Smit identifies elsewhere in this volume as a major, though perhaps implied, project underpinning Adler's *oeuvre*. While Reus-Smit is skeptical that a theory of practice (and of its cognitive evolution) can underwrite cosmopolitan values,

the phenomenology of cognitive evolution can ground the moral character of social orders in bodily and sensory space, where freedom and
constraint, pleasure and pain and satisfaction and frustration all dwell.
These experiential states are ethically compelling terms for normative
theory, and clarify the relationship between cognitive evolution and the
attainment of the good – at least on some conceptions.[67] In particular, it is
a space in which empathy and acknowledgment gain perceptual and
affective qualities, and resolve as more basic emotions. These are definable
and help operationalize Adler's conception of bounded progress. They
offer a *fourth* route to a middle ground, distinct from three approaches
Reus-Smit suggests in this volume – not order, not right and not the
transcendental conditions of practice, but a language of considerable
normative and descriptive flexibility. Phenomenology lets us talk about
people and the world in ways that are acutely and vividly of ethical
meaning, invoking common experiences that admit of empathy and
demand engagement in ways that languages of rights and orders do not.

Second, phenomenology may present a substantive *demonstration* of
common humanity, by emphasizing the dynamics of experience shared
by all, and by rendering human sensation, emotion and perception as
a common condition of possibility for more culturally specific practices. One of the more ethically meaningful dimensions of cognitive
evolution is the shared experience of learning as part of the process of
effective action and human flourishing. For Dewey, it is clear that
cognitive evolution will be part of any process of progress, however
bounded or humble in conception. Through the phenomenology of
cognitive evolution, we arrive at universal or cosmopolitan definitions
of confronting resistance in the world, of experimentation, and of
collective inquiry in practice. By meeting others with the statement
"we all struggle," we may cross different communities of practice
with the basic material of acknowledgment – to use Adler's language –
needed to develop broader or deeper shared political trajectories.

This implication of the phenomenology of cognitive evolution sheds
light on sympathetic projects in political and ethical theory. Simone Weil
argued for a common humanity based on the recognition even strangers
have of one-another's suffering, using the example of our apparent

---

[67] It may also be suggestive of some meta-ethical theories over others; the
phenomenological basis for cognitive evolution I outline here may make it
harder to do deontological ethics than one of virtue or consequence. That
discussion, however, lies outside the remit of this chapter.

obligation to render basic aid should we come across a person in abject distress and should we possess the ready means to assist.[68] This primitive ethical obligation, which in Weil's view precedes determinations of membership within particular moral communities, has been taken up by Linklater as a potential basis for a sociology of global morals.[69] Taking Weil's argument to refer to "certain emotional and expressive capacities which revolve around mutually intelligible concerns about the vulnerabilities of the body,"[70] and reading it alongside Frankfurt School interests in giving voice to those suffering, Linklater uncovers the possibility of a learned, corporeal solidarity across communities.[71] Emmanuel Levinas is another sympathetic thinker, whose phenomenology begins not with the self but with the other, meaning that experience begins not with being but with duty.[72] As with Weil, the basis for ethics here lies in recognizing human vulnerability – what Levinas sees as the human face's implicit injunction of "Thou shall not kill"[73] – and feeling obliged to care at a primitive, affective level. Applied to cognitive evolution, it suggests the possibility of communities of practice capable of recognizing and navigating the "*mauvaise conscience*" that Levinas proposes, with some communities established to resist it, override it, so as to commit violence, and others to institutionalize it.

I do not claim that the addition of phenomenology resolves the problem of how to ground even a modest conception of progress, nor any kind of cosmopolitanism, but I think it clarifies how a theory of cognitive evolution might go some of the way toward doing so. I have thus tried to flesh out (so to speak) Adler's normative project, which I consider to be one of the most important and also one of the most elusive of the tasks he takes up in his book.

Conclusion: Phenomenology in an Age of "Post-Truth"

In this chapter I have discussed what phenomenology can offer to the project of theorizing cognitive evolution in IR. I began by surveying the positions of two pragmatist phenomenologists, Dewey and

---

[68] Weil 1952.   [69] Linklater 2007.   [70] Ibid., 192.
[71] Linklater (2011) also cites Norbert Elias on the development of increased public aversion to violence, and would later develop this empirical analysis of a cosmopolitan emotional instinct in his history of the cosmopolitan harm principle.
[72] Levinas 1989; see also Bergo 2017.   [73] Levinas 1985, 89.

Merleau-Ponty, and connected their arguments to those Adler makes in his seminal book. Both philosophers approach emotion and sensation in ways that seem to account for the start and end – the trigger and *telos* – of the causal mechanisms of cognitive evolution. Beyond this, I have also argued that phenomenology accounts for the micro-foundations and materiality of cognitive evolution, while also connecting conceptions of it to ongoing IR research on ontological security. Finally, I have argued that phenomenology provides an important link between the descriptive and normative aspects of theorizing cognitive evolution, making it possible to talk about common humanity through the shared and universal aspects of experience. While there remains much to be said about phenomenology, both on this subject and in IR more generally, I hope to have established the meta-theoretical and normative value of including it within the project of theorizing cognitive evolution.

Yet I thus want to offer some more concrete concluding remarks about what this means for the practical task of going out and making sense of international politics. There are some clear implications to introducing phenomenology to the theory of cognitive evolution: greater attention to sensation, emotion and corporeality through psychological, psychoanalytic and affect-oriented approaches to conceptualizing, measuring and explaining outcomes of interest.[74]

One concrete example of this is the recent epistemic fracturing of political discourse into a state of "post-truth" – the epistemological condition Crawford, in this volume, identifies with growing normlessness and tribalistic anti-immigrant xenophobia. "Post-truth" was *Oxford Dictionary*'s 2016 "word of the year,"[75] and arises out of high-profile abandonment of facts by the Trump (2016) presidential and pro-Brexit campaigns, which together dominated news cycles in the United States and the United Kingdom[76]. It refers to a moment where politicians and some media outlets claiming demonstrable falsehoods that nonetheless penetrate public opinion (particularly in communities on the political far-right) because of their emotional resonance rather

---

[74] This is perhaps best exemplified in Elias's (1994) melding of psychogenetic and sociogenetic forces in accounting for the role of disgust and bodily regulation in *The Civilizing Process*.

[75] Their definition for post-truth is "relating to or denoting circumstances in which objective facts are less influential in shaping public opinion than appeals to emotion and personal belief."

[76] McIntyre 2018, 2.

than their evidentiary soundness. Yet while lying or "bullshitting"[77] is not a new phenomenon in political rhetoric, there is something deeper at work here: partisans for reactionary conservatism and nationalism seem not just unconcerned when their claims are undermined by evidence; they genuinely seem to believe their claims even when starkly disconfirming evidence is right in front of them.[78]

Post-truth is the outcome of several mechanisms of cognitive evolution. It arises from competition between communities of practice, but it also appears to be the *genesis* of a new community of practice as well, since it is not just a function of the rise of new populist insurgents but of the fracturing of a previously more unified discursive sphere. In addition to these "socio-cultural" mechanisms, there is at least one "agentic" process at work as well – evolution in socially generated reflection and judgment.[79] Post-truth is thus the cognitive evolution of a community of inquiry that increasingly has learned to find facts and evaluate claims in ways at odds with normal journalism and scholarship. Yet while these mechanisms offer a sociological account of how it is that political knowledge and discourse have become so fractured, they do not account for a critical link between institutional change and the perceptual, affective forces that could explain post-truth not just as a change in discourse, but a change in embodied cognition. A definitive quality of post-truth is that epistemic confidence is determined not by methodological procedures of investigation but by immediate emotional and political resonance.

While commentators lament post-truth as the demise of a practical correspondence view of facts, as statements that either do or do not describe the real state of things, its affective dimensions imply something more than lies or "bullshit" is behind the phenomenon. While some American pundits have suggested that "facts have a Well-Known liberal bias,"[80] this is only partially correct; rather it is that liberal

---

[77] On bullshit, defined as instrumental speech unconcerned with the truth rather than designed to deliberately dissemble, see Frankfurt's eponymous book (2005) on the subject.

[78] A recent monograph by McIntyre (2018) reviews and discusses post-truth, including some of the cognitive biases and media history responsible for this outcome. For the sake of brevity, and also in order to focus on deeper evolutionary processes, I will not reproduce this here.

[79] All of these mechanisms are drawn from Adler (2019).

[80] See, for example, Paul Krugman's December 8, 2017 editorial in *The New York Times*, available online at www.nytimes.com/2017/12/08/opinion/facts-have-a-well-known-liberal-bias.html. Accessed October 10, 2018.

politics are advantaged by a way of evaluating the world embedded in many institutions of governance and, indeed, in scientific research. Rather, truth is determined based on what *is experienced* as most apt, consistent and agency-enhancing. Through a focus on feelings of anxiety and satisfaction, and on perceptions and projections of bodily engagement, phenomenology sheds light on what forms of agency are at play. The structural bases for post-truth are easier to diagnose than the ways agency propel (or resist) it, and the remedy is a theory of cognitive evolution that includes the ways truth is experienced – and how that experience does or does not differ from the experience of expedient or empowering fantasy. This sort of understanding of post-truth, or simply of epistemic judgment more generally, emerges most clearly through a phenomenology of cognitive evolution.

References

Acuto, Michele and Simon Curtis. 2014. Assemblage Thinking and International Relations. In *Reassembling International Theory*, edited by Michele Acuto and Simon Curtis, 1–15. London: Palgrave Macmillan.

Adler, Emanuel. 2019. *World Ordering: A Social Theory of Cognitive Evolution*. Cambridge: Cambridge University Press.

Adler, Emanuel and Vincent Pouliot. 2011. International Practices. *International Theory* 3(1): 1–36.

Åhäll, Linda. 2019. Feeling Everyday IR: Embodied, Affective, Militarising Movement as Choreography of War. *Cooperation and Conflict* 54(2): 149–66.

Åhäll, Linda and Thomas Gregory. 2015. *Emotions, Politics, and War*. New York: Routledge.

Alexander, Thomas M. 1987. *John Dewey's Theory of Art, Experience, and Nature*. Albany: State University of New York Press.

Barnett, Michael and Raymond Duvall. 2005. Power in International Politics. *International Organization* 59(Winter): 39–75.

Bennett, Andrew. 2013. The Mother of All Isms: Causal Mechanisms and Structured Pluralism in International Relations Theory. *European Journal of International Relations* 19(3): 459–81.

Bergo, Bettina. 2017. Emmanuel Levinas. In *The Stanford Encyclopedia of Philosophy* (Fall 2017 ed.), edited by Edward N. Zalta. https://plato.stanford.edu/archives/fall2017/entries/levinas/.

Büger, Christian and Frank Gadinger. 2014. *International Practice Theory: New Perspectives*. London: Palgrave.

Carman, Taylor. 2008. *Merleau-Ponty*. New York: Routledge.

Deudney, Daniel. 2000. Geopolitics as Theory: Historical Security Materialism. *European Journal of International Relations* 6(1): 77–107.

Dewey, John. 1916. *Democracy and Education*. New York: Macmillan.

Dewey, John. 1929. *Experience and Nature*. London: George Allen & Unwin.

Dewey, John. 1939a. *Art as Experience*. New York: Capricorn Books.

Dewey, John. 1939b. *Logic: The Theory of Inquiry*. New York: Henry Holt.

Dewey, John. 1987. *The Later Works, 1925–1953 (Volume 10: 1934)*, edited by Jo Ann Boydston. Carbondale: Southern Illinois University Press.

Dittmer, Jason. 2017. *Diplomatic Material: Affect, Assemblage, and Foreign Policy*. Durham: Duke University Press.

Drieschova, Alena. 2017. Pierce's Semeiotics: A Methodology for Bridging the Material-Ideational Divide in IR Scholarship. *International Theory* 9 (1): 33–66.

Drieschova, Alena. 2019. A Role for Phenomenology in IR Scholarship. In *Science, Technology, and Art in International Relations*, edited by J. P. Singh, Madeline Carr and Renée Marlin-Bennett. New York: Routledge.

Elias, Norbert. 1994. *The Civilizing Process: Sociogenetic and Psychogenetic Investigations*. Oxford: Blackwell.

Evers, Miles M. 2020. Just the Facts: Why Norms Remain Relevant in an Age of Practice. *International Theory* 12(2): 220–30.

Frankfurt, Harry G. 2005. *On Bullshit*. Princeton: Princeton University Press.

Giddens, Anthony. 1979. *Central Problems in Social Theory: Action, Structure, and Contradiction in Social Analysis*. Berkeley: University of California Press.

Gross, Neil. 2009. A Pragmatist Theory of Social Mechanisms. *American Sociological Review* 74(3): 358–79.

Guzzini, Stefano. 2011. Securitization as a Causal Mechanism. *Security Dialogue* 42(4–5): 329–41.Hall, Todd H. and Andrew G. Ross. 2015. Affective Politics after 9/11. *International Organization* 69(4): 847–79.

Harnisch, Sebastian. 2012. Conceptualizing in the Minefield: Role Theory and Foreign Policy Learning. *Foreign Policy Analysis* 8(1): 47–69.

Higate, Paul. 2012. The Private Militarized and Security Contractor as Geocorporeal Actor. *International Political Sociology* 6(4): 355–72.

Hildebrand, David L. 2008. *Dewey: A Beginner's Guide*. Oxford: Oneworld.

Hopf, Ted. 2010. The Logic of Habit in International Relations. *European Journal of International Relations* 16(4): 539–61.

Hutchison, Emma. 2016. *Affective Communities in World Politics.* Cambridge: Cambridge University Press.

Hutchison, Emma and Roland Bleiker. 2014. Theorizing Emotions in World Politics. *International Theory* 6(3): 491–514.

Jackson, Patrick Thaddeus. 2004. Hegel's House, or "People Are States Too." *Review of International Studies* 30(2): 281–87.

Kahler, Miles. 1998. Rationality in International Relations. *International Organization* 52(4): 919–41.

Kestenbaum, Victor. 1977. *The Phenomenological Sense of John Dewey: Habit and Meaning.* Atlantic Highlands: Humanities Press.

Kinnvall, Catarina. 2004. Globalization and Religious Nationalism: Self, Identity, and the Search for Ontological Security. *Political Psychology* 25 (5): 741–67. https://doi.org/10.1111/j.1467-9221.2004.00396.x

Knopf, Jeffry W. 2003. The Importance of International Learning. *Review of International Studies* 29(2): 185–207.

Koschut, Simon. 2017. Discourse and Emotions in International Relations. *International Studies Review* 19(3): 481–87.

Kurki, Milja. 2008. *Causation in International Relations: Reclaiming Causal Analysis.* Cambridge: Cambridge University Press.

Laing, Ronald D. 1969. *The Divided Self.* London: Penguin.

Levinas, Emmanuel. 1985. *Ethics and Infinity.* Pittsburgh: Duquesne University Press.

Levinas, Emmanuel. 1989. Ethics as First Philosophy. In *The Levinas Reader,* edited by Seán Hand. Oxford: Blackwell.

Levy, Jack S. 1994. Learning and Foreign Policy: Sweeping a Conceptual Minefield. *International Organization* 48(2): 279–312.

Levy, Jack S. 1997. Prospect Theory, Rational Choice, and International Relations. *International Studies Quarterly* 41(1): 87–112.

Linklater, Andrew. 2007. Towards a Sociology of Global Morals with Emancipatory Intent. *Review of International Studies* 33(2): 135–50.

Linklater, Andrew. 2011. *The Problem of Harm in International Politics.* Cambridge: Cambridge University Press.

Mac Ginty, Roger. 2017. A Material Turn in International Relations: The 4x4, Intervention and Resistance. *Review of International Studies* 43(5): 855–74.

McDermott, Rose. 2004. *Political Psychology in International Relations.* Ann Arbor: University of Michigan Press.

McDermott, Rose. 2014. The Body Doesn't Lie: A Somatic Approach to the Study of Emotions in World Politics. *International Theory* 6(3): 557–62.

McIntyre, Lee. 2018. *Post-Truth.* Cambridge, MA: MIT Press.

Mercer, Jonathan. 2006. Human Nature and the First Image: Emotion in International Politics. *Journal of International Relations and Development* 9(3): 288–303.

Merleau-Ponty, Maurice. 2002. *Phenomenology of Perception*. New York: Routledge.

Mitzen, Jennifer. 2006. Ontological Security in World Politics: State Identity and the Security Dilemma. *European Journal of International Relations* 12 (3): 341–70.

Pratt, Simon Frankel. 2016. Pragmatism as Ontology, Not (Just) Epistemology: Exploring the Full Horizon of Pragmatism as an Approach to IR Theory. *International Studies Review* 18(3): 508–27. htt ps://doi.org/10.1093/isr/viv003.

Pratt, Simon Frankel. 2017. A Relational View of Ontological Security in International Relations. *International Studies Quarterly* 61(1): 78–85.

Pratt, Simon Frankel. 2020. From Norms to Normative Configurations: A Pragmatist and Relational Approach to Theorizing Normativity in IR. *International Theory* 12(1): 59–82.

Reus-Smit, Christian. 2014. Emotions and the Social. *International Theory* 6 (3): 568–74.

Ross, Andrew A. G. 2006. Coming in from the Cold: Constructivism and Emotions. *European Journal of International Relations* 12(2): 197–222.

Ross, Andrew A. G. 2019. Emotion and Experience in International Relations. In *Parsing the Passions: Methodology and the Study of Emotion in World Politics*, edited by Eric Van Rythoven and Mira Sucharov. New York: Routledge.

Schmidt, Sebastian. 2014. Foreign Military Presence and the Changing Practice of Sovereignty: A Pragmatist Explanation of Norm Change. *American Political Science Review* 108(4): 817–29.

Searle, John R. 1995. *The Construction of Social Reality*. New York: The Free Press.

Sil, Rudra and Peter J. Katzenstein. 2010. Analytic Eclecticism in the Study of World Politics: Reconfiguring Problems and Mechanisms across Research Traditions. *Perspectives on Politics* 8(2): 411–31.

Solomon, Ty. 2014. The Affective Underpinnings of Soft Power. *European Journal of International Relations* 20(3): 720–41.

Standal, Øyvind F. and Kenneth Aggerholm. 2016. Habits, Skills and Embodied Experiences: A Contribution to Philosophy of Physical Education. *Sport, Ethics and Philosophy* 10(3): 269–82.

Steele, Brent J. 2008. *Ontological Security in International Relations: Self-Identity and the IR State*. London: Routledge.

Stein, Janice Gross. 1994. Political Learning by Doing: Gorbachev as Uncommitted Thinker and Motivated Learner. *International Organization* 48(2): 155–83.

Stein, Janice Gross. 2002. Psychological Explanations of International Conflict. In *Handbook of International Relations*, edited by Walter Carlsnaes, Thomas Risse and Beth A. Simmons, 293–308. London: Sage.

Sucharov, Mira and Eric Van Rythoven. 2019. *Methodology and Emotion in International Relations: Parsing the Passions*. New York: Routledge.

Waltz, Kenneth N. 1979. *Theory of International Politics*. New York: McGraw-Hill.

Weil, Simone. 1952. *The Need for Roots: Prelude to a Declaration of Duties Towards Mankind*. London: Routledge and Kegan Paul.

Weinert, Mathew S. 2018. Reading World Society Phenomenologically: An Illustration Drawing upon the Cultural Heritage of Humankind. *International Politics* 55(1): 26–40.

Wendt, Alexander. 1987. The Agent-Structure Problem in International Relations Theory. *International Organization* 41(3): 335–70.

Wendt, Alexander. 1999. *Social Theory of International Politics*. Cambridge: Cambridge University Press.

Wight, Colin. 2006. *Agents, Structures, and International Relations: Politics as Ontology*. Cambridge: Cambridge University Press.

5 Narratives in Cognitive Evolution

The Importance of Discourse in Meaning-Making Processes

MAÏKA SONDARJEE

We live by stories, we also live in them. One way or another we are living the stories planted in us early or along the way, or we are also living the stories we planted – knowingly or unknowingly – in ourselves. We live stories that either give our lives meaning or negate it with meaninglessness. If we change the stories we live by, quite possibly we change our lives.[1]

Since his doctoral dissertation under the supervision of Ernst Haas, Emanuel Adler has always had an interest in learning processes.[2] Coupled with a concern with progress,[3] communitarian ontology[4] and a proficiency in sociological conceptions of practices,[5] his newest theoretical endeavor is a processual theory of cognitive evolution. As the introduction of this volume made clear, cognitive evolution is a collective-learning process happening within and between communities of practice, through action in their surrounding environment. Analytically, Adler seeks to explain how individuals, knowledge and practices enacted by communities are intertwined in a process of constant evolution.

Rather than finding fissures in the wall of this theoretical house, this chapter has two interrelated purposes. First, it explores one of the vistas for research suggested by the editors of this volume in the introduction, concerning communication and discourse. It recommends the inclusion of the concept of narratives to Adler's framework, as a meaning-making process of cognitive evolution. The overall argument is that adding narratives to cognitive evolution has the potential to strengthen Adler's processual ontology. To explain the concept of narrative, I briefly present the case of the evolution of the World Bank practices and narrative in the 1990s, from an expertocracy stance toward a more

[1] Nigerian storyteller Ben Okri, quoted in T. King 2003, 153.
[2] Adler 1991, 1992.   [3] Adler and Crawford 1991.
[4] Adler and Barnett 1998; Adler 2005, 2008.   [5] Adler and Pouliot 2011.

inclusive institution. Second, this chapter explains that by adding narratives to the cognitive evolution story, its "becoming" ontology could become the most important contribution of Adler's latest work for the field of International Relations (IR). It presents this ontology as a radical alternative to both substantialist and relational approaches. This chapter thus aims to show that cognitive evolution and narratives are complementary because they both rest on a becoming ontology, giving to the latter the potential to strengthen Adler's ontology in empirical research. Furthermore, adding discourse to a cognitive evolution framework has the potential to theorize better how *meaningful* knowledge evolves.

Cognitive Evolution and Discourse

In a similar vein to Alena Drieschova's chapter on materiality in this volume, this chapter points at Adler's insufficient acknowledgment of a crucial part of social reality. The importance of discourse and discursive processes in collective learning is greatly under-theorized in Adler's magnum opus. While Adler makes clear that he wants to depart from post-structuralist or postmodern approaches, discourse made the cut in Adler and Pouliot's definition of international practices. Practices are "socially meaningful patterned actions that in being performed more or less competently, simultaneously embody, act out, and possibly reify background knowledge and discourse in and on the material world."[6] In most practice-oriented approaches, discourse can be seen either as a part of the communal resources actors draw on when enacting a practice, such as routines, sensibilities or background knowledge; or discourse can be seen as a type of practice, that is, discursive practices.

Putting discourse in a sidenote is revealing of an assumption most scholars have in IR: what people do is more important than what they say. Of course, what people do and what they learn is essential. However, what they say about what they do and learn, and what they say caused them to act is also important.[7] Echoing researchers looking at discourse as generative rather than as representation, I assume that what people say is useful to understand intentionality, as well as past and future trajectories of actions.[8] As per Charles Taylor

---

[6] Ibid., 6.   [7] Bruner 1986, 16.   [8] Milliken 1999; Hansen 2006; Epstein 2011.

seminal argument, we are "self-interpreting animals" as much as we are actants in the world, and this self-interpretation does not "cause" our actions but makes us experience the world in a certain way, therefore guiding our actions.[9]

This chapter is not meant to present all the ways in which discourse could have been taken into account in cognitive evolution, or all the discursive mechanisms that could explain cognitive evolution, nor is it to present an extensive literature review of discursive theories in IR.[10] Doing a review work would not be useful for the purpose of this book. Instead, I seek to suggest a way to integrate one form of discourse (narratives) to cognitive evolution as a way to complement Adler's becoming ontology.

Cognitive evolution involves "an active process of redefinition or reinterpretation of reality – what people consider real, possible and desirable – on the basis of new causal and normative knowledge."[11] How do narratives fit in this definition? On the one hand, in *World Ordering: A Social Theory of Cognitive Evolution*, Adler focuses much more on the evolution of "meaningful" knowledge rather than simply "knowledge." Having recognized that knowledge does not come in a substantial form, as a thing to be grasped, there is a need to theorize how actors interpret and give meaning to new causal and normative knowledge. Their collective narrative helps to understand how they interpret meaning. On the other hand, how one acquires new knowledge and what one looks at in the world depend on how he or she interprets it and talks about it. Collective actors do not act only following experience and new knowledge, but also following how they interpret this experience and how they attribute meaning to it discursively.[12]

It is important to note that discourse, in our case narrative, is not only a type of practice. Discourse is necessary for *all* practices to be meaningful. As Iver B. Neumann argues, practices are discursive not only because they involve speech acts, but also because practices "cannot be thought 'outside of' discourse."[13] His study of diplomacy, dating from almost two decades ago, was not only a plea to bring back practices in the linguistic turn, but also a call on scholars to

---

[9] Taylor 1985.
[10] For that sort of work, refer to Milliken 1999; Schmidt 2010; Epstein 2011; or Martel 2017.
[11] Adler and Barnett 1998, 43.   [12] Patterson and Monroe 1998, 330.
[13] Neumann 2002, 628.

combine meaning with the study of practices. Neumann's suggestion was that this combination should be done in a dynamic interplay integrated in the concept of culture. In this chapter, I am making a similar plea for the cognitive evolution nascent agenda: scholars need to conceptualize the interplay between discourse and practice to understand the evolution of what makes sense for actors to do and to learn in a given situation. I suggest that this can be done through the concept of ontological narrative, precisely because it is a discursive form that shows becoming processes.

Narratives

Philosophers of History first conceptualized narratives as forms of representations: representational templates used to order the chaos of lived experience.[14] Historians and scholars of literary art rather reduced narratives to their simplest expression, as stories and their telling, or a "manner of speaking about events, whether real or imaginary."[15] Narrative psychologists believe that people view themselves and others in terms of narratives, as in stories of success and failure, development and decline,[16] and more recently, rationalist political scientists represented narratives as a discursive "thing" that individuals and organizations can use strategically.[17] At the methodological level, narrative inquiry assumes that people lead storied lives that they communicate in the narrative form, and researchers' task is to describe those lives and write narratives of experience.[18]

Most importantly, in IR, poststructuralist and postmodern scholars have studied a variety of historical representation as regimes of truth. As Kevin C. Dunn explains: "Societies discursively produce, circulate, and consume representations of (events), constructing what are often called 'regimes of truth' or 'knowledge'."[19] Dunn and others have forcefully argued that concepts and actors in IR, such as the state, anarchy or the Orient, are not essentialized entity but ongoing processes created through discursive structures.[20] However, most of these scholars avoid assessing the evolution, or changing character of representations in time. They focus on bracketed meaning-making

---

[14] Mink 1966.   [15] White 1980.   [16] Sugiman et al. 2008.
[17] Roselle, Miskimmon and O'Loughlin 2014.   [18] Clandinin 2006.
[19] Dunn 2008.   [20] Doty 1993.

processes, or the meaning of a given historical representations in time but not the evolution of a given situation or concept in a storyline.[21] Therefore, only narratives, as a specific form of discourse, have the potential to illustrate a becoming ontology. Furthermore, while the postmodern standpoint often leads to the argument that observers can never definitely know reality, ontological narratives could be studied pragmatically as "existing" meaning-making device used by actors in the international sphere.

This chapter shifts from these poststructural, representational, rationalist and methodological views already existing in IR scholarship toward an ontological understanding of social narratives. As will be explained in the second section of this chapter, exploring narratives this way has the potential to strengthen Adler's processual ontology. I define ontological narratives as hermeneutic and symbolically negotiated understandings of past, present or future action. Ontological narratives tell stories of becoming in which people (through individual narratives) and organizations (through social narratives) make sense of events by assembling and integrating them in stories that subsequently become part of their identity. In other words, experience is constituted and understood through narratives, and ontological narratives are used to define who we are, which is at the basis of knowing what to do.[22] Looking at refugees' actions would not be enough to understand why and how they act. How they define their journey, how they reconstruct their history and where their expectations are leading them are crucial questions to understand their "practice" as refugees.[23]

A narrative is a form of discourse that is not primarily, and not even necessarily, verbalized. Narratives, even collective ones, play out in people's mind and actions and can often only be reconstructed analytically through artificial means (ethnography, post hoc interviews or archive analysis). In some cases, "scholars study stories that are not necessarily conveyed in a specific text [or through public discourse], but rather encapsulate people's perceptions of stories assessed through [post hoc] questions."[24] To reconstruct a collective actor's narrative, one has to listen to the public speeches of its leaders, what individual actors have to say about it, what is written in its reports, memos and proceedings, but also what justifications, reasons and expectations

[21] Dunn 2003.   [22] Somers and Gibson 2017, 38.
[23] See Crawford, this volume.   [24] Shenhav 2015, 22.

individuals in that organization give for their actions at a given point in time.

Because narratives provide "a moral compass" to make practical judgments, it is often more tacit than verbalized.[25] It is difficult to distinguish between narrative mode of thought and narrative discourse, and trying to do so would even be a vain enterprise.[26] The goal of the researcher is thus to reconstruct a discourse that has not necessarily been previously verbalized. Bueger, for example, reconstructed the narrative of Somali pirates through publicly available interviews, and found a discourse that was not verbalized apart from these interviews. He was able to recognize that pirates organized themselves around a "grand narrative" of piracy as a legitimate practice of protecting borders against foreign intruders, rather than defining themselves as thieves and criminals.[27] This is important not to understand what people have "in their minds" but to understand the becoming process of a collective actor, that is, the evolution of what an actor considers legitimate to do. Beverly Crawford explains in her chapter in this volume that narratives can also be created and supported by communication on social media.

Precisely, Frank Fischer refers to narratives as "cognitive scheme" that imposes a "coherent interpretation of the whirl of events and actions that surrounds us."[28] People, he says, are guided by the narrative they have constructed in giving meaning to the evolving social reality they are embedded in. Narratives help individuals and collective actors to make sense of the world and constitute their social identities in a process of becoming. In the piracy case, while it would not be misleading *per se* to analyze pirates as thieves, it would be incomplete because it is not the reasons they themselves have for doing what they do at a certain point in time.

Practices and Narratives

How are practices and narratives related? The relationship between practices and narratives is a constitutive one in which neither has ontological nor temporal precedence. Neither is prior, because a community's practice would be illegible without an associated

---

[25] Bueger 2013, 1817.   [26] Bruner 1991, 5.   [27] Bueger 2013.
[28] Fischer 2003, 163; see also Shenhav 2015, 11.

discourse. As meaning-making process, narratives do not "cause" a given practice, but they give reasons for it.[29] Without a coherent narrative, a practice falls in the empty category of routinized act. But at the same time, while understanding "makes practice possible," practices also largely carry the understanding.[30] So without practices, a discourse is empty words.

Some scholars see narratives in an instrumental manner, as something created *a priori* and promoted *by* a practice[31]. Ontological narratives, on the other hand, are normative template for making practical judgments or negotiating moral dilemmas that are created while a practice is performed. They help individuals or organizations adjust to new situations or to explain past deeds. They are visible during the enactment of a practice; they are built, sustained and modified in the course of action, not only in language. Therefore, processes of understanding or interpretation of reality follow a "tightly interwoven nexus of doings and sayings in which neither the doings nor the sayings have priority."[32] A narrative is not only how people reconstruct their process of becoming – their past, present and expectations about the future – but also how they act according to this process.

Narrative and practice are co-constituted in three main ways. First, formulating narratives about one's practices amounts to what Schatzki calls giving the world intelligibility, that is, how the world makes sense and what actions make sense to perform in a given situation.[33] At the heart of all practice theories, he argues, is the idea that practices are the site where understanding is structured and intelligibility articulated. Giving the world intelligibility in organizing it in stories about how we become ourselves is at the basis of how we act. An organization's ontological narrative gives its actions intelligibility, that is, it specifies what makes sense to do in XYZ situation. Narratives therefore do not create practices or knowledge in a causal fashion; they dynamically enable a practice to unfold as it does. "Although people are always able and prepared to do a variety of things, at a given moment they invariably carry out those actions that are signified to them as the ones to perform."[34] On the one hand, practices of non-proliferation are what they are because of what states do, but also because of what states say

---

[29] Bruner 1991, 7.   [30] Taylor 2004.
[31] Roselle, Miskimmon and O'Loughlin 2014.   [32] Schatzki 1996, 112.
[33] Ibid., 111.   [34] Ibid., 118.

and believe about the effectiveness of performing non-proliferation. On the other hand, if states were only talking about non-proliferation but not acting conformingly *at all*, discourse would not cause non-proliferation by itself. The usefulness of narratives in understanding the action's intelligibility for an organization is to point at *the reasons* rather than the *causes* for a practice.

Second, the evolution of a narrative does not cause a given repertoire of practices in the traditional sense because practices are often already in motion when discourse shifts at higher levels in the organization. A shift in narrative participates in the acceleration, multiplication, scaling up and institutionalization of existing practices. An evolving narrative opens up spaces of possibilities for new practices and new knowledge to emerge and for existing practices to gain traction inside an organization. It legitimizes and gives tools to advocates of new practices, and gives everyone a variation in the world intelligibility. It signals to sub-communities inside an organization that it is okay to go in this or that direction, and can even be associated to new grants, tools, power or a rise in the hierarchy of the organization for those who adopt certain practices.

For example, the shift in how the World Bank talks about itself as a more open institution, its mission and its practices in the 1990s corroborated already existing, even if sometimes marginal, tendencies toward local appropriation and inclusion of local actors. In other words, the shift in discourse in the 1990s legitimized initiatives and new practices already in motion and empowered those who were initiating those practices. Therefore, an organization's discursive shift does not cause but has a "signaling effect" to internal staff and to external audiences. It has the power to legitimize patterns already existing, or reinforce an ethos in place in some sub-communities.

Third, changes in practices can make a new discourse more coherent, acceptable and resilient, thus reinforcing the change in narrative. A leader or an organization's managing team will be unsuccessful in changing a narrative if practices do not follow. If marginal practices become more frequent, they will strengthen an organization's narrative. A narrative is thus dependent on action to become more legitimate and be recognized as an institution's ontological narrative. The relationship between narratives and practices is thus a co-constitutive and self-reinforcing one. Additionally to giving action intelligibility (specification of what makes sense to do), evolution in practices and narratives reinforce and enable each other to be sustained in time, become more broadly accepted and get institutionalized.

The World Bank's Narrative

The case of the World Bank since the 1980s is a case where the evolution in narrative was essential for the multiplication of practices, and empowered staff to redefine how they made sense of the world and how to act in a range of situations. In the 1990s and the 2000s, the narrative of the Bank evolved from defining itself as an outside expert institution toward picturing the inclusion of local actors as crucial to development practices. That is, the Bank management and employees started to talk about how open the organization is and should be to external voices from borrowing governments, NGOs, citizens and other stakeholders. The Bank's narrative about the necessity to be more open and to be a listening institution evolved concurrently to practices of participation in various quarters.[35]

The Bank's discourse about itself in the 1980s was that the "external expert stance" was a deeply embedded part of their understanding of how to produce results. Yet, in some teams, staff members were already starting to operate under a participatory mindset, either with participatory rural appraisal,[36] bottom-up planning[37] or including disadvantaged groups in specific social projects.[38] The accepted practice of US-trained economists was to elaborate structural adjustment plans in Washington, D.C., to help governments who, they would say, did not have the required expertise. Their narrative in relation to that practice was that "the project sponsors and designers [need to] place themselves outside the local system they are investigating and about which they are making decisions."[39] Most economists at the Bank believed that the best way to trigger development was to help countries with a deeply needed expertise. A senior Bank economist recalls that the hegemonic discourse was "we tell them what to do, we are right and they are wrong, and they don't know anything."[40]

---

[35] This is not a statement on the successfulness or the meaningfulness of these practices. But practices since the 1980s top-down Washington Consensus evolved and there were multiple attempts to include local governments, citizens and NGOs, albeit unsuccessful or less-than-meaningful ones.

[36] Chambers 1994. [37] Cernea 1992.

[38] Operations Policy Department 1994. [39] World Bank 1996b.

[40] Interview 20, July 17, 2017.

In the 1990s, the narrative started to shift toward the Bank saying that it needed to be more open, and not repeat mistakes of the past such as applying top-down, one-size-fits-all policies. In his first address to the Board of Governors at the Annual Meetings of the Bank and the IMF in 1995, the recently appointed Bank President James Wolfensohn stated that the Bank must be ready to listen to criticisms and to "learn from others," and spoke of a need to "go beyond arrogance in the development business."[41] In a speech to senior staff one year after he took office, he declared the advent of "a new atmosphere of change": "We are open. We are flexible. We want to listen."[42] These were unprecedented shifts in discourse at the management level. From attributing the success of projects on the quality of the Bank's staff or its capacity to cope with crises in the 1980s, Bank managers and staff started to attribute success to projects that have the governments and/or civil society "on board": "[Projects success] depend on the context of ownership by the country. There are some really good ones with lots and lots of ownership that have helped countries absorb and used billions of dollars."[43] This concept of ownership became much closer to inclusion and consultation than empowerment throughout the 2000s, but the shift is still considered by most Bank staff members as major in the history of the organization. In sum, the narrative of the Bank as told by official discourse and employees went from an "old-fashioned thinking"[44] or "traditional economic perspective"[45] toward more openness, inclusiveness, and "client-focused" discourse.[46]

This narrative did not evolve in a vacuum. A repertoire of practices also evolved since the 1980s, mainly in three areas: [1] inclusion of borrowing governments in policymaking; [2] communicating with NGO and [3] participation of citizens in projects. First, while the structural adjustment and the associated Policy Framework Papers are infamously associated inside and outside the Bank as embodying a one-size-fits-all set of conditionalities, the subsequent poverty reduction strategy papers (PRSPs) needed borrowing governments to write their developmental plans, or at least sign it off and participate in its writing in a more concrete way. Governments ended up writing programs they felt would please the donors, so macroeconomic policies did

[41] Speech James Wolfensohn, October 10, 1995, p. 38.   [42] Mallaby 2006, 147.
[43] Interview 20, July 17, 2017; Interview 31, November 6, 2017.
[44] Interview 39, November 14, 2017.   [45] Interview 41, November 21, 2017.
[46] Interview 33, November 7, 2017.

not change tremendously between the two periods,[47] but the programs are largely seen as being more successful in the 2000s than in previous decades. When senior officials at the Bank remember the structural adjustment period, they don't point at the inappropriateness of policies, but at the top-down structure of the conditionalities attached to them: "the real problem with this is not that it was the wrong policies, but it was the wrong people designing them."[48] As a senior Bank official puts it, "you can take the horse to the water, but you will not make it drink."[49] While the content was not drastically different, the practice of writing the development plans changed when the Policy Framework Papers were replaced by the PRSPs. While the former was written by Bank staff in Washington, D.C., the other was written in the country, with advice from Bank staff.

Second, practices of communication and consulting with NGOs evolved since the 1980s from the Bank seeing them as enemies to nuisance to useful partners. In the 1980s, Bank representatives were simply "not allowed" to talk to civil society actors. The NGO leader Warren Nyamugasira remembers that in the early 1990s, they "could not speak unless spoken to. The whole structure was designed to underline the dependence of the Africans upon the donors."[50] In the 1980s, the Bank was very opaque regarding its projects and internal communication. As a senior official recalls, "there was no transparency and no project documents could be released to NGOs."[51] By 2001, there were 70 NGO officers for a total of 90 resident missions, and there were as many as 120 by the end of 2007. In the 2000s, the Bank kept on formalizing tools for staff to routinized NGOs consultations in their practices, such as multiple guidelines and sourcebooks.[52] According to the Bank website, the involvement of NGO in Bank policymaking went from 21 percent in 1990 to 82 percent in 2012.[53]Third, while some small-scale participatory initiatives emerged in the 1980s, involving citizens in projects became standard practice only in the 1990s. In December 1990, the Bank-wide Learning Group on Participatory Development was created and financed by the Swedish government with a trust of $1.3 million, with the main goal to

[47] Interview 28, August 15, 2017.   [48] Ibid. Mallaby 2006.
[49] Interview 20, July 17, 2017.   [50] Cited in Mallaby 2006, 448.
[51] Interview OHP Robert Goodland, January 26, 2005.
[52] Civil Society Team 2000; NGO and Civil Society Unit 2000.
[53] www.worldbank.org/en/about/partners/civil-society#2.

mainstream participatory approaches in the Bank. The Learning group had to develop and document twenty Bank-supported operations considered as participatory, and help Bank staff to learn from these initiatives and move toward greater popular participation.[54] In 1996, the learning group published a *Participation in Practice* handbook to review how participation was making its way into the practices of various country teams, detailing fifteen cases of Bank projects that integrated participatory practices.[55] That same year, the Bank published its official Sourcebook on participation, which gave guidelines, practice pointers, tools and formal techniques for Bank staff to promote citizens participation[56] On a larger scale, while the Bank tried to institutionalized broad-based participation in the writing of PRSPs by borrowing countries, the results were very unequal and often factitious participation process unfolded. Many country teams reproduced the techniques laid out in Bank sourcebooks, making broad-based participatory processes very similar from one country to the other. Yet, as argued by many Bank managers, the PRSP "catalyzed a concept which is the participation of broad national stakeholders, and how that affects national development priorities. [...] The PRSP process was an important part of softening the ground and enabling governments to accept the premise that citizens have a much larger role than just being users of services."[57] The type of broad-based participation included in the PRSP may have disappeared, but Bank staffs still regularly organize citizens' consultations as part of their daily practice.

Did the narrative of openness cause the practices of participation to multiply or did the changes in practices created a shift in narrative? While the narrative and the practice shifts happened roughly in the same period, neither its narrative nor its practices had temporal nor ontological precedence over the other, that is, they co-constituted each other. The shift in how Bank leaders, officials, report writers and staff were talking about the Bank, its mission and its purpose corroborated with already existing tendencies toward more inclusion of local actors in various practices. Through these new practices, they believed they were making their organization more open and inclusive. In giving the world and the Bank mission a different intelligibility, the shift in narrative legitimized initiatives and practices already in motion and

---

[54] Bhatnagar and Williams 1992, 1.   [55] World Bank 1996a.
[56] World Bank 1996b.   [57] Interview 15, July 16, 2017.

opened up possibilities for new practices to emerge. The relationship was one of mutual reinforcement and legitimization.

In short, the evolution of the narrative had a "signaling effect" for internal staff. As one senior Bank official puts it, the official discourse gave employees "strong sense of what is correct, what is right" to do or not to do.[58] While this new discourse did not change the practices of Bank staff overnight, and while practices of participation existed at the Bank before the ontological narrative changed, it gave a sense amongst Bank staff members that the president and the management "was willing to push the Bank into new territory in terms of the imperative of increasing participatory approaches."[59] The shift in narrative was thus important in "shaping the patterns" or "shifting the ethos" more than in causing a change in operational practices *per se*[60]. Many Bank staff members mentioned that the shift in discourse at various levels "created an atmosphere" of openness, which in turn created more internal debates about the organization's practice.[61] This discursive shift hence did not have an independent effect on practices, but gave legitimacy and visibility to a certain type of practices inside the Bank.

As explained by a Bank senior manager, the change happening simultaneously in many quarters was not directly linked to what the Bank management and official publications would say. "It isn't that the Bank thought all of a sudden, 'Hey, isn't consultation a good idea?' or that Mr. Wolfensohn said, 'Hey, you guys need to do some consultation for once and all!'"[62] A senior economist confirmed that new discourse at the top did not force her to change her practices but gave her practice more legitimacy.[63] This is crucial to understand how discourse gave meaning and legitimacy to practices, thus encouraging cognitive evolution. For some staff members, the practice shift toward more communication and partnership with NGOs, for example, was partly due to the fact that senior management were giving the signal that "working with NGOs is okay" and partly because country-level staff recognized that "success depends on being able to reach out at the local level and that NGOs have a way of doing that."[64] The evolution in narrative did not cause a change in practice but was a necessary

---

[58] Interview 39, November 14, 2017.   [59] Interview 15, July 16, 2017.
[60] Interview 41, November 21, 2017 and Interview 31, November 6, 2017.
[61] Interview 41, November 21, 2017.   [62] Interview 26, July 24, 2017.
[63] Interview 39, November 14, 2017.
[64] Interview OHP Alexander Shakow, March 19–20, 2002.

condition for the multiplication of practices of openness and formal tools, as well as for their institutionalization.

Cognitive Evolution and Becoming

Adding ontological narratives would not only fit Adler's framework, but strengthen it. This move would illustrate and potentially give methodological tools to study Adler's becoming ontology in the real world. With a general move toward relational ontologies in the field of IR, a comprehensive and clear becoming ontology would have the potential to shift current understandings of world politics. Twenty years after Patrick Jackson and Daniel Nexon[65] defined for IR scholars "processual relationalism," and a few years after David McCourt[66] pointed at a practice-relational turn, Adler is suggesting a distinctive theory of entities, relations and practices as processes. While it is often assumed that processual relationalism and the practice/relational turn are better equipped to explain processual change than substantial theories of world politics, taken on their own terms, they are all about relations before they are about evolution. On the one hand, many IR scholars who adopt processual relationalism still center the analysis on relations rather than processes.[67] On the other hand, some relational approaches are simply better equipped to explain static outcomes than changing ones.[68]

Somehow taking sides with Alex Wendt's *Quantum Mind and Social Science* (2015), Adler's theoretical innovation is to emphasize *becoming processes* rather than either substances or relations. His becoming ontology, on which he has been working since the early 1990s (even since his childhood as he often says!), considers everything to be in flux, as a permanent process of change and evolution.[69] Adopting neither side, such an ontology views both relations and substances as *processes of becoming*. Building on complexity theory and evolutionary constructivism, Adler sees stability as requiring constant fluctuations, or as Prigogine would put it, "order through fluctuations." This order

---

[65] Jackson and Nexon 1999.   [66] McCourt 2016.
[67] Enloe 2014; Adler-Nissen 2015; Pratt 2016.
[68] Hafner-Burton, Kahler and Montgomery 2009; Mérand, Hofmann and Irondelle 2011.
[69] Adler 1991, 43.

through fluctuation, and the importance of past and future times in the present, could be conceptualized through ontological narratives.

Echoing Qin Yaqing[70] work grounded in Chinese philosophy, I argue that it is important to distinguish processual ontologies, based on "relations in motion," from both substantive and relational ones. Processual ontologies, of which becoming ontology is but one example, have their own dynamics and understand differently how change happens. For this reason, a becoming ontology of IR should be distinguished from both substantial and relational alternatives. Adler proposes an ontological middle ground, as it were, considering both relations and substances as important, but explaining both as processes. I will briefly define and analytically separate theories of substance, relations and processes/becoming, in order to highlight Adler's contribution. This should illuminate how narratives fit a processual ontology more than any other type of discourse, and could solve one of cognitive evolution theory's shortcomings, that is, an under-theorization of discourse and communication.

Substantialism

Most IR theories are implicitly substantialist, maintaining that the primitive units of analysis are things, beings, entities or essences. Entities (states, norms, capabilities, organizations) predate interaction, and relations are reduced to their existence between entities. Structural realists, neoliberal internationalists, many critical theorists and even most norm-oriented constructivists see states, states interests, power, domination or norms as mostly fixed "things."[71]

Substantialism relies on basic intuitions about the world. Human basic instinct tells the story of a world made of things: trees, books, cars, people, treaties, borders, norms or interests. When one sees the Blue Danube, no one says "look at that perpetual flowing of the water," but "look at how fast the river is flowing."[72] A similar tweak of the mind happens when we think that "the wind is blowing," that "the US is signaling" or that "they adopted an anti-slavery norm." However, the wind, states and norms are not things; they are evolving processes that we conveniently reduce to static conditions. This procedure of reductionism is an analytical tool preventing us from

[70] Yaqing 2009.   [71] Emirbayer 1997, 284.   [72] Elias 1978, 111–12.

122 Narratives in Cognitive Evolution

understanding the continually evolving character of the world. Reification is a basic reflex of the mind, and gives more coherence and stability to the world, as well as more ontological security. Substantialism's main flaw, despite its clear appeal to scholars of world politics, is its struggle to explain change, and especially endogenous change. Notably, substantialist theories are often unable to explain change between systems (feudal to early state system), change within systems (shifts in the balance of power in a multipolar system) or the fall of the Berlin wall.

Relationalism

Borrowing from relational sociology, relational scholars in IR reject substantialism. It is self-explanatory that they see relations, that is, configurations of ties or recurrent social interactions between individual or collective agents, as the building blocks of the social world.[73] Society does not possess relations, but *is* relations: "society is not a space 'containing' relations, or an arena where relations are played. It is rather the very tissue of relations."[74] Relational sociologists usually agree on two precepts: in the beginning there are relations, and subjects and objects are defined relationally.[75] There are no pre-given units or entities existing without the transactional context within which they are embedded.[76] It would be unreasonable, for example, to define the owner of the means of production or the proletarian without defining capitalism, much like slaves/master, hunter/hunted or mother/child. A good example is Cynthia Enloe's work on how diplomatic wives' unpaid labor participates in promoting national interests and sustaining a hierarchical systemic order between the global North and the global South.[77] Such an understanding of the role of these women in diplomacy would have been impossible if taken in isolation from their relations with their husbands and their relationships with men in general.

The difference between processual and relational theories is that the latter does not necessarily focus on change. A scholar centering her analysis on static relations would not be fundamentally incoherent. Social relations can be (simultaneously or not) a process or an outcome

---

[73] See McCourt 2016 for an up-to-date review of relationalism in IR.
[74] Donati 2015, 87.   [75] Ibid.   [76] Emirbayer 1997, 287.   [77] Enloe 2014.

of that process. As an emergent effect of a process, a social relation can be a reality (a "thing") existing between two or more agents.[78] If it represents a stable connection between various positioned actors, it can be defined as a social structure upon which the system as a whole is based. Relational sociology can therefore be better at explaining stability than change, or relations without evolution.

As one seminal example, Bourdieu very clearly adopts a relational sociology in that social classes are understood in their location in a social field made of hierarchical relations.[79] There is no doubt that for Bourdieu, "the real is the relational."[80] Relations are fundamental in Bourdieu's world, yet not evolving interactions or intersubjective links between individuals, but "objective relations, which exist independently of individual consciousness and will."[81] Bourdieusian theories of IR are therefore better equipped to explain stability because a field is "either a structure in formation or already formed and imposing itself on agents as recipients."[82] Because Bourdieusian IR sees the structure as the distribution of power among individuals, relative to their position in a given field, structures are imposed on agents at least in some ways.[83] This structure, once formed, is hard to change endogenously. Bourdieu's practical sense, based on the habitus and position in the field, is also highly taken-for-granted and mostly unreflexive once internalized, because it is based on material conditions of existence more than reflexive background knowledge.[84] Indeed, an individual's habitus is mainly the product of its belonging to a social class and through education, creating a stability that is very uneasy to change.[85] Yes, the habitus can change, but actors remain in a field of very stable objective relations: "social reality *is* relational, but only habitus *becomes*, and only partly so."[86] Change in a Bourdieusian framework is therefore possible in the form of movement in the position of things, not a constant becoming of reality.

Despite a trend of dynamic actor-network theory (ANT)[87], ANT as a research program also favors relations over becoming processes. ANT scholars can emphasize change over stability in looking at "the complex and heterogeneous micro-organizational processes involved

---

[78] Donati 2015, 90.   [79] Bourdieu 1990. See also Renault 2016, 22.
[80] Bourdieu and Wacquant 1992, 97.   [81] Ibid.
[82] King 2000; Bigo 2011, 239.   [83] Bourdieu 1994.   [84] Bourdieu 1972, 256.
[85] Bourdieu 1994, 257.   [86] Adler 2019, 57.
[87] Somers 1994; Lapid and Kratochwil 1997.

in the ongoing enactment of social reality,"[88] but ANT can also see configuration of ties as the static structure between concrete entities. Many network theorists, for example, focus on relations as "structural properties of network,"[89] and how these networks have stable effect on actors' hierarchies or positions.

Processes in Becoming

A becoming ontology assumes that both entities and relations are processes in constant evolution. While Jackson and Nexon emphasize the changing character of relations in processual relationalism, as previously explained, not all relational theories are processual ones. Processual relationalism comes from a desire to prioritize relations over substances, therefore sitting uncomfortably in between relational and processual ontologies. I argue that Adler offers the first fully fledged processual IR ontology. His theoretical innovation is to see relations, entities, practices and knowledge as being all in a constant state of becoming.

Since Heraclitus, philosophers of processes have focused exclusively on the dynamic character of relations. As such, a primarily processual ontology is distinct from both substantial and relational approaches. In processual ontologies, "the interrelated elements exist nowhere else than in their interrelations so that the elements are no longer external to their relations (as in substantial ontologies) [and] their interrelation is nothing else than the development of their own activity so that the relation does not have any kind of ontological priority over the elements (as in relational ontologies)."[90] At the heart of a processual ontology is the assumption that relations, as well as the elements they link, are in a constant process of becoming.

A process of becoming does not refer to changes in one specific thing, but to changes in the general condition of things; it involves not only one event, but various events, and events exist "only in and through processes."[91] A becoming ontology is a commitment to an even more fundamentally processual nature of the real than any type of relationalism. Processes are not simply relations; they are sets of "relations in

---

[88] Chia 1996, 59, cited in Adler 2019, 61.
[89] Hafner-Burton, Kahler and Montgomery 2009, 559.   [90] Renault 2016, 21.
[91] Rescher 1996, 38.

motion," or "ongoing interactive relations, embedded in social practice and producing social meaning."[92] At the heart of this ontology is the idea that entities and relations are in a constant state of becoming. As per Emirbayer's (processual) relational sociology, relations are "preeminently dynamic in nature as unfolding, ongoing processes rather than as static ties among inert substances."[93]

The French philosopher Emanuel Renault argues that the distinctive aspect of processual ontologies is that the dawn or the end point of a relation or substance is nothing but moments of becoming.[94] This does not mean that relational and substantial properties are subordinated to processes, but that they are made of processes. Neither does this mean that "things" do not exist. Most things appear stable, but such seemingly persistent things are in fact dynamic organizations made of continuous interaction of manifolds of processes.[95] In other words, entities are instantiations of processes or analytically separated moments in the course of a process. Heraclitus was right to say that we cannot step in the same waters twice, but we can certainly step twice in the same river, if it is seen as a reified, metastable entity.[96]

Adler's cognitive evolution is making such a move toward a becoming ontology, one that is primarily concerned with processes and evolution. After a thorough literature review going back to Heraclitus and passing by Hegel, Whitehead, Bergson and others, Adler's major point of anchor is Nicholas Rescher's assertion that "becoming" means reality is made of processes constantly being reshaped "in an ongoing development proceeding through the operation of a dialectic that continually blends conflicting opposites into a unitary but inherently unstable fusion."[97] Knowledge, especially, is not a "thing" or a "fixed or stable make-up," but is in fact processual in nature.[98]

Not unlike his earlier work on security communities and international practices, Adler holds a belief that institutions, organizations and polities are made of practices in motion, dynamic background knowledge and transactions among practitioners and between practitioners and their environment. "Institutions, organizations, and polities, which are usually associated with essences and 'being' ontology, actually become as a result of practices' processes, background

---

[92] Yaqing 2009, 9.   [93] Emirbayer 1997, 289.   [94] Renault 2016, 22.
[95] Rescher 1996, 51.   [96] Ibid., 52.   [97] Ibid., 13.   [98] Ibid., 134.

knowledge, and transactions between practitioners and between them and the wider world or environments."[99] Change, for Adler, is not just a sporadic happening, but the main condition of social reality. He thus develops a theory against substantial or "being" theories of change that analyze change in terms of a movement in the position or the essence of things such as rational choice theories, structural theories,[100] but also against static relational theories such as ANT or constructivist sequential theories of norm change. To use Wendt's terminology, what we see as things are only processes that collapse into thingness.[101]

While Adler considers becoming as a condition of the social world, he seeks to conceptualize change and stability as part of the same ontology, as an alternative to theories exclusively studying change[102] or stability[103]. Practices are the focal point of both continuity and change because they are the vehicles of reproduction, but stability is often an illusion created by the recursive nature of practices; new ways of thinking and doing emerge continuously from practices in which meanings are never inherently fixed or stable.[104] I will explain later in this chapter how narratives help explain the evolution of the meaning actors attribute to what they are supposed to do in a given situation.

To summarize, Adler's becoming ontology highlights five features:[105] (a) *processes* and *relations* are at the basis of what entities become; (b) *time* and *duration*, namely, the open-ended creative emergence of consciousness and social reality; (c) *the construction of social facts*; (d) *propensities* for something to become rather than the determination of something that *is* and (e) *immanence*, or the preservation of the past in the present, the latter of which is also creatively "pulled" forward by expectations of the future.

Becoming and Narratives

This ontological discussion highlighted Adler's main theoretical innovation. This chapter's suggestion of adding narratives to cognitive evolution is one way to operationalize becoming processes while addressing his lack of engagement with discourse. I suggested narratives as a discursive addendum to cognitive evolution precisely because

---

[99] Adler 2019, 46.   [100] Wallerstein 1974; Waltz 1979; Gilpin 1981.
[101] Wendt 2015.   [102] Holsti 1998   [103] Keohane 1984.
[104] Adler and Pouliot 2011, 16.   [105] Adler 2019.

in explaining how actors see themselves in time; it also fits a becoming ontology. Through narratives, actors come to make sense of the world in a processual manner, because people make choices and decide to deal with new problems on the basis of projections, expectations and memories associated with their narrative. Narratives are diachronic: collective actors are in a constant process of building their narrative, and to understand themselves as changing subject. In doing so, they are accounting not only for what they are doing, but what they did and what they will do. Through telling stories about themselves, they are making a connection between the past, present and future: they are always in becoming. Despite what Dunn[106] argues, narratives do not necessarily assume linearity, but rather the prevalence of time (both past and future) in the present. The shift in discourse at the World Bank did not show the shift that had necessarily happened or was happening at the moment, but showed expectations for the future, hopes for more openness and where the Bank should be heading.

Looking at communities' narrative especially has the potential to operationalize cognitive evolution's process of immanence, that is, the preservation of the past in the present, both being mobilized in our expectations for the future.[107] It does so because a narrative refers to where you have been and where you are going, in bringing memories and past mistakes into the present, as well as expectations for the future. In Etienne Wenger's terminology, narratives refer to the trajectory of an actor because "it brings the past and the future into the experience of the present."[108] Wenger uses the example of apprentices in traditional apprenticeship, who are not only learning skills, but are exposed to possible futures. Narratives refer to how actors mobilize a sense of who they are and where they come from, and develop a sense of trajectory that expands their identity in time.[109] This understanding of temporality is crucial because this is how narratives can strengthen a becoming ontology. A becoming ontology does not only look at the future of an actor, but integrates the past, the present and the future in a novel vision of temporality. Similarly, social narratives help us understand how actors themselves give a sense of their evolution, and integrate their past present and future actions. This is why the concept of narrative could help to operationalize Adler's becoming ontology and

---

[106] Dunn 2008, 78.   [107] Adler 2019, 199, 232.   [108] Wenger 2000, 241.
[109] Lave and Wenger 1991.

apply it productively in empirical research, as in the case of the World Bank, refugees or pirates.

Conclusion

Constructivist, poststructuralist and postmodern scholars in IR, but also rationalist ones, have integrated discourse or narrative in their understanding of the social world, either as forging identities or as instrumental to reaching a goal. As suggested by the editors of this volume in their introduction, further research should be done on communication in cognitive evolution processes, because if learning takes places in joint participation in a community, communication with each other must happen in various forms.[110] For example, what is the relationship between communities' public justifications and cognitive evolution?[111] Or how is progressive change linked to deliberative processes? This move to include communication as part of cognitive evolution would position Adler's framework as more comprehensive and having the potential to become a new important paradigm in IR.

While rationalist schools of thought in IR have used the concept of instrumental narrative and poststructuralist ones have explained how discourse give meaning to the world, cognitive evolution would benefit from a theorization of how ontological narratives participate in becoming processes. I demonstrated in this chapter that narratives complement well Adler's becoming ontology because of its potential to explain how meaning-making processes are in a constant state of becoming. Narratives open an important window onto how practices are given legitimacy and are able to multiply and disseminate in communities. Discourse is essential in understanding the complexity of practices, and even more the becoming complexity of cognitive evolution processes.

References

Adler, Emanuel. 1991. Cognitive Evolution: A Dynamic Approach for the Study of International Relations and Their Progress. In *Progress in Postwar International Relations*, edited by Emanuel Adler and Beverly Crawford, 43–88. New York: Columbia University Press.

[110] Pouliot, Kornprobst and Ish-Shalom, this volume.   [111] Kornprobst 2014.

Adler, Emanuel. 1992. The Emergence of Cooperation: National Epistemic Communities and the International Evolution of the Idea of Nuclear Arms Control. *International Organization* 46(1): 101–46.

Adler, Emanuel. 1997. Seizing the Middle Ground: Constructivism in World Politics. *European Journal of International Relations* 3(3): 319–63.

Adler, Emanuel. 2005. *Communitarian International Relations. The Epistemic Foundations of International Relations*. London: Routledge.

Adler, Emanuel. 2008. The Spread of Security Communities: Communities of Practice, Self-Restraint, and NATO's Post–Cold War Transformation. *European Journal of International Relations* 14(2): 195–230.

Adler, Emanuel. 2019. *World Ordering: A Social Theory of Cognitive Evolution*. Cambridge: Cambridge University Press.

Adler, Emanuel and Michael Barnett. 1998. *Security Communities*. Cambridge: Cambridge University Press.

Adler, Emanuel and Beverly Crawford, eds. 1991. *Progress in Postwar International Relations*. New York: Columbia University Press.

Adler, Emanuel and Vincent Pouliot, eds. 2011. *International Practices*. New York: Cambridge University Press.

Adler-Nissen, Rebecca. 2015. Conclusion: Relationalism or Why Diplomats Find International Relations Theory Strange. In *Diplomacy and the Making of World Politics*, edited by Jacob O. Sending, Vincent Pouliot and Iver B. Neumann, 1–30. Cambridge: Cambridge University Press.

Bhatnagar, Bhuvan and Aubrey C. Williams, eds. 1992. Participatory Development and the World Bank: Potential Directions for Change. World Bank Discussion Papers 183. Washington, DC: World Bank.

Bigo, Didier. 2011. Pierre Bourdieu and International Relations: Power of Practices, Practices of Power. *International Political Sociology* 5(3): 225–58.

Bourdieu, Pierre. 1972. *Esquisse d'une théorie de la pratique. Précédé de «Trois études d'éthnologie kabyle»*. Paris: Éditions du Seuil.

Bourdieu, Pierre. 1990. *The Logic of Practice*, translated by Richard Nice. Stanford: Stanford University Press.

Bourdieu, Pierre. 1994. *Raisons pratiques. Sur la théorie de l'action*. Paris: Éditions du Seuil.

Bourdieu, Pierre and Loic Wacquant. 1992. *An Invitation to Reflexive Sociology*. Chicago: Chicago University Press

Bruner, Jerome S. 1986. *Actual Minds, Possible Worlds*. Cambridge, MA: Harvard University Press.

Bruner, Jerome. 1991. The Narrative Construction of Reality. *Critical Inquiry* 18(1): 1–21.

Bueger, Christian. 2013. Practice, Pirates and Coast Guards: The Grand Narrative of Somali Piracy. *Third World Quarterly* 34(10): 1811–27.

Cernea, Michael M. 1992. The Building Blocks of Participation: Testing Bottom-Up Planning. World Bank Discussion Papers 166. Washington, DC: World Bank.

Chambers, Robert. 1994. The Origins and Practice of Participatory Rural Appraisal. *World Development* 22(7): 953–69.

Chia, Robert. 1996. The Problem of Reflexivity in Organizational Research: Towards a Postmodern Science of Organization. *Organization* 31(1): 31–59.Chia, Robert. 1999. A "Rhizomic" Model of Organizational Change and Transfor-mation: Perspective from a Metaphysics of Change. *British Journal of Management* 10(3): 209–27.

Civil Society Team. 2000. *Consultations with Civil Society. A Sourcebook.* Washington, DC: World Bank.

Clandinin, D. Jean. 2006. Narrative Inquiry: A Methodology for Studying Lived Experience. *Research Studies in Music Education* 27 (1): 44–55.

Collier, Paul and Jan Willem Gunning. 1999. The IMF's Role in Structural Adjustment. *Economic Journal* 109(459): F634–51.

Connelly, F. M. and D. Jean Clandinin. 1990. Stories of Experience and Narrative Inquiry. *Educational Researcher* 19(5): 2–14.

Donati, Pierpaolo. 2015. Manifesto for a Critical Realist Relational Sociology. *International Review of Sociology – Revue Internationale de Sociologie* 25(1): 86–109.

Doty, Roxanne L. 1993. Foreign Policy as Social Construction: A Post-Positivist Analysis of US Counterinsurgency Policy in the Philippines. *International Studies Quarterly* 37(3): 297–320.

Dunn, Kevin C. 2003. *Imagining the Congo: The International Relations of Identity.* New York: Palgrave MacMillan.

Dunn, Kevin C. 2008. Historical Representations. In *Qualitative Methods in International Relations. Research Methods Series*, edited by Audie Klotz and Deepa Prakash, 78–92. London: Palgrave MacMillan.

Elias, Norbert. 1978. *What Is Sociology?*, translated by Stephen Mennell and Grace Morrissey. New York: Columbia University Press.

Emirbayer, Mustafa. 1997. Manifesto for a Relational Sociology. *American Journal of Sociology* 103(2): 281–317.

Enloe, Cynthia H. 2014. *Bananas, Beaches and Bases: Making Feminist Sense of International Politics*, 2nd ed. Berkeley: University of California Press.

Epstein, Charlotte. 2011. Who Speaks? Discourse, the Subject and the Study of Identity in International Politics. *European Journal of International Relations* 17(2): 327–50.

Fischer, Frank. 2003. *Reframing Public Policy: Discursive Politics and Deliberative Practices*. New York: Oxford University Press.

Gilpin, Robert. 1981. *War and Change in World Politics*. Cambridge: Cambridge University Press.

Hafner-Burton, Emilie M., Miles Kahler and Alexander H. Montgomery. 2009. Network Analysis for International Relations. *International Organization* 63(3): 559–92.

Hansen, Lene. 2006. *Security as Practice. Discourse Analysis and the Bosnian War*. New York: Routledge.

Holsti, K. J. 1998. The Problem of Change in International Relations Theory. *Working Paper* #26. Institute of International Relations: University of British Columbia.

Jackson, Patrick Thaddeus and Daniel H. Nexon. 1999. Relations before States: Substance, Process and the Study of World Politics. *European Journal of International Relations* 5(3): 291–332.

Keohane, Robert O. 1984. *After Hegemony: Cooperation and Discord in the World Political Economy*. Princeton: Princeton University Press.

King, Anthony. 2000. Thinking with Bourdieu against Bourdieu: A "Practical" Critique of the Habitus. *Sociological Theory* 18(3): 417–33.

King, Thomas. 2003. *The Truth about Stories: A Native Narrative*. Toronto: Anansi Press.

Kornprobst, Markus. 2014. From Political Judgements to Public Justifications (and Vice Versa): How Communities Generate Reasons Upon Which to Act. *European Journal of International Relations* 20(1): 192–216.

Lapid, Yosef and Friedrich Kratochwil. 1997. *The Return of Culture and Identity in IR Theory*. Boulder: Lynne Rienner.

Lave, Jean and Etienne Wenger. 1991. *Situated Learning. Legitimate Peripheral Participation*. Cambridge: Cambridge University Press.

Mallaby, Sebastian. 2006. *The World's Banker: A Story of Failed States, Financial Crises, and the Wealth and Poverty of Nations*. New York: Penguin Press.

Martel, Stéphanie. 2017. *Le rôle du discours dans la construction de l'ASEAN comme communauté de sécurité*. PhD Thesis. Montreal: Université de Montréal.

McCourt, David. 2016. Practice Theory and Relationalism as the New Constructivism. *International Studies Quarterly* 60(3): 475–85.

Mérand, Frédéric, Stéphanie C. Hofmann and Bastien Irondelle. 2011. Governance and State Power: A Network Analysis of European Security. *Journal of Common Market Studies* 49(1): 121–47.

Miller-Adams, Michelle. 1999. *The World Bank: New Agendas in a Changing World*. London: Routledge.

Milliken, Jennifer. 1999. The Study of Discourse in International Relations: A Critique of Research and Methods. *European Journal of International Relations* 5(2): 225–54.

Mink, Louis O. 1966. The Autonomy of Historical Understanding. In *Philosophical Analysis and History*, edited by William H. Dray, 160–92. New York: Harper & Row.

Neumann, Iver B. 2002. Returning Practice to the Linguistic Turn: The Case of Diplomacy. *Millennium* 31(3): 627–51.

NGO and Civil Society Unit. 2000. *Consultations with Civil Society Organizations: General Guidelines for the World Bank Staff.* Washington, DC: World Bank Social Development Department.

Nielson, Daniel L., Michael J. Tierney and Catherine E. Weaver. 2006. Bridging the Rationalist–Constructivist Divide: Re-engineering the Culture of the World Bank. *Journal of International Relations and Development* 9(2): 107–39.

Operations Policy Department. 1994. *The World Bank and Participation.* Washington, DC: World Bank.

Patterson, Molly and Kristen Renwick Monroe. 1998. Narrative in Political Science. *Annual Review of Political Science* 1(1): 315–31.

Pratt, Simon. 2016. A Relational View of Ontological Security in International Relations. *International Studies Quarterly* 61(1): 78–85.

Renault, Emmanuel. 2016. Critical Theory and Processual Social Ontology. *Journal of Social Ontology* 2(1): 17–32.

Rescher, Nicholas. 1996. *Process Metaphysics: An Introduction to Process Philosophy.* Albany: State University of New York Press.

Roselle, Laura, Alister Miskimmon and Ben O'Loughlin. 2014. Strategic Narrative: A New Means to Understand Soft Power. *Media, War and Conflict* 7(1): 70–84.

Schatzki, Theodore Richard. 1996. *Social Practices. A Wittgensteinian Approach to Human Activity and the Social.* Cambridge: Cambridge University Press.

Schmidt, Vivien. 2010. Taking Ideas and Discourse Seriously: Explaining Change through Discursive Internationalism as the Fourth "New Internationalism." *European Political Science Review* 2(1): 1–25.

Shenhav, Shaul R. 2015. *Analyzing Social Narratives.* London: Routledge.

Somers, Margaret R. 1994. The Narrative Constitution of Identity: A Relational and Network Approach. *Theory and Society* 23(5): 605–49.

Somers, Margaret R. and Gloria Gibson. 2017. Reclaiming the Epistemological "Other": Narrative and the Social Construction of Identity. In *Social Theory and the Politics of Identity*, edited by Craig Calhoun, 37–99. Hoboken: Wiley-Blackwell.

Sugiman, Toshio, Kenneth J. Gergen, Wolfgang Wagner and Yoko Yamada, eds. 2008. *Meaning in Action: Constructions, Narratives, and Representations.* Tokyo: Springer Japan.

Taylor, Charles. 1985. *Human Agency and Language: Philosophical Papers.* Cambridge: Cambridge University Press.

Taylor, Charles. 2004. *Modern Social Imaginaries.* Durham: Duke University Press.

Wallerstein, Immanuel. 1974. The Rise and Future of the World Capitalist System: Concepts for a Comparative Analysis. *Comparative Studies in Society and History* 16(4): 387–415.

Waltz, Kenneth. 1979. *Theory of International Politics.* Long Grove: Waveland Press.

Wendt, Alexander. 2015. *Quantum Mind and Social Science.* Cambridge: Cambridge University Press.

Wenger, Etienne. 2000. Communities of Practice and Social Learning Systems. *Organization* 7(2): 225–46.

White, Hayden. 1980. The Value of Narrativity in the Representation of Reality. *Critical Inquiry* 7(1): 5–27.

World Bank. 1996a. Participation in Practice: The Experience of the World Bank and Other Stakeholders. *World Bank Discussion Paper* 333. Washington, DC: World Bank.

World Bank, 1996b. *The World Bank Participation Sourcebook.* Washington, DC: World Bank.

Yaqing, Qin. 2009. Relationality and Processual Construction: Bringing Chinese Ideas into International Relations Theory. *Social Sciences in China* 30(3): 5–20.

6 | Cognitive Evolution and the Social Construction of Complexity

PETER M. HAAS

Adler's work exemplifies constructivist studies of global governance. Such work focuses on the social construction of collective understandings, and how they may change over time through shifts in collective framing which shape international governance arrangements by defining and redefining identity, community, interests, an understanding of the world and appropriate institutions for conducting negotiations.[1] In terms of cognitive *evolution*, the generation of new ideas and practices comes from various communities, subject to the systemic constraints which provide for social selection.[2] As such, constructivist theorizing is analytically prior to conventional estimates of interests and capabilities in International Relations (IR).

In this chapter I look at international efforts to govern complexity, since the 1960s. The environment as an issue area is the leading edge of the cresting wave of the recognition of complexity, and its attendant challenges for global governance. The aggregate process of governance is one of cognitive evolution, as actors collectively imagined the environment in terms of complexity, and that the primary agents have been ecological epistemic communities.

Complexity has become the organizing principle of contemporary world politics.[3] Complexity goes beyond mere complex interdependence,

My thanks to the Troika for their editorial guidance, and to the participants at the Toronto and Vienna workshops for their feedback on earlier drafts and for exposing me to fresh perspectives and a process of self-reflective learning. Thanks always to Manolo for our collaboration and discussions over the years, and his complementary but slightly different perspective on social learning and global governance. Thanks also to the WZB and Graduate Institute Geneva for providing hospitable environments while I revised this chapter.
[1] Berger and Luckmann 1967; E. B. Haas 1975, 1990; Onuf 1989; P. Haas 1992; Ruggie 1998.
[2] Adler and Haas 1992.
[3] MacNeill, Winsemius and Yakushiji 1991; Jervis 1997; Farrell & Newman 2018; Orsini et al. 2019.

by establishing new parameters shaping collective action through a multiplicity of interlinkages between issues and actors, and more profoundly between natural and social systems.[4] Namely, actors are increasingly aware of the uncertainty implicit in the world, and surrounding their practices and others' practices. As discussed later, such complexity implies emergent properties of the system, as well as eschewing ambitious large-scale irreversible projects.

While complexity now characterizes world politics more generally, as a social fact and as a material structure, it is also widely encountered in specific issue areas including security, International Political Economy (IPE), environment and development. Confronting environmental challenges has led to a broader shift to recognizing the interplay between these issue areas which had previously been regarded as operating in isolation. In short, complexity requires interpretation for decision makers. The analytic question here relates to agency: who provides such interpretation and with what effect?

I look at how actors – practitioners, experts and the array of "stakeholders" – recognized and responded to this ontological transition. Epistemologically, a compelling answer requires process tracing and actor-level studies[5] to determine how the anomalous world was recognized and governed, as interests remained ambiguous and had to be constructed. Governance is a constantly moving target. It is more of a project than a thing, which changes according to newly consolidated norms and causal understandings regarding the domain of governance.

The question is how was complexity socially constructed, *for* and *by* decision makers, so that it could be governed internationally. Basically, there were two approaches to governing complexity. The first is a full front holistic approach to recognizing inter-issue effects combined with efforts to mitigate the driving forces behind complexity which was developed by communities of practice. The second approach was an incremental one intended to develop new regimes to govern discrete issues in new comprehensive ways. The incremental approach prevailed over the comprehensive strategy. Over time the discrete governance efforts catalyzed into a set of common practices across different functional domains, leading to the institutionalization of the practices and of

[4] Choucri 1993.
[5] Methodologically, this claim relates to Crawford's chapter and Adler's conclusion, this volume.

the reliance on scientific experts to guide them. Epistemic communities promoted the incremental approach, whereas communities of practice were associated with the comprehensive approach.

Again, with Adler I accept that responses and learning do not occur automatically (his early reliance on Popper's 3rd world[6] was appropriately dropped because it lacked a mechanism by which dusty ideas would move from the library to the policy world).

Practices and ideas are mutually constitutive, or co-productive. At times this occurs through internal relations, à la Wendt[7], and before him Bertell Ollman[8] and Anthony Giddens.[9] But idea and practice formation also have independent or endogenous dynamics, and thus cognitive evolution occurs at a higher scale of abstraction where developments in each must be reconciled.[10] My concern about communities of practice, mentioned later, derives from an interest in trying to disentangle the independent influences of ideas and practices.[11] Practices thus must reflect consensual ideas as well as embodying them. In order for ideas to be established and institutionalized as consensual they require agents working on their behalf (or agents using ideas for their own purposes). To my mind ideas are partially decomposable from practices, and often analytically prior.

Agency and Cognitive Evolution

Cognitive evolution involves agency. Two groups are involved in cognitive evolution: communities of practice and epistemic communities. While communities of practice are primarily an analytic category, epistemic communities are both an analytic category as well as corresponding to real collectivities of self-identified actors.

It seems difficult to operationalize communities of practice. They are assemblages of actors who share common goals, loose understandings and common practices.[12] The practices are both internal to the community, and help define it in a Bourdieusian sense, as well as being projected onto the policy space they hope to influence or are actively involved in.

---

[6] Adler 1991.   [7] Wendt 1987, 1992.   [8] Ollman 1971.   [9] Giddens 1984.
[10] Ezhrahi 1980; Campbell 1993; Ansell and Weber 1999; Haas and Haas 2002.
[11] Adler and Pouliot 2011, 10. This is connected to Sondarjee's discussion of narratives and practices in this volume.
[12] Wenger 1998.

Communities of practice enjoy similar characteristics to social movements.[13] Because of the combination of practice, habitus and prior communitarian beliefs, it is *ex ante* impossible to tease out the effects, or presence of the core beliefs of the community and the practices in which they engage because they are all presumed to coexist. Because the notion of a community of practice tends to be static and diachronic, we know that there are a group of people involved in a common project, but we cannot tease out their common beliefs and socialized habits, presuming that they have both without verifiable evidence.[14] While they may overlap in practice, it is difficult to ascertain confidently which is which without clearer conceptual boundaries.

Whereas epistemic communities are more like communities (*Gemeinschaft*) in the sense that they have common internalized beliefs; communities of practices are more like social groups (*Gesellschaft*) unified by common social practices but where the more organic or essentialist constitutive elements are less clear.

To some extent communities of practice, at least when most influential, include epistemic communities among their members. Conversely, epistemic communities may exist independently of communities of practice. We can imagine three overlapping categories: communities of practice which include epistemic communities, epistemic communities and communities of practice without epistemic communities.

The question I pursue in this chapter is by what means does cognitive evolution occur in representing complexity for decision makers. That is, who is involved in cognitive evolution, and by what means do their ideas become institutionalized into social practices. I argue that this is through epistemic communities and a delegation model, rather than through communities promoting practice and concurrent changes in practices and understandings through engaged deliberation between networks of practitioners, analysts and other actors. In this instance I contrast the influence of two distinct groups: epistemic communities promoting incremental approach to governing complexity, and a community of practice promoting an integrated approach to governing complexity.

---

[13] For careful studies differentiating social movements from other concepts see Djelic and Quack 2010; Dunlop and Radaelli 2012, and from advocacy coalitions see Sabatier and Jenkins-Smith 1993.
[14] See also Pratt's insistence on the need for phenomenology as an approach in this volume.

Complexity as Ontology

Complexity is the defining feature of contemporary world politics.[15] Complexity has analytic features, many of which have been identified by work on wicked problems[16] and super wicked problems,[17] as well as the standard work on complexity theory.[18]

Recent studies of international environmental politics apply complexity theory to characterize the political landscape of international environmental politics, including regime complexes, and politics more broadly. Regime complex literature,[19] though, tends to focus on the effects of different types of networks within and between regimes, rather than applying complexity theory per se to explain network creation and aggregate practices.

Power requires a nuanced understanding within a framework of complexity.[20] In addition to its material dimensions, power also rests on shared conceptual foundations, which steer collective practices. The source of such influence depends on the collective beliefs and understandings of those providing framing advice to decision makers, which is essentially Weberian in nature because it rests on voluntary social deference based on social facts of the legitimacy of expert advice. Thus, influential epistemic actors exercise power by shaping discourses and informing actor interests.[21] In turn, such influence remains constrained by the institutional pressures on knowledge-based communities to choose research questions, receive funding and to be subject to governmental harassment, such as climate change scientists have encountered recently in the United States.[22]

Philippe LePrestre identifies the following characteristics of complex systems: multiple agents, connections between agents and multiple scales, networks linking the agents, inherently intertwined and indeterminate connections between physical and social systems, with extensive feedback loops and nonlinearities, and hierarchies of interrelated institutions at different organizational scales. Governance may be

---

[15] La Porte 1975; Simon 1981; Perrow 1984; Jervis 1997; Ansell and Weber 1999.
[16] Rittel and Webber 1973.   [17] Levin et al. 2012.
[18] Ladyman, Lambert and Wiesner 2013; Boulton, Allen and Bowman 2015, 36.
[19] Raustiala and Victor 2004; Alter and Meunier 2009; Biermann et al. 2009; Keohane and Victor 2011.
[20] Katzenstein and Seybert 2018. See also the chapter by Guzzini in this volume.
[21] Adler, Emanuel and Bernstein 2005; Allan 2017.
[22] Oreskes and Conway 2010; Bradley 2011.

adaptive and self-organizing with emergent properties following from path-dependent processes and tipping points.[23]

Oran Young offers a complementary but shorter list of clusters of characteristics of complex systems:

Four principal clusters of features, which often interact with one another, present challenges to those seeking to design and operate governance arrangements capable of producing sustainable results of a large scale: (i) connectivity, or tight coupling among system components, (ii) thresholds, triggers and nonlinear patterns of change, (iii) dynamic and direction processes, and (iv) emergent properties and the frequency of surprises.[24]

The environment as an issue area captures (or even instantiates) many of these general features of IR, and thus makes for a valuable laboratory for its study and developing more generalizable insights for IR.[25] As early as 1963 Lynton Caldwell mused:

Would the perspective gained by looking at the way in which our society shapes it surroundings give us insight into relationships between specific social, economic, or political problems – into interrelationships between the parts and the whole? ... The proposition that "environment" may be a useful focus for public policy purposes is advanced primarily for reasons of exploration – not advocacy.[26]

The environment is the camel's nose into complexity in several ways. It provides an empirical venue for investigating social responses to complexity, as environmental issues reflect the characteristics of complex systems, and international environmental issues were some of the first to be recognized and addressed on those terms. Because the environment is so inextricably linked to other areas of international governance, as the environment cannot be addressed without heeding the other sources of environmental threats, and environmental conditions affect other areas of human existence so widely for good and ill, addressing environmental complexity gives rise to broader patterns of global governance. Environmental ideas are also inherently holistic and ecological, and thus provide a cognitive evolutionary impulse for integrating complex global issues.[27] For this reason Paul Shepherd called

---

[23] Le Prestre 2016, 136–48.   [24] Young 2017, 4.
[25] Caldwell 1963; Sprout and Sprout 1971, 1972.   [26] Caldwell 1963, 132–33.
[27] Alker and Haas 1993.

the environment a subversive topic and ecology the "subversive science."[28]

International governance of complexity is difficult in the absence of a single source of authority responsible for governing these issues, or capturing their interconnections. Unanticipated consequences of actions are common, and surprises are frequent features of world politics. There is a disconnect between actors' intended consequences and actual outcomes.

Order – that is governance – is possible without ideas, but it is likely to be unstable without the support of organizing ideas and understandings. Dominant countries devote significant resources to enforcing and maintaining order, rather than resting that order on the legitimacy of the procedures and ideational foundations by which it was developed and maintained.[29] Between chaos and order lie ideas.

The variety of regimes coming out of World War II is clear, each with its own distinct and discrete policy community (or epistemic community or community of practice), but no clear attention is paid to why issues were understood to take the forms for which they were governed. Discrete regimes for discrete problems were the name of the game. From the perspective of dominant social epistemologies, such decoupling was based on a dominant reductionist Newtonian view of the world.[30] From an agentic perspective it was due to the different array of actors, interests and capabilities associated with each issue which accounts for the differences between regimes and governance arrangements for each issue. The relative strength of different communities helps to account for the variation in design, resources and influence of the variety of functional agencies and regimes.[31] Yet as Newton gave way to Einstein little attendant change has appeared in governance philosophy or theory.

Surprisingly little theoretically informed work exists about the initial creation of governance institutions for international complexity.[32] While there has been speculation about the effects of regime fragmentation, and the possible reasons for harmonization between regimes, the genesis question remains largely unanswered, and the dynamics of regime linkage remain contested between rationalists[33]

---

[28] Sears 1964.   [29] Franck 1990.   [30] Kern 2003; Wendt 2015.
[31] Keohane and Nye 1977.
[32] See Acheson 1969; Gardner 1980; Braithwaite and Drahos 2000; Mazower 2012; Held, Hale and Young 2013.
[33] Lake 2020.

and constructivists[34]. The reasons for institutional decay and elimination also remain only partially investigated.[35]

For constructivists, and for my argument, regimes remain disjointed because different actors and ideas were deployed at the outset of each regime, combined with path dependence so that they persist in their different forms. The only pressure for harmonization occurs with major systemic shocks, when decision-making choices get elevated to the top levels of national bureaucracies where geopolitical doctrines get applied across the board.[36] Decisions are made more incrementally by mid-level bureaucrats at the interstices of history.

Overly simplified, two sets of groups have been engaged with seeking to interpret complexity for governance since the 1960s. The first is made up of a number of communities of practice associated with complexity theory, who tried to govern complex systems through a frontal assault in which they would deploy new norms and holistic management. The second is an epistemic community operating by stealth, which sought to gradually create comprehensive governance approaches to the environment, and to foster a dense network of linkages between environmental and development activities. Governing individual issues through regimes, they have helped crystallize a broader network or archipelago of interlinked governance efforts that spread beyond the environment as traditionally understood and a new global governance agenda that looks at relations between the physical environment and socioeconomic systems.

Addressing Complexity Head on with Complexity Theory

The first response to the recognition of global complexity in the 1960s emerged from complexity theorists, academics, private sector individuals and NGOs who sought to apply concepts from complexity theory to the governance of complexity. That is, they tried to integrate communities of practice with decision makers to yield governance efforts which directly addressed complexity either through advocating fundamentally new modes of production and consumption (following the Limits to Growth vision) or to try to devise complex integrated

---

[34] Haas and Haas 1995.
[35] Shanks, Jacobson and Kaplan 1996; Debre and Dijkstra 2020; Eilstrup-Sangiovanni 2020.
[36] Holsti 1992; Ikenberry 2001.

management approaches which would both capture the multiple inter-linkages between social, physical and political systems as well as include communities of practice in collective reflection in order to yield an ongoing process of continuous collective learning.

Many communities of practice informed by complexity theories have tried to create holistic governance designs for the environment, which treat the environment as being inextricably interconnected to social issues. These groups tend to offer two key elements to their analysis: that because of the interpenetration of social and ecological systems, norms are impossible to escape (either in terms of the concepts applied or the distributional effects of proposed policies); and because of the dense causal textures that connect social and ecological issues, a concerted and holistic governance structure is required. They have called for a uniform and simultaneous frontal assault on all issues.

Underlying the common approach has been complexity theory and general systems theory,[37] focused by Boulding's apt metaphor of a "spaceship earth" needing holistic guidance.[38] Pristine nature no longer exists. All ecosystems are subject to some degree of human intervention[39] so the normative or ethical question is which level of equilibrium is desirable, with what distributional effects. Consider sustainability. There are many multiple possible equilibria for sustainable consumption: the question is how are allocative consumption decisions to be distributed between and within countries?[40]

The leading edge of recognition of complexity and its parameters comes from studies of human–environment relations by geographers, and later by complexity theorists and then world historians. Attention has moved from looking at the local or regional level and on resource degradation or scarcity to global-level ecosystem degradation.

Interestingly, while this literature has been organized and promoted by scholars and practitioners and NGOs aspiring to be policy networks and social movements, their influence has been modest at best.

There is long-standing research on local human interference with natural systems and environmental degradation as a consequence of human activities, as well as ways in which human societies relied on

---

[37] Churchman and Ackoff 1950; Churchman 1984.   [38] Boulding 1966.
[39] Vitousek et al. 1997.
[40] Galtung 1973; Cole 1977; Freeman and Jahoda 1978; Agarwal and Narain 1991.

environmental resources for sustainability.[41] Early studies that recognized the impact of Greek pastoral practices on erosion and the decline of agriculture,[42] studies of how Roman military expansionism destroyed Mediterranean forests[43] and the recognition of local air pollution in Medieval England. George Perkins Marsh, a forester and diplomat, observed systematic deforestation in Italy as a consequence of human activity, thus noting that environmental conditions could be directly affected by patterns of social behavior.[44] Subsequent studies by geographers offered broader historical documentation of human impacts on the environment, and indeed, its *transformation.*[45] Others offered cautionary tales of civilizational collapse due to environmental abuses,[46] while others documented the extent of human dependence on environmental resources, in particular the spread of crops.

Understanding spread with the era of western exploration. Exploration and colonization by the west led to the gradual understanding of a natural history, which varies across the globe and is subject to influence by humans.[47] Scientific studies accompanied colonial expansion,[48] although the accumulation of scientific knowledge about the rest of the world could not be collapsed into political expansionism. Natural historians, including such people as Darwin, Lewis and Clark and von Humboldt, collected specimens and observations that set the foundations for understanding evolutionary dynamics, and appreciating human interference in natural systems, as well as the contributions of natural systems to what we now call human sustainability.

Malthusian informed views looked at the effects of finite resource endowments on economic growth and on national security. Jevons expressed concern about coal scarcity[49] as early as 1865, followed by worries about the "population explosion,"[50] threats to the global commons[51] and the Limits to Growth.[52][53]

The United States environmental movement popularized many of these arguments.[54] It revealed how the United States had eliminated what we would now call biodiversity through the systematic hunting of

---

[41] See also Drieschova in this volume.   [42] Hughes 1975.
[43] Braudel 1979, 1984.   [44] Marsh 1965.
[45] Thomas 1956; Turner II et al. 1990.   [46] Diamond 2005.
[47] Burke 2012, 12–17, ch 14.   [48] Crosby 1986.   [49] Jevons 1865.
[50] Ehrlich and Ehrlich 1968, 2004.   [51] Hardin 1968.
[52] Meadows et al. 1971, 1992; Woodwell 1985.
[53] Sondarjee, this volume, would refer to these as narratives.   [54] Osborn 1949.

buffalo and passenger pigeons in the nineteenth century, and the indiscriminate and unreflective use of dichlorodiphenyltrichloroethane (DDT) in the twentieth.[55] These arguments significantly influenced a generation of transformative activists and policymakers.[56]

With the 1972 United Nations Conference on the Human Environment (UNCHE) and the Limits to Growth debate (LTG), attention moved to global effects of national economic activities.[57] They recognized the extensive impact on terrestrial systems from human practices, as well as such activities as ways in which commerce contribute to invasive species and the degradation of global ecosystems. World historians studied the large-scale social activities which had systematic effects on global ecosystems, thus moving beyond the focus on resource scarcity.[58]

A global, ecological and complex perspective came into being concurrently,[59] although with little direct communication with the previous line of thinking. It looked at the mutual interconnections and co-constitutive effects between physical and natural systems. Vernadsky introduced the idea of biogeochemistry,[60] seeing the world as an interconnected set of physical ecosystems. Along with Teilhard de Chardin, physical systems were seen as essentially intertwined with social systems. Social systems contributed to environmental states, and vice versa. Braudel and the French Annales School further advanced such a research program.[61] Vaclav Smil's magisterial studies have tried to deal with environmental and social systems together.[62] Stephen Toulmin artfully combined this effort to unify the social with the natural, by looking at how social beliefs shaped aggregate practices, their effect on the environment and the environment's effect on societies. But most fundamentally he looked at how human understanding about these interconnections could change, and thus steer movements to mitigate stresses and greater sustainability.[63] Thus a focus on reflexivity was introduced to understand the complex interconnections between physical and social systems.

The focus here is on interactive effects within issues, between issues and between natural and social systems writ large. "Global catastrophic

[55] Carson 1962.   [56] Speth 2004, 2008; Deudney and Mendenhall 2016.
[57] Vitousek et al. 1997.
[58] Ponting 1992; McNeill 2000; Manning 2003; McNeill and McNeill 2003; Christian 2004.
[59] Alker and Haas 1993.   [60] Vernadsky 1944.
[61] Braudel 1977, 1979, 1982, 1984.   [62] Smil 1993, 2006.   [63] Toulmin 1990.

risks are parts of extremely complicated causal networks."[64] Moreover, because of an attention to social systems, the question becomes how do social systems recognize the consequences (and causes) of their activities, and change them?

Concerns about global risk have raised the prospect of the collapse of environmental systems, leading to social collapse unless coordinated international responses are taken.[65] Recent studies of the Anthropocene and the Great Acceleration[66] point to large-scale ontological social transformations in production, consumption and long-distance trade. Global ecological boundaries are being stressed, and human societies need to quickly appreciate the threats and devise effective responses. The World Economic Forum sees a world of interpenetrated risks from discrete functional areas of activity, with the need for better planning to identify and reduce the interactive effects which can lead to runaway disasters for physical and social systems.[67]

Such a unified view has returned attention to the role of institutions as mediating factors (or even causal factors) between the social and physical domains. For instance, the LTG failed to recognize the powerful role of markets at sending price signals to trigger technological innovations.[68] The recent peak oil argument evaporated in the face of technological changes and fracking. However, the members of the community of practice continued to cling to their Malthusian beliefs, even in the face of recurrent falsifications of their predictions. The famous wager between Paul Ehrlich and Julian Simon about resource scarcity as measured by mineral prices, which Ehrlich lost, failed to sway any of the members of the community.[69]

A plethora of US research programs and research challenges were initiated to study aspects of global change. The Consortium for International Earth Science Information Network initiated a conceptually ambitious program for linking social and physical system dynamics, including learning feedback within social systems.[70] Documenting the physical impacts on social systems. Understanding the social dynamics which lead to social

---

[64] Global Challenges Foundation 2016, 72.
[65] Kasperson and Kasperon 2001; Bostrom and Cirkovic 2008; Woodwell 2016.
[66] Crutzen 2003; Rockstrom et al. 2009; Biermann, Wijkman and Rockstrom 2012; Biermann et al. 2012.
[67] World Economic Forum 2016.   [68] Kaysen 1972.   [69] Sabin 2013.
[70] Consortium for International Earth Science Information Network (CIESIN) 1992.

impacts on the environment. Decision theories about policies for address-ing, and for learning and social adjustments. The US National Academy of Sciences organized several committees on global change research and the human dimensions of global environmental change, giving rise to fairly extensive reports that looked at patterns of interactions between human and natural systems.[71] Along with other previous social science efforts,[72] these described large-scale social trends and their impacts on the environ-ment, along with treatments of how societies relied on the environment for resources and for healthy ecosystems, although they tended to conclude with pleas for further research on decision-making and a better under-standing of how societies would learn about these relationships and adapt to increasing environmental stress.[73] The International Human Dimensions Program on Global Environmental Change gave rise to a systematic research program which overlapped with the Earth Systems Governance Network, giving rise to studies of social dynamics and responding to global environmental change.[74]

These broad ideas about direct approaches to governing complexity and environmental issues have been embraced and pursued by a number of communities of practice.

World Orders Models Project

The World Orders Models Projects (WOMPs) of the 1960s and 1970s called for normatively self-conscious holistic approach to global gov-ernance, of which environmental governance was a part. Through a number of reports[75] the WOMPs forged a transnational group of scholars and global *savants*. It was envisioned by its organizers as a social movement as well as an academic exercise, seeking to promote social change through its reflective study. Despite high-profile reports and extensive internal deliberations, it has not had widespread impact, and its overall mission dissipated after the decline of the New International Economic Order project at the UN and the popularity of state-led international economic governance.

---

[71] Stern et al. 1992; National Research Council 1999.
[72] Jacobson and Price 1990.   [73] Brewer and Stern 2005.
[74] Young, King and Schroeder 2008; Biermann and Pattberg 2012; Uhrqvist and Linner 2015.
[75] de Seynes 1972; Kothari 1974; Falk 1975; Galtung 1980.

Club of Rome

The Club of Rome, in a series of reports, pointed to the meshing of social and physical systems, and the need to find ways of bringing them into a greater state of balance.[76] The most influential of the Club of Rome Reports was the Limits to Growth Report, which at the very least contributed to widespread public concern worldwide about the environmental crisis, twelve million copies were sold worldwide, and reinforced pressure for the first UN Conference on the environment in 1972. The Club of Rome has had surprisingly little impact, despite its high profile and elite membership. Perhaps this is due to its primary mission of funding reports rather than conducting intensive and reflexive deliberations within its own organization.

IHDP and Future Earth

Earth system scientists have tried to combine their research with policy reliance. As earth system sciences matured,[77] international institutionalized research programs were organized to harness researchers and to mobilize funding. The International Geosphere-Biosphere Programme (IGBP) from 1999–2015[78] and the International Human Dimensions Program (IHDP) fronted much of this work, until they were combined with DIVERSITAS into Future Earth in 2016, and reorganized around a loosely articulated set of "knowledge-action networks." While the IGBP tended to focus on research on physical earth systems, and the IHDP focused on the social institutions and the interplay between natural and social systems in global environmental governance.[79] Future Earth is self-consciously a community of practice, aspiring to develop policy-relevant ideas for sustainability through coordinated interactions with a variety of researchers, stakeholders and practitioners. It promotes transdisciplinary research combining a wide variety of non-state stakeholders in formulating research questions and conducting research. It remains hamstrung by funding shortfalls and organizational challenges in trying to operationalize institutional patterns for organizing communities of practice.

---

[76] Onuf 1983; King and Schneider 1991; MacNeill et al. 1991.
[77] Schlesinger 1991; Melillo, Field and Moldan 2003.   [78] Kwa 2005, 923–32.
[79] Young, King and Schroeder 2008.

Addressing Complexity through Stealth by Ecological Epistemic Communities

An ecologically informed epistemic community has played an instrumental role in articulating and disseminating, and at times implementing, holistic approaches for dealing with discrete environmental issues.[80] Over time as individual problems have been addressed, decision makers have learned to recognize the connections between issues, leading to a more densely governed policy space.

While they reflect an ecological perspective,[81] the ecological perspective is grounded on ecological science. A rather large intellectual history and historiography of ecology tells a consistent story of its core beliefs and development.[82] All concur on the analytically prior ecological perspective or viewpoint which informs the work, as well as its core focus on networks and uncertainty. C. H. Waddington, a major evolutionary biologist, acknowledged that his causal theorizing could not be separated from a prior "metaphysical" belief in the holistic nature of the world which preselected an orientation for cybernetic modeling of natural phenomena and a preference for dynamic ecological models, or what we would now call a prior ontology.[83]

A number of prominent ecologists make this point. George Van Dyne writes "understanding ecosystems means understanding interactions among components. Each component is influenced by others."[84] Eugene Odum makes the same point.[85]

Alexander von Humboldt (1769–1859) was one of the first to encourage scientific study of the earth as a single entity, along with British geologist James Hutton (1726–1797). The term "ecology" was coined by Ernst Haeckel (1834–1919) in 1866 to refer to

the investigation of the total relations of the animal to its inorganic and to its organic environment; including above all, its friendly and inimical relations with those animals and plants with whom it comes directly or indirectly into contact – in a word, ecology is the study of all those complex interrelations referred to by Darwin as the conditions of the struggle for existence.[86]

---

[80] Haas 2015.
[81] Sprout and Sprout 1971, 1972; Dahlberg 1983; Pirages 1983.
[82] McIntosh 1985; Worster 1987; Botkin 1990; Hagen 1992; Golley 1993.
[83] Waddington, 1975, 1–11.   [84] Van Dyne 1969, 7.   [85] Odum 1977.
[86] McIntosh 1985, 7–8.

Russian Academician Vladimir Vernadsky (1863–1945) was the first to apply a global level of analysis to the study of ecosystems and to systematically include humanity in an analysis of global change, both as a cause (or source) of change in global ecosystems, and as a source of constructive intervention in their operation. By focusing on the biosphere, he attracted attention to a geographic space broader and deeper than the territorial dimensions traditionally understood in public and academic discourse, along with the extent to which humanity was deliberately and unconsciously changing the face of the planet through interfering with chemical cycles.[87] Borrowing from de Chardin, he referred to the "noosphere" to focus attention on how collective views of human–nature interactions co-evolved along with physical changes in the world.[88] His work is now widely hailed as the intellectual precursor of much of the more rigorous scientific ecological work.[89]

His ideas diffused to France, and later to the United States. His book on the biosphere was translated to French in 1929 and was available in Europe. His son brought his father's work to the attention of the noted American Geologist G. Evelyn Hutchinson at Yale. Hutchinson solicited a key paper from Venadsky on geochemistry, which was published in the Transaction of the Connecticut Academy of Sciences,[90] and arranged to have one of Vernadsky's articles translated for the prestigious American scientific journal *American Scientist*,[91] thereby bringing biogeochemistry to the attention of many American scientists. The scholars involved were relatively insulated from political pressures, and were able to develop the concepts independently of state-driven projects.

A highly placed academician under Lenin and Stalin, Vernadsky helped establish a number of scientific laboratories, including a biogeochemical laboratory in 1928, which he directed until 1941. The laboratory operated outside the direct oversight of the Russian administration, despite Vernadsky's "essentially liberal and anti-Marxist" ideas.[92] His views were accepted by other scientists because they "provided a scientific rationale for a conservation program hostile to arid development and supportive of wilderness preservation" as well

---

[87] Yanshin and Yanshina 1988.   [88] Vernadksy 1945.
[89] Bailes 1981; Lapo 1987; Yanshin and Yanshina 1988.   [90] Vernadsky 1944.
[91] Vernadksy 1945.   [92] Bailes 1981.

as "providing tangible and symbolic islands of autonomy from the state – under the control of the scientific community – while at the same time propounding the view that scientists, owing to their eco-logical expertise, should play a central role in economic planning and resource management."[93] The scientists were purged in the 1930s, when "holistic ecological doctrines that asserted limits to humans' ability safely to transform nature were now to be regarded not only as flawed but as devised by the class enemies of Soviet Socialism."[94]

In the United States the scholarly studies of systems ecology flour-ished in the 1960s under the direction of Eugene Odum at the University of Georgia at Athens, where researches developed the notions of ecosystems and social systems based upon energy flows and borrowed from cybernetics. Odum published the highly successful and influence *Fundamentals of Ecology* in 1953, which legitimated the field of study within American academia and attracted a generation of students. The United States Atomic Energy Commission (AEC) and Oak Ridge National Laboratories solicited his expertise, and funded his work for the monitoring of groundwater radiation and assessment of its effects.

The International Biosphere Program (IBP) from 1964 to 1974 helped to institutionalize ecological science in fifty-eight countries worldwide, although at the expense of often neglecting local contexts in order to apply a universal research template.[95] In the United States it provided the foundations for stable funding and discretionary control over its own research. The US component of the IBP received 40–50 million dollars over the lifetime of the program, largely from the NSF.

In the 1980s the broad ecological perspective was refined into more policy-oriented work, particularly by Buzz Holling, consistent with the broader ecological perspective or viewpoint. Edward Ploman wrote:

The basic assumption and models in the classic scientific tradition appear, in the light of the new perspectives, to be mechanistic, closed, and reductionist. In the new emerging approaches, instability, openness, fluctuation, disorder, fuzziness, and creativity are built into scientific representations of reality, as are contradiction, ambiguity, and paradox. There is in these new approaches a fundamental shift from the simple to the complex, from structure to

[93] Weiner 1990, 71.   [94] Ibid., 73.
[95] Blair 1977; Golley 1993; Kwa 2005; Aronova, Baker and Oreskes 2010.

process ... . The implications are far reaching. Rationality is no longer identified with certainty, nor probability with ignorance. Complexity and unpredictability are recognized as intrinsic features of systems as diverse as the world climate and the human brain. Complex systems are seen as evolving in an evolutionary process which both stochastic and deterministic factors play a vital role.[96]

Henry Regier and Elizabeth Bronson amplified some of implications of this perspective.

Humans cannot really manage an ecosystem; they may be able to manage their own influences with an ecosystem especially if they control those influence as their human sources. Careful humans adapt to and make use of non-human nature so as not to cripple the natural generative and regenerative processes that contribute to self-integration. Limits on sustainability are interpreted conservatively in order to leave a margin of safety for the inevitable unexpected events ... . The relevant science is strongly contextual, historical, comparative, and predictive.[97]

Holling developed these orientations into a set of ecological management principles.[98] They were quickly applied to the management of specific systems, including marine management[99] and resource management.[100] This work developed an early vision of sustainable use which was orthogonal to major existing dichotomies in traditional dichotomy in American resource management and environmentalism of preservationists and conservationists, and Cornucopians and Malthusians.

Maurice Strong celebrated an ecological approach to management as the animating philosophy behind UNCHE, and the dominant policy paradigm which the United Nations Environment Programme (UNEP) would help to apply to international law and resource management.[101] The new epistemic community replaced the prior policy elites of neo-classical economists and resource managers throughout the UN system as the presumptive environmental experts because the World Bank and General Agreement on Tariffs and Trade (GATT) failed to take the new issue seriously, and only submitted perfunctory papers to UNCHE. They did not play significant roles at the conference, and lost the

---

[96] Ploman 1985, 8.   [97] Regier and Bronson 1992, 112–13.
[98] Holling 1978.
[99] Vallega 1992; Cicin-Sain and Knecht 1998; Costanza et al. 1998.
[100] Savory 1988; Costanza 1991.   [101] Strong 1973.

epistemological high ground to Strong's preferred ideas and idea brokers.

The epistemic communities associated with ecological management were recruited to work for international intuitions, and helped shaped governance arrangements for tropical forestry management (who would focus on keystone species), conservation policy (focusing on preserving habitats) and pollution control (by applying comprehensive and cautious approaches based on critical loads and ecosystem loading for air and oceans). Rather than making strategic choices, the institutions chose experts who were regarded as having relevant knowledge for the issues at hand. In the absence of multiple competing epistemic communities, the ecological group was the only game in town, as is further seen later when ecological thinkers replaced economists and conservation economists at the World Bank and other international institutions in the early 1970s before and immediately after UNCHE.

The ecological ideas were applied in a variety of projects on behalf of the institutions in which they had become embedded. In terms of species conservation, early efforts reflected the ecological approach to ecosystems governance, stressing inputs from local stakeholder in the protection of habitats of endangered species.[102] The International Union for the Conservation of Nature (IUCN) and UNEP crafted the 1980 World Conservation Strategy, which anticipated many of the sustainable development guidelines for natural resource conservation. UNESCO developed the Man and the Biosphere Program in 1971 to protect endangered species in developing countries, applying the revolutionary approach of creating concentric zones of use in habitats and involving local farmers and nomads in resource management.[103] It now includes 669 sites in 120 countries worldwide, including 16 transboundary sites.[104]

Ecological approaches to pollution control were widely applied by UNEP through its international law-making activities to protect regional seas and the stratospheric ozone layer.[105] More broadly, the effects of the ecological epistemic ideas were diffused more widely through national- and international-level institutions.[106] As most national governments developed national environmental agencies they were staffed by the available experts, many of whom were drawn from or were

---

[102] Holdgate 1999; Macekura 2015.
[103] di Castri 1976; di Castri et al. 1981; Schleper 2017.   [104] UNESCO, n.d.
[105] Haas 1992; Tolba and Rummel-Bulska 1998; Haas 2021.
[106] Meyer 1997; Haas 2015.

sympathetic to the epistemic community.[107] Subsequently they made foreign and domestic environmental policies which reflected the eco-logic perspective.[108] International institutions, most notably UNEP and the World Bank after 1997, helped transfer resources so that governments could build domestic institutional capacity, conduct domestic monitoring and verification and acquire pollution monitoring and control technology. Formal environmental impact assessment requirements and comprehensive coastal zone management became increasingly common world by the 1990s, promoted by UNEP, the World Bank and US AID.[109] International legal commitments within environmental regimes (multilateral environmental agreements) helped impel and consolidate these two-level dynamics, by introducing comprehensive commitments, new ideas and providing mechanisms for signaling commitments.[110]

Most of these efforts were to apply more holistic governance approaches to discrete environmental issues: conservation or pollution. Surprising few links were drawn between environmental issues. Gradually links were drawn between environmental protection and other global issues, though, such as the burgeoning environment and development agenda, environment and security agenda and sustainability with the sustainable development goals. Gradually concerns about the use of foreign aid to promote economic development in the third world were linked to considerations about environmental externalities; as were concerns about climate change with security consequences from environmental refugees.

Communities of practice have also been involved in governing discrete environmental issues. Four projects have been discussed in the international environmental politics literature, one of which has been effective.

Certification Schemes

Nonmarket-based certification schemes by communities of MNCs, NGOs, stakeholders (such as organic farmers, coffee brokers, timber brokers, fishers and various commodity coops) and the occasional academic have developed collective voluntary guidelines and independent

---

[107] Urpelainen and Aklin 2014.   [108] Busch, Jörgens and Tews 2005.
[109] Sorensen 1993; Gilpin 1995; Sorensen 1997; Cicin-Sain and Knecht 1998.
[110] Haas 2015.

certification schemes for the sustainable production of such commodities as timber, forest products fish and coffee.[111]

Corporate Environmental Self-Monitoring

Extensive efforts at establishing corporate environmental monitoring processes have also occurred through corporate communities of practice.[112] Despite establishing ISO guidelines with which many companies seem to comply, such efforts are organizational, and are loosely connected to changes in corporate behavior or environmental outcomes.

UN Institutional Reform

UN institutional reforms have also been animated by communities of practice, although with relatively little success. From 1997 to 2012 communities of practice composed of academics, NGOs and practitioners met often to develop ways to improve UNEP's effectiveness at promoting environmental protection and sustainability within the UN system.[113] Despite a variety of imaginative proposals, UNEP ultimately received modest institutional changes at the 2012 Rio Plus 20 Conference.[114]

International Environmental Lawyers

A small cadre of international environmental lawyers, working in governments and UNEP, helped craft the core elements of many of the salient international environmental treaties developed since 1972, establishing key procedural obligations in the language of Brunnee and Toope. Contini and Sand[115] identified the core structures of environmental treaties which ecological epistemic communities helped to fill with their technical understanding of the operation of particular international ecosystems. The standard practice for environmental treaties became black and gray lists with appended science panels.[116] However, there remained a wide variation in the

---

[111] Cashore 2004; Bartley and Smith 2010; Auld 2014.
[112] Prakash and Potoski 2006.   [113] Biermann and Bauer 2005.
[114] Bernstein 2013.   [115] Contini and Sand 1972.
[116] Lang, Neuhold and Zemanek 1991; Szell 1991; Lang 1992.

design of the dozens of treaties signed since the 1970s, with the treaties reflecting the initial structures being ones in which epistemic communities played a strong role. That is, the lawyers tried to promote a common design across the board, whereas the variation in attendant practices depended upon the active involvement of epistemic communities.

Unlike the community of practice of international lawyers described by Brunnee and Toope,[117] which had a uniform constitutive effect on diplomacy, the impact on international environmental law has been much more nuanced and differentiated. The practice of uniform but differentiated obligations resulted more from hard diplomatic bargaining than interactions with lawyers. The underlying norms of international environmental law and practice remain contested, with the extent to which states will accept limitations on sovereignty disputed and contradictory within soft law.[118]

Explaining Variation

Why were epistemic communities more successful than communities of practice at shaping the global governance agenda for addressing complexity? The epistemic communities enjoyed greater authority and institutional access than did the communities of practice. Moreover, their message was less threatening to traditional actors. While the epistemic communities operated through delegation, and hence their advice was taken up based on the social authority enjoyed by the epistemic communities, the communities of practice were asking people (and states) to fundamentally change their attitudes and behavior (Bernstein talks about "structural fit"). Thus subversive ideas transmitted by groups who enjoyed closer institutional ties to decision makers prevailed over radical ideas about systemic transformation which echoed from outside the hallways of power (again, see Guzzini's chapter on power). Their power and influence rested on their reputation for epistemic authority. They were largely insulated from institutional influence because of a sense of urgency and the absence of contending expert perspectives, and thus able to operate as agents with a wide degree of discretion.

---

[117] Brunnee and Toope 2011.   [118] Bernstein 2001.

Conclusion: Progress and Cognitive Evolution

Dramatic changes in collective attitudes and practices about complexity have occurred. These changes span changes in institutions, in practices, and in social understandings. Social understandings include new more comprehensive approaches to public policy which take account of interconnections between issues as well as changes in the philosophy of science used in IR. Thus, increasing efforts to govern complexity accompany changes in understanding and studying complexity. However, these changes have occurred and actors have developed new reflective understandings which became gradually institutionalized. Rather than systemic *autopoesis* and self-correction it is a much more contingent, haphazard and a slow process.

The collective consciousness has changed to reflect an awareness of the flaws of modern progress and the collateral damage sustained through neglecting interconnections between issues.[119] Understanding began with environmental governance, and then spread to recognize the links between environmental conditions and other issues, such as environment and security, environment and trade, environment and aid, environment and human rights and so on.

New understandings about complexity, institutionalized through the processes of epistemic communities educating decision makers, and through an interactive pragmatic process of academics working with decision makers, have led to new broader appreciations of the challenges of complexity and the application of more comprehensive interconnected policy approaches to coping with global complexity.[120] This collective move toward recognizing ecological complexity involved moving away from linear thinking to more integrated or holistic thinking. Larry Summers, when president of Harvard University, said that the true mission of the university was to train students to think in terms of long causal chains. This shift in collective understanding occurred through the institutionalization of new ideas, doctrines and understandings about complexity.

Recognizing and governing complexity has been a contingent process. Alternate approaches always existed, and alternative ways of resolving complexity have always been possible. The current system remains fragile and subject to reversal. For instance, ecological

---

[119] Radkau 2008; Deudney and Mendenhall 2016.   [120] Haas and Haas 2009.

management approaches to dealing with environmental threats served as the foundations for the UNCHE action plan and institutional design. Yet ecological management was by no means the only conceptual option available to decision makers. After all, economists continued to dominate within the major economic institutions. What happened at UNCHE was that the World Bank simply didn't take the new issue of global environmental protection seriously, and submitted one contracted background paper to the conference. In the face of weak economic proposals for environmental mitigation, the relatively weaker ecological perspective was able to prevail.

Environmental governance has given rise to an increasingly broad appreciation of complexity. Epistemic communities have played a stronger role in this history than have communities of practice. As states became increasingly intertwined in a growing number of international environmental regimes they came to appreciate the complex texture of environmental governance and of international relations as a whole. As states have become increasingly aware of complexity – through their own exposure to ideas from epistemic communities and academics, and institutionalization through participation in international environmental regimes – they have learned about the nature and challenges of global complexity, and grown increasingly willing to defer to epistemic communities. While globalization and complexity haven't been tamed, some of the most egregious externalities and collateral damage have been recognized and ameliorated.

And yet the hermeneutic circle remains broken.[121] While decision makers have developed a new approach to dealing with environmental issues within the lens of complexity, IR theorizing about world politics and the dynamics of such puzzling and reimagining world order has not kept up. IPE and security studies remain focused on conventional accounts of behavior (with the notable exception of[122])

These changes in collective practice and understanding are also signs of progress.[123] International environmental conditions where the epistemic communities were involved have improved. Ecological ideas have been embedded in the plethora of national and international

---

[121] Green and Hale 2017.   [122] Oatley 2019.
[123] If we think of progress as replacing hard problems with more politically tractable problems this changing agenda may be less progressive. Its progress rests on the development of institutional capabilities, collective understandings and concrete improvements on the ground.

environmental bodies established since 1972. And, as a consequence of the embedded of these ideas in collective governance structures the collective global governance agenda has stretched from recognizing discrete problems to recognizing the connections between issues within the sustainable development tent adopted at Rio Plus 20 in 2012, as seen by the recent environment plus agenda of environment and development, trade and environment, security and environment, and even justice and the environment and the adoption of the Sustainable Development Goals.

References

Acheson, Dean. 1969. *Present at the Creation: My Years at the State Department*. New York: Norton.

Adler, Emanuel. 1991. Cognitive Evolution. In *Progress in Postwar International Relations*, edited by Emanuel Adler and Beverly Crawford, 43–88. New York: Columbia University Press.

Adler, Emanuel and Steven Bernstein. 2005. Knowledge in Power: The Epistemic Construction of Global Governance. In *Power in Global Governance*, edited by Michael Barnett and Raymond Duvall, 294–318. Cambridge: Cambridge University Press.

Adler, Emanuel and Peter Haas. 1992. Conclusion: Epistemic Communities, World Order, and the Creation of a Reflective Research Program. *International Organization* 46(1): 367–90.

Adler, Emanuel and Vincent Pouliot. 2011. *International Practices*. Cambridge: Cambridge University Press.

Agarwal, Anil and Sunita Narain. 1991. *Global Warming in an Unequal World: A Case of Environmental Colonialism*. New Delhi: Centre for Science and Environment.

Aklin, Michaël and Johannes Urpelainen. 2014. The Global Spread of Environmental Ministries: Domestic-International Interactions. *International Studies Quarterly* 58(4): 764–80.

Alker, Hayward. R. and Peter M. Haas. 1993. The Rise of Global Ecopolitics. In *Global Accord: Enviornmental Challenges and Global Responses*, edited by Nazil Choucri, 133–71. Cambridge, MA: MIT Press.

Allan, Bentley. 2017. From Subjects to Objects: Knowledge in International Relations Theory. *European Journal of International Relations* 24(4): 841–64.

Alter, Karen. J. and Sophie Meunier. 2009. The Politics of International Regime Complexity. *Perspectives on Politics* 7(1): 13–24.

Ansell, Cristopher K. and Steven Weber. 1999. Organizing International Politics: Sovereignty and Open Systems. *International Political Science Review* 20(1): 73–93.

Aronova, Elena, Karen S. Baker and Naomi Oreskes. 2010. Big Science and Big Data in Biology: From the International Geophysical Year through the International Biological Program to the Long Term Ecological Research (LTER) Network, 1957–Present. *Historical Studies in the Natural Sciences* 40(2): 183–224.

Auld, Graeme. 2014. *Constructing Private Governance: The Rise and Evolution of Forest, Coffee, and Fisheries Certification.* New Haven: Yale University Press.

Bailes, Kendall E. 1981. Science, Philosophy and Politics in Soviet History: The Case of Vladimir Vernadskii. *The Russian Review* 40 (3): 278–99.

Bartley, Tim and Shawna N. Smith. 2010. Communities of Practice as Cause and Consequence of Transnational Governnace. In *Transnational Communities: Shaping Global Economic Governance*, edited by Marie-Laure Djelic and Sigrid Quack, 347–74. Cambridge: Cambridge University Press.

Berger, P. L. and Luckmann, T. (1967). *The Social Construction of Reality.* New York: Doubleday Anchor.

Bernstein, Steven. 2001. *The Compromise of Liberal Environmentalism.* New York: Columbia University Press.

Bernstein, Steven. 2013. Rio+20: Sustainable Development in a Time of Multilateral Decline. *Global Environmental Politics* 13(4): 12–21.

Biermann, F. K. W., Kenneth Abbott, Karin Backstrand, Steven Bernstein, Michelle M. Betsill, Harriet Bulkeley, Ben Cashore and Peter M. Haas. 2012. Navigating the Anthropocene: Improving Earth System Governance. *Science* 335(6074): 1306–07.

Biermann, Frank and Steffen Bauer, eds. 2005. *A World Environment Organization: Solution or Threat for Effective International Environmental Governance?* Farnham: Ashgate.

Biermann, Frank and Philipp Pattberg, eds. 2012. *Global Environmental Governance Reconsidered.* Cambridge, MA: MIT Press.

Biermann, Frank, Philipp Pattberg, Harro van Asselt and Faribord Zelli. 2009. The Fragmentation of Global Governance Architectures: A Framework for Analysis. *Global Environmental Politics* 9(4): 14–40.

Blair, W. Frank. 1977. *Big Biology.* New York: Stoudsburg, Dowde, Hutchingson & Ross.

Bostrom, Nick and Milan M. Cirkovic, eds. 2008. *Global Catastrophic Risks.* Oxford: Oxford University Press.

Botkin, Daniel B. 1990. *Discordant Harmonies.* Oxford: Oxford University Press.

Boulding, Kenneth E. 1966. The Economics of the Coming Spaceship Earth. In *Environmental Quality in a Growing Economy*, edited by Henry Jarrett and Kenneth E. Boulding, 3–14. Baltimore: Johns Hopkins University.

Boulton, Jean G., Peter M. Allen and Cliff Bowman. 2015. *Embracing Complexity: Strategic Perspectives for an Age of Turbulence*. 1st ed. Oxford: Oxford University Press.

Bradley, R. S. 2011. *Global Warming and Political Intimidation*. Amherst: University of Massachusetts Press.

Braithwaite, John and Peter Drahos. 2000. *Global Business Regulation*. Cambridge: Cambridge University Press.

Braudel, Fernand. 1977. *Afterthoughts on Material Civilization and Capitalism*. Baltimore: Johns Hopkins University Press.

Braudel, Fernand. 1979. *The Structures of Everyday Life*. New York: Harper and Row.

Braudel, Fernand. 1982. *The Wheels of Commerce*. New York: Harper and Row.

Braudel, Fernand. 1984. *The Perspective of the World*. New York: Harper and Row.

Brewer, Garry D. and Paul C. Stern, eds. 2005. *Decision Making for the Environment: Social and Behavioral Science Research Priorities*. Washington, DC: National Academies Press.

Brunnée, Jutta and Stephen J. Toope. 2011. Interactional International Law and the Practice of Legality. In *International Practices*, edited by Emanuel Adler and Vincent Pouliot, 108–36. Cambridge: Cambridge University Press.

Burke, Peter. 2012. *A Social History of Knowledge: From the Encyclopedia to Wikipedia*. Cambridge: Polity.

Busch, Per-Olof, Helge Jörgens and Kerstin Tews. 2005. The Global Diffusion of Regulatory Instruments: The Making of a New International Environmental Regime. *The Annals of the American Academy of Political and Social Science* 598(1): 146–67.

Caldwell, Lynton K. 1963. Environment: A New Focus for Public Policy? *Public Administration Review* 23(3): 132–39.

Campbell, Donald T. 1993. Evolutionary Epistemology. In *Evolutionary Epistemology, Rationality, and the Sociology of Knowledge*, edited by Gerard Radnitzky, W. W. Bartlet and Karl Popper. Chicago: Open Court.

Carson, Rachel. 1962. *Silent Spring*. New York: Houghton Mifflin.

Cashore, Benjamin William, Graeme Auld and Deanna Newsom. 2004. *Governing Through Markets: Forest Certification and the Emergence of Non-State Authority*. New Haven: Yale University Press.

Choucri, N. 1993. *Global Accord*. Cambridge, MA: MIT Press.

Christian, David. 2004. *Maps of Time*. Berkeley: University of California Press.

Churchman, C. West. 1984. *The Systems Approach*. New York: Delacorte Press.

Churchman, C. West and Russel L. Ackoff. 1950. *Methods of Inquiry: An Introduction to Philosophy and Scientific Method*. St Louis: Educational.

Cicin-Sain, Biliana and Robert W. Knecht. 1998. *Integrated Coastal and Ocean Management: Concepts and Practices*. Washington, DC: Island Press.

Cole, Sam. 1977. *Global Models and the International Economic Order*. Oxford: Pergamon. Consortium for International Earth Science Information Network (CIESIN).

Contini, Paolo and Peter H. Sand. 1972. Methods to Expedite Environmental Protection: International Econstandards. *American Journal of International Law* 66(1): 37–59.

Costanza, Robert, ed. 1991. *Ecological Economics: The Science and Management of Sustainability*. New York: Columbia University Press.

Costanza, Robert, Francisco Andrade, Paula Antunes, Marjan van den Belt, Dee Boersma, Donald F. Boesch, Fernando Catarino, et al. 1998. Principles for Sustainable Governance of the Oceans. *Science* 281(5374): 198–99.

Crosby, Alfred W. 1986. *Ecological Imperialism: The Biological Expansion of Europe, 900–1900*. Cambridge: Cambridge University Press.

Crutzen, Paul. 2003. How Long Have We Been in the Anthropocene. *Climatic Change* 6: 251–57.

Dahlberg, Kenneth A. (1983). Contextual Analysis: Taking Space, Time, and Place Seriously. *International Studies Quarterly* 27(3): 257–66.

de Seynes, Philippe. 1972. Prospects for a Future Whole World. *International Organization* 26(1): 1–17.

Debre, Maria Josepha and Hylke Dijkstra. 2020. Institutional Design for a Post-liberal Order: Why Some International Organizations Live Longer than Others. *European Journal of International Relations* 27(1): 311–39.

Deudney, Daniel and Elizabeth Mendenhall. 2016. Green Earth: The Emergence of Planetary Civilization. In *New Earth Politics: Essays from the Anthropocene*, edited by Simon Nicholson and Jinnah Sikina, 43–72. Cambridge, MA: MIT Press.

di Castri, Francesco. 1976. International, Interdisciplinary Research in Ecology. *Human Ecology* 4(3): 235–46.

di Castri, Francesco, Malcom Hadley, et al. 1981. MAB: The Man and the Biosphere Program as an Evolving System. *AMBIO* 10(2–3): 52–57.

Diamond, Jared. 2005. *Collapse: How Societies Choose to Succeed or Fail*. New York: Penguin.

Djelic, Marie-Laure and Sigrid Quack. 2010. *Transnational Communities: Shaping Global Economic Governance*. Cambridge: Cambridge University Press.

Dunlop, Claire A. and Claudio M. Radaelli. 2012. Systematising Policy Learning. *Political Studies* 61(3): 599–619.

Ehrlich, Paul and Anne Ehrlich. 1968. *The Population Bomb*. San Francisco: Sierra Club Books.

Ehrlich, Paul and Anne Ehrlich. 2004. *One with Ninevah: Politics, Consumption and the Human Future*. Washington, DC: Island Press.

Eilstrup-Sangiovanni, Mette. 2020. What Kills International Organisations? When and Why International OrganisationsTerminate. *European Journal of International Relations* 27(1): 281–310.

Ezhrahi, Yaron. 1980. Utopian and Pragmatic Rationalism: The Political Context of Scientific Advance. *Minerva* 18(1): 111–31.

Falk, Richard A. 1975. *A Study of Future Worlds*. New York: Free Press.

Farrell, H. and A. L. Newman. 2018. Linkage Politics and Complex Governance in Transatlantic Surveillance. *World Politics*, 70(4),515–54.

Franck, Thomas M. 1990. *The Power of Legitimacy Among Nations*. New York: Oxford University Press.

Freeman, Christopher and Marie Jahoda. 1978. *World Futures*. New York: Universe.

Galtung, Johan. 1973. "The Limits to Growth" and Class Politics. *Journal of Peace Research* 10(1/2): 101–14.

Galtung, Johan. 1980. *The True Worlds: A Transnational Perspective*. New York: Free Press.

Gardner, Richard N. 1980. *Sterling-Dollar Diplomacy in Current Perspective: The Origins and the Prospects of our International Economic Order*. New York: Columbia University Press.

Giddens, Anthony. 1984. *The Constitution of Society: Outline of the Theory of Structuration*. Berkeley: University of California.

Gilpin, Alan. 1995. *Environmental Impact Assessment*. Cambridge: Cambridge University Press.

Global Challenges Foundation. 2016. *Global Catastrophic Risks*. Oxford: Global Challenges Foundation.

Golley, Frank B. 1993. *A History of the Ecosystem Concept in Ecology*. New Haven: Yale University Press.

Green, Jessica F. and Thomas N. Hale. 2017. Reversing the Marginalization of Global Environmental Politics in International Relations: An Opportunity for the Discipline. *PS: Political Science and Politics* 50(2): 473–79.

Haas, Ernst B. 1975. Is There a Whole in the Hole? *International Organization* 29(3): 827–76.

Haas, Ernst B. 1990. *When Knowledge is Power*. Berkeley: University of California Press.

Haas, Peter M. 1992. Introduction: Epistemic Communities and International Policy Coordination. *International Organization* 46(1): 1–37.

Haas, Peter M. 1992. Banning Chlorofluorocarbons: Epistemic Community Efforts to Protect Stratospheric Ozone. *International Organization* 46(1): 187–224.

Haas, Peter M. 2021. Epistemic Communities and International Environmental Law. In *Oxford Handbook of International Environmental Law*, 2nd ed., edited by Lavnya Rajamai and Jacqueline Peel. Oxford: Oxford University Press.

Haas, Peter M. 2015. *Epistemic Communities, Constructivism and International Environmental Politics*. London: Routledge.

Haas, Peter M. and Ernst B. Haas. 1995. Learning to Learn: Improving International Governance. *Global Governance* 1(3): 255–84.

Haas, Peter M. and Ernst B. Haas. 2002. Pragmatic Constructivism and the Study of International Institutions. *Millennium* 31(3): 573–602.

Haas, Peter M. and Ernst B. Haas. 2009. Pragmatic Constructivism and the Study of International Institutions. In *Pragmatism in International Relations*, edited by Harry Bauer and Elisabetta Brighi, 103–23. London: Routledge.

Hagen, Joel B. 1992. *The Entangled Bank: Origins of Ecosystem Ecology*. Brunswick: Rutgers University Press.

Hardin, Garett. 1968. The Tragedy of the Commons. *Science* 162(1968): 1243–48.

Held, David, Thomas Hale and Kevin Young. 2013. *Gridlock: Why Global Cooperation is Failing When We Need It Most*. Cambridge: Polity.

Holdgate, Martin. 1999. *The Green Web*. London: Earthscan.

Holling, C. S., ed. 1978. *Adaptive Environmental Assessment and Management*. New York: Wiley.

Holsti, K. J. 1992. *Peace and War: Armed Conflicts and International Order 1648–1989*. Cambridge: Cambridge University Press.

Hughes, J. Donald. 1975. *Ecology in Ancient Civilizations*. Albuquerque: University of New Mexico Press.

Ikenberry, G. J. 2001. *After Victory: Institutions, Strategic Restraint, and the Rebuilding of Order after Major Wars*. Princeton: Princeton University Press.

Jacobson, Harold K. and Martin F. Price. 1990. *A Framework for Research on the Human Dimensions of Global Environmental Change*. Paris: International Social Science Council.

Jervis, R. 1997. *System Effects*. Princeton: Princeton University Press.

Jervis, Robert. 1997. *System Effects: Complexity in Social and Political Life*. Princeton: Princeton University Press.

Jevons, William Stanley. 1865. *The Coal Question*. London: MacMillan.

Kasperson, Jeanne X. and Roger E. Kasperon, eds. 2001. *Global Environmental Risk*. Tokyo: United Nations University Press.

Katzenstein, Peter J. and Lucia A. Seybert. 2018. *Protean Power: Exploring the Uncertain and Unexpected in World Politics*. Cambridge: Cambridge University Press.

Kaysen, Carl. 1972. The Computer that Printed out W*O*L*F*. *Foreign Affairs* 50(3): 660–68.

Keohane, Robert. O. and Joseph. S. Nye. 1977. *Power and Interdependence: World Politics in Transition*. Boston: Little, Brown.

Keohane, Robert O. and David G. Victor. 2011. The Regime Complex for Climate Change. *Perspectives on Politics* 9(1): 7–24.

Kern, Stephen. 2003. *The Culture of Time and Space 1880–1918*. Cambridge, MA: Harvard University Press.

King, Alexander and Bertrand Schneider. 1991. *The First Global Revolution: A Report by the Council of the Club of Rome*. New York: Pantheon Books.

Kothari, Rajni. 1974. *Footsteps into the Future: Diagnosis of the Present World and a Design for an Alternative*. New York: Free Press.

Kwa, Chunglin. 2005. Local Ecologies and Global Science. *Social Studies of Science* 35(6): 923–50.

La Porte, Todd R. 1975. *Organized Social Complexity: Challenge to Politics and Policy*. Princeton: Princeton University Press.

Ladyman, James, James Lambert and Karoline Wiesner. 2013. What is a Complex System? *European Journal for Philosophy of Science* 3(1): 33–67.

Lake, David A. 2020. The Organizational Ecology of Global Governance. *European Journal of International Relations*, online first.

Lang, Winfried, Hanspeter Neuhold and Karl Zemanek. 1991. *Environmental Protection and International Law*. Boston: Graham.

Lang, Winfried. 1992. Diplomacy and International Law Making: Some Observations. *Yearbook of International Environmental Law* 3(1): 108–22.

Lapo, Audrey. 1987. *Traces of Bygone Biospheres*. Moscow: Mir.

Le Prestre, Philippe. 2016. *Global Ecopolitics Revisited*. London: Routledge.

Levin, Kelly, Benjamin Cashore, Steven Bernstein and Graeme Auld. 2012. Overcoming the Tragedy of Super Wicked Problems. *Policy Sciences* 45 (2): 123–52.

Macekura, Stephen J. 2015. *Of Limits and Growth: The Rise of Global Sustainable Development in the Twentieth Century*. Cambridge: Cambridge University Press.

MacNeill, Jim, Pieter Winsemius and Taizō Yakushiji. 1991. *Beyond Interdependence: The Meshing of the World's Economy and the Earth's Ecology*. New York: Oxford University Press.

Manning, Patrick. 2003. *Navigating World History*. London: Palgrave.

Marsh, George Perkins. [1865]1965. *Man and Nature*. Cambridge, MA: Harvard University Press.

Mazower, Mark. 2012. *Governing the World: The Rise and Fall of an Idea, 1815 to the Present*. New York: Penguin.

McIntosh, Robert P. 1985. *The Background of Ecology*. Cambridge: Cambridge University Press.

McNeill, J. R. 2000. *Something New Under the Sun: An Environmental History of the Twentieth-Century World*. New York: W. W. Norton.

McNeill, John R. and William H. McNeill. 2003. *The Human Web: A Bird's-Eye View*. New York: W. W. Norton.

Meadows, Donella H., Dennis L. Meadows, et al. 1971. *The Limits to Growth: A Report for the Club of Rome's Project on the Predicament of Mankind*. New York: Universe Books.

Meadows, Donella. H., Dennis L. Meadows, et al. 1992. *Beyond the Limits*. Post Mills: Chelsea Green.

Melillo, Jerry M., Christopher B. Field and Bedrich Moldan, eds. 2003. *Interactions of the Major Biogeochemical Cycles: Global Change and Human Impacts*. Washington, DC: Island Press.

Meyer, John W., David John Frank, Ann Hironaka, Evan Schofer and Nancy Brandon Tuma. 1997. The Structuring of a World Environmental Regime, 1870–1990. *International Organization* 51(4): 623–51.

National Research Council, et al. 1999. *Our Common Journey: A Transition Toward Sustainability*. Washington, DC: National Academy Press.

Oatley, Thomas. 2019. Toward a Political Economy of Complex Interdependence. *European Journal of International Relations* 25(4): 957–78.

Odum, Eugene P. 1977. The Emergence of Ecology as a New Integrative Discipline. *Science* 195(4284): 1289–993.

Ollman, Bertell. 1971. *Alienation: Marx's Conception of Man in Capitalist Society*. Cambridge: Cambridge University Press.

Onuf, Nicholas G. 1983. Reports to the Club of Rome. *World Politics* 36(1): 121–46.

Onuf, Nicholas G. 1989. *World of Our Making: Rules and Rule in Social Theory and International Relations*. Columbia: University of South Carolina Press.

Oreskes, Naomi and Erik M. Conway. 2010. *Merchants of Doubt*. New York: Bloomsbury Press.

Orsini, A., P. Le Prestre, P. M. Haas, M. Brosig, P. Pattberg, O. Widerberg and D. Chandler. 2019. Forum: Complex Systems and International Governance. *International Studies Review* 22(4): 1008–38.

Osborn, Fairfield. 1949. *Our Plundered Planet*. Boston: Little, Brown.

Perrow, Charles. 1984. *Normal Accidents: Living with High Risk Technologies*. New York: Basic Books.

Pirages, Dennis. 1983. The Ecological Perspective and the Social Sciences. *International Studies Quarterly* 27(3): 243–55.

Ploman, Edward W. 1985. Introduction. In *The Science and Praxis of Complexity*, edited by Shūhei Aida, 1–24. Tokyo: United Nations University.

Ponting, Clive. 1992. *A Green History of the World*. New York: St. Martin's Press.

Prakash, Aseem and Matthew Potoski. 2006. *The Voluntary Environmentalists*. Cambridge: Cambridge University Press.

Radkau, Joachim. 2008. *Nature and Power: A Global History of the Environment*. Cambridge: Cambridge University Press.

Raustiala, Kal and David G. Victor. 2004. The Regime Complex for Plant Genetic Resources. *International Organization* 58(2): 311–44.

Regier, Henry A. and Elizabeth A. Bronson. 1992. New Perspectives on Sustainable Development and Barriers to Relevant Information. *Environmental Monitoring and Assessment* 20(2–3): 111–20.

Rittel, Horst W. J. and Melvin. M. Webber (1973). Dilemmas in a General Theory of Planning. *Policy Sciences* 4(2): 155–69.

Rockstrom, John, W. Steffen, K. Noone, A. Persson, F. S. I. Chapin and E. F. Lambin. 2009. A Safe Operating Space for Humanity. *Nature* 461: 472–75.

Ruggie, John G. 1998. What Makes the World Hang Together? Neo-Utilitarianism and the Social Constructivist Challenge. *International Organization* 52(4): 855–85.

Sabatier, Paul A. and Hank C. Jenkins-Smith, eds. 1993. *Policy Change and Learning: Advocacy Coalition Approach*. Boulder: Westview Press.

Sabin, Paul. 2013. *The Bet: Paul Ehrlich, Julian Simon, and Our Gamble over Earth's Future*. New Haven: Yale University Press.

Savory, Allan. 1988. *Holistic Resource Management*. Washington, DC: Island Press.

Schleper, Simone. 2017. Conservation Compromises: The MAB and the Legacy of the International Biological Program, 1964–1974. *Journal of the History of Biology* 50(1): 133–67.

Schlesinger, William H. 1991. *Biogeochemistry: An Analysis of Global Change*. San Diego: Academic Press.

Sears, Paul B. 1964. Ecology: A Subversive Subject. *Bioscience* 14(7): 11–13.

Shanks, Cheryl, K. Harold, H. K. Jacobson and Jeffrey H. Kaplan. 1996. Inertia and Change in the Constellation of International Governmental Organizations. *International Organization* 50(4): 593–627.

Simon, Herbert A. 1981. *The Sciences of the Artificial*. Cambridge, MA: MIT Press.

Smil, Vaclac. 1993. *Global Ecology*. London: Routledge.

Smil, Vaclac. 2006. *Transforming the Twentieth Century*. Oxford: Oxford University Press.

Sorensen, Jens. 1993. The International Proliferation of Integrated Coastal Zone Management Efforts. *Ocean & Coastal Management* 21(1–3): 45–80.

Sorensen, Jens. 1997. National and International Efforts at Integrated Coastal Management: Definitions, Achievements, and Lessons. *Coastal Management* 25(34): 3–41.

Speth, James Gustave. 2004. *Red Sky at Morning: America and the Crisis of the Global Environment*. New Haven: Yale University Press.

Speth, James Gustave. 2008. *The Bridge at the Edge of the World*. New Haven: Yale University Press.

Sprout, Harold and Margaret Sprout. 1971. *Toward a Politics of Planet Earth*. New York: Van Nostrand Reinhold.

Sprout, Harold and Margaret Sprout. 1972. The Ecological Viewpoint – and Others. In *The Future of the International Legal Order*, edited by Cyril E. Black and Richard A. Falk, 569–606. Princeton: Princeton University Press.

Stern, Paul C., Oran R. Young, et al., eds. 1992. *Global Environmental Change: Understanding the Human Dimensions*. Washington, DC: National Academy Press.

Strong, Maurice F. 1973. One Year after Stockholm: An Ecological Approach to Management. *Foreign Affairs* 51(4): 690–707.

Szell, Patrick. 1991. The Development of Multilateral Mechanisms for Monitoring Compliance. In *Environmental Protection and International Law*, edited by Winfried Lang, Hanspeter Neuhold and Karl Zemanek, ch. 7. London: Graham and Trotman.

Thomas, William L., ed. 1956. *Man's Role in Changing the Face of the Earth*. Chicago: University of Chicago Press.

Tolba, Mostafa K. and Iwona Rummel-Bulska. 1998. *Global Environmental Diplomacy*. Cambridge, MA: MIT Press.

Toulmin, Stephen. 1990. *Cosmopolis: The Hidden Agenda of Modernization*. New York: Free Press.

Trotmanjndrey, V. 1987. *Traces of Bygone Biospheres*. Moscow: Mir.

Turner II, B. L., William C. Clark, Robert W. Kates, John F. Richards, Jessica. F. Matthews and William B. Meyer, eds. 1990. *The Earth as Transformed by Human Action*. Cambridge: Cambridge University Press.

Uhrqvist, Ola and Björn-Ola Linnér. 2015. Narratives of the Past for Future Earth: The Historiography of Global Environmental Change Research. *Anthropocene Review* 2(2): 159–73.

UNESCO. *Man and the Biosphere Programme*. Unesco.org. www.unesco.org/new/en/natural-sciences/environment/ecological-sciences/man-and-biosphere-programme/. Accessed April 14, 2017.

Vallega, Adalberto. 1992. *Sea Management: A Theoretical Approach*. London: Elsevier Applied Science.

Van Dyne, George M., ed. 1969. *The Ecosystem Concept in Natural Resource Management*. New York: Academic Press.

Vernadsky, Vladimir I. 1944. Problems of Geochemistry. *Transactions of the Connecticut Academy of Arts and Sciences* 35: 487–517.

Vernadksy, Vladimir I. 1945. The Biosphere and the Noosphere. *American Scientist* 33(1): 1–12.

Vitousek, Peter, Harold A. Mooney, et al. 1997. Human Domination of the Earth's Ecosystems. *Science* 277(5325): 494–99.

Waddington, Conrad H. 1975. *The Evolution of an Evolutionist*. Ithaca: Cornell University Press.

Weiner, Douglas R. 1990. Prometheus Rechained: Ecology and Conservation. In *Science and the Soviet Social Order*, edited by Loren R. Graham, 71–93. Cambridge, MA: Harvard University Press.

Wendt, Alexander. 1987. The Agent-Structure Problem in International Relations Theory. *International Organization* 41(3): 335–70.

Wendt, Alexander. 1992. Anarchy Is What States Make of It: The Social Construction of Power Politics. *International Organization* 46(2): 391–425.

Wendt, Alexander. 2015. *Quantum Mind and Social Science: Unifying Physical and Social Ontology*. Cambridge: Cambridge University Press.

Wenger, Etienne. 1998. *Communities of Practice*. Cambridge: Cambridge University Press.

Woodwell, George, M. 1985. On the Limits of Nature. In *The Global Possible: Resources, Development, and the New Century*, edited by Roberto Repetto, 47–65. New Haven: Yale University Press.

Woodwell, George M. 2016. *A World to Live In*. Cambridge, MA: MIT Press.

World Economic Forum. 2016. *The Global Risks Report*. Geneva: World Economic Forum.

Worster, Donald. 1987. *Nature's Economy*. Cambridge: Cambridge University Press.

Yanshin, A. L. and F. T. Yanshina. 1988. The Scientific Heritage of Vladimir Vernadsky. *Impact of Science on Society* 38(3): 283–96.

Young, Oran R. 2017. *Governing Complex Systems: Social Capital for the Anthropocene*. Cambridge, MA: MIT Press.

Young, Oran R., Leslie A. King and Heike Schroeder, eds. 2008. *Institutions and Environmental Change: Principle Findings, Applications, and Research Frontiers*. Cambridge, MA: MIT Press

7 | Refugees and Their Allies as Agents of Progress

Knowledge and Power in Forbidden Boundary Regions

BEVERLY CRAWFORD AMES

Since Antiquity, the treatment of migrants has been the barometer of whether our common humanity is acknowledged. It measures the extent to which "the other" is dehumanized or included in the fold of humanity. Only by the mid-twentieth century had the international community begun to acknowledge and protect the humanity of the displaced. The twenty-first century, however, has witnessed a landslide of events threatening that progress. Walls and fences built to keep out asylum seekers multiplied from eleven countries when the Berlin Wall collapsed to more than seventy countries in 2018. In 2017, 68.5 million people found themselves displaced by war, discrimination, disaster, famine, torture and oppression. How was twentieth-century progress in protection of forced migrants achieved and why has it unraveled?

To find answers I look to Emanuel Adler's cognitive evolution (CE) theory and his focus on progress. Adler argues that progress in international relations depends upon practices – like implementing treaty-based promises of refugee protection – that enhance "human interests across borders." He speaks of progress as "acknowledging our common humanity" – the humanity of those not only across borders but also *those who cross over borders* and those who live between borders without the security of a community that would offer them legal protection. CE theory provides an array of knowledge-based practices which *could* lead to this acknowledgment but would not necessarily do so. The foundation of CE theory is epistemological security – the validity of what we collectively consider knowledge. Without that security, CE – whether progressive or not – cannot take place. For progress to be achieved epistemological security must be assured and practices that embody "ethical

169

collective knowledge"[1] must diffuse widely. A number of authors in this volume have elaborated on, extended and critiqued Adler's idea of progress, and, by extension, the concept of "regress."[2]

Through the lens of Adler's theory, I examine the fate of forced migrants to ask whether and how international progress has been achieved. *How those of us living under the protection of citizenship rights treat forced migrants without those rights provides a yardstick for determining whether or not global change is moving in the direction of progress.* Focusing on the forcibly displaced, I define "acknowledgment of our common humanity" as the growing number and quality of practices that treat all displaced persons as "our fellow humans" by extending to them and enforcing the same human rights that citizens of secure, democratic states enjoy. I examine the historical development of those practices and show how "better practices," leading to that acknowledgment replaced practices that fell short. I look to refugees and their allies as the agents of that progress.

I base my discussion on the assumption that progress can be achieved in international relations. In Old School terms, I am on the side of the "idealists" in the "realist-idealist" debate in International Relations (IR) theory[3] and stand squarely in the liberal intellectual tradition. More recent debates, which remind me of epicycles in the Ptolemaic (as opposed to Copernican) scientific tradition, which debate elaborate solutions to the wrong problem, treat progress in IR as a contested concept. While some scholars are skeptical about whether progress can be achieved at all, others take a more positive view and focus on *how* and under what conditions progress in IR – whether civilizational, institutional, moral, minimal, limited, contingent or bounded, can be achieved.[4] Following Adler and his concept of "bounded progress," my focus is more akin to the latter.

Adler's CE theory begins with the establishment of "communities of practice" – in this case, those communities who make the initial decision to seek, offer and/or deny refuge. These communities are established when actors share "background knowledge," introduce new

---

[1] Adler 1991, 2019, and this volume.
[2] See also Pouliot, Kornprobst and Ish-Shalom, Drieschova, Pratt, Haas, Reus-Smith and Sondarjee, all this volume.
[3] Carr 1939, 1964; Wendt 1992.
[4] See, for example, Elman and Elman eds. 2003; Price 2008; Barnett 2009; Linklater 2010, 2011; Deudney and Mendenhall 2016; Ikenberry 2018.

knowledge, acquire and exercise performative and/or deontic power, and learn, unlearn and relearn together. CE is possible when these communities become agents of change. An environment of growing interdependence and epistemological security is necessary to facilitate their interaction and agency. They must share a common reality and be motivated to interact. Through interaction, they create new practices. Over time, some communities die out and new ones are established. Political, educational, and, at times, religious authorities, possess the deontic power to assign status and function to some practices and not others. If their favored practices are widely diffused and institutional- ized, they can embed new practices in the social order and gradually restructure social consciousness.

For Adler, this process can result in tentative progress only when communities of practice become repositories of *ethical* collective know- ledge, create *shared meanings* about the value of human worth, create *better practices* to act on those shared meanings, have the *power* to institutionalize and diffuse those practices and *expand* the boundaries of those communities. This was the process by which the practice of slavery was discarded and former slaves were acknowledged to be full human beings. In some parts of the world, however, slavery has made a comeback. That comeback provides a warning: progress is reversible.

Adler's theory does not offer a detailed examination of how CE can retreat from a tentative march to progress. A discussion of practices surrounding refugee protection in the current "post-truth era" offers clues about the path that such a retreat could take. I define "post-truth" practices as those that embody contempt for knowledge, distrust of those who produce knowledge and the use of the methods of science and scholarship to discredit facts and those who produce them. I argue that when these practices come to dominate the vernacular, they pro- duce an environment in which *normlessness* threatens to shape dis- course and action, and the epistemological security upon which CE depends, is weakened and can be destroyed. When epistemological security is wounded, progress is endangered.

A case study of refugees and their fate is an apt subject to examine the utility of CE theory and the strength of ethical practices that can lead to progress. To the extent that the humanity of the alien "other" is acknow- ledged and the suffering of forced migrants is alleviated,[5] *this case*

---

[5] Barnett and Stein 2017.

provides a measure of the resilience of the liberal social order. An examination of the evolution of practices of refugee protection allows a glimpse into the arena of contestation between nationalist and liberal internationalist norms, practices and communities of practice. It allows us to analyze how practitioners have reached across boundaries between communities to negotiate terms that acknowledge refugees' humanity. It allows us to trace the processes of social learning by which opposing communities of practice are able to strike (or not strike) compromises that would define those terms. It allows us to examine how the practices of the refugees themselves may contribute to the social learning process when they claim their own humanity in the act of flight while living between and across dangerous and forbidden boundaries where their humanity has been denied. A study of the refugee experience illustrates how they and their allies can create a community of practice based on a culture of resilience and how they can become agents of change to spur the institutionalization and cross-boundary diffusion of practices that acknowledge their humanity.

A case study of refugee protection also provides insight into "post-truth" practices of communities and political authorities that challenge the theory of CE and endanger progress. In the wake of a weakening of traditional nationalist and liberal internationalist values, the rise of these communities with their norm-breaking power threatens to sap the human appetite for evidence-based claims – in this case, claims involving refugees and their impact on host societies. These communities – now fashionably called "tribes" – relish and amplify the denial of facts and distrust of liberal democratic institutions for the sake of excluding what they consider "alien" communities from any recognition of their moral worth and entitlement to human rights. This denial and distrust weakens epistemological security, the foundation upon which CE theory rests.

In the following section, I describe how the moral dialogue between national and international communities redefined the goals of each community and expanded their boundaries. I then turn to a discussion of how, in the current era, both CE and progress are endangered when "post-truth" practices become so extreme and powerful that they threaten to cutoff that debate. I conclude by asking whether the debate and the historical practices of refugee protection can be sustained and whether CE theory can hold in a period of epistemological insecurity.

How "Better Practices" Led to Widespread Acknowledgment of Forced Migrants' Humanity

The history of refugee protection begins with those whose humanity was denied – slaves, serfs, women, minorities – and their instinctive search for sanctuary where their humanity will be acknowledged. That search is the first indicator that refugees themselves are agents of change. The potential for acknowledging their humanity is intertwined with authorities' changing responses to them at particular historical moments. Sometimes contact with refugees calmed fears and permitted a welcoming environment. Often the decision to offer sanctuary was a calculated move to gain or retain political power. Most often it originated in the authorities' belief that only co-ethnics or co-religionists should be treated as fully human.[6] Only in the twentieth century did the international community come to agree that *all* refugees possessed human rights and therefore deserved refuge as they themselves would deserve it if forced to flee. Based on that agreement, twentieth-century practices aspired to bring all forced migrants into the realm of humanity no matter their ethnicity or religion.

The early twentieth century had witnessed the dissolution of empires and the escalation of fiercely defended borders between modern European nation states. Nation states' territorial control under the Westphalian system had long permitted legal exclusion of outsiders from state territory. Millions fleeing war and expulsion from newly created states found themselves in a no-man's-land between dangerous and forbidden borders and unwelcome beyond them. As ethnic nationalism within state borders gained dominance, minorities were expelled, and enlightenment ideas about the "natural rights" of man were relegated to the pit of hopeless idealism. There were no international ethical standards or practices acknowledging the human rights of the expelled or obliging neighbors to offer refuge.

The creation of the League of Nations provided forced migrants the first opportunity in history to avail themselves of international protection. After the 1917 Russian Revolution, the new Soviet government had forced millions of its anti-communist enemies into exile. It did not join the League, and most members regarded it with enmity. Those fleeing or exiled from the regime scattered throughout Europe. At first,

---

[6] For this history see Crawford 2018.

anti-communist movements and governments believed that the Russian refugees were counterrevolutionaries who might be able to overthrow the new communist government. The Yugoslav and Czechoslovak governments aided them, in the belief that they might help destroy the Communist enemy. But hope of a counterrevolution faded, and they too launched campaigns of expulsion, ejecting Russians onto their neighbors' territory, angering them and thereby creating tensions among League members. For the fledgling League, solving the refugee problem would quell this simmering tension and would help solidify the League's status.

In response to the Russian refugee crisis, the League Council created a High Commission for Refugees (HCR). That job of High Commissioner fell to Dr. Fridtjof Nansen, a respected explorer with cosmopolitan and humanitarian sensibilities informed by Enlightenment ideas of human equality. His mandate was "to coordinate the action of governments and private organizations for the relief of Russian refugees." With little financial support for the HCR from the League, Dr. Nansen successfully raised funds from other voluntary humanitarian organizations and together with these allies, developed practices to aid the displaced.

Nansen initiated two innovations to alleviate the refugee crisis, and both became widely diffused practices. He first recognized that a practical obstacle to bringing forced migrants into the realm of humanity was the absence of a passport. Displaced Russians in 1903 had described this absence succinctly: "Man consists of a body, soul, and a passport." In other words, a man without a passport is only two-thirds human – a body and soul but without the rights of a national (human) community to protect them.[7] Although a passport was primarily an instrument of state control over its borders, for the holder it signified citizenship under that state's protection. States were obligated to respect the rights of alien passport holders as (human) citizens of neighboring states. For this reason, Nansen created an international "Nansen passport," under the auspices of the League for displaced people. If apprehended, displaced persons holding Nansen passports could appeal to the League, which had consular offices in most member states. Second, Nansen convinced League members to resettle over one million displaced people in their countries. Previously, member

---

[7] Stoessinger 1956, 3.

states from Europe to Asia had accepted the displaced for temporary labor but had resisted their resettlement. But when Nansen offered League financing, many states agreed to his resettlement scheme. Thus, they too became unwitting refugee allies.

The refugees themselves became "accidental" agents of progress. They were forced to defy boundaries, refuse to be and locked out and own their entitlement to be treated as human. *To be able to endure in the dangerous space between borders and on foreign soil, they had to embrace their own worth as human beings while those around them refused to acknowledge it.* As Frederick Douglass stated, "A man who will not fight for himself . . .is not worth being fought for by others . . . . The limits of tyrants are prescribed by the endurance of those whom they oppress."[8] Refugees who found reservoirs of courage and resilience inside themselves in their flight from tyranny represented a challenge to tyranny itself. In the act of seeking refuge and enduring, they both proclaimed their own humanity and forced others to acknowledge it. This act was, in Adler's terms, endowed with meaning and was the first important step on the path to progressive CE. Beginning with the flight from the Soviet Union, refugees changed social consciousness over the course of the twentieth century about who has the right to be called human and treated as a human being.

When he became High Commissioner for Refugees, Nansen never suspected that he, the League of Nations, member states, private charities and the refugees themselves had together created what would become the foundation of a modern social order of international refugee protection. He also could not know what would come next: a flood of Armenian refugees from the 1922 Ottoman massacres. The pre-World War I Armenian genocide had received little international attention. But the creation of the League now enabled a solution to the nightmare of those who had escaped a new onslaught of atrocities. The League Council authorized the HCR to solve the Armenian "refugee crisis" with the tools it had developed for the Russians. It granted "refugee status" to the displaced and charitable organizations helped finance the effort to aid and resettle them. When the funds were spent, Nansen charged richer refugees a "tax" for the Nansen passport, which would fund the passports of the poorer ones.

[8] Douglass 1857.

But in a world of sovereign states, the Nansen passport failed to gain deontic power. Armenians, for example, who were resettled in Syria had faced what Syrian refugees today experience in Greece: appalling living conditions spawning disease, semi-starvation and detention. When the Soviet Union annexed Armenian territory, calling it Erivan, many of the displaced chose to be repatriated there where they could enjoy the (human) rights of citizenship. For them, the Nansen passport offered no real protection and would eventually be abandoned.

The nightmare of war and redrawing of boundaries in the 1920s gave birth to new displaced persons who needed assistance: Assyrians, Bulgarians, Chaldeans, Syrians and Kurds. Although long-term solutions to their plight remained elusive, the HCR provided immediate assistance as tangible acknowledgment of their humanity. With each crisis, the League extended refugee status to new displaced communities and established new offices, geographically diffusing its accumulated knowledge and practices.

By the time Nansen died in 1930, his work had created new communities of humanitarian practice focused on the protection of the displaced. He also had amassed a new cadre of allies: The International Labor Organization provided refugees with work permits; the Epidemics Commission of the League provided refugees with health care. These allies and others enabled even wider diffusion of the practice of aiding the displaced and acknowledging their humanity. *Importantly, however, neither Nansen's innovations nor the League's assistance was extended to people of color.* Standard works on the League of Nations are silent with regard to millions of displaced Africans and Asians. Indeed, they were not recognized as human at all, even by European and Russian refugees. Even before the rise of dictatorships, the practice of protecting refugees became a practice of protecting white people.[9]

In 1933, these new practices were institutionalized in a convention relating to the International Status of Refugees.[10] The convention contained a new and crucial innovation, the principle of *non-refoulement*, which obligated states "not to refuse entry to refugees at the frontier of their countries of origin" nor to send refugees back to their home countries. Signed by nine countries, it applied only to Russian and Armenian refugees, but the *non-refoulement* principle

---

[9] Tate 1943; Vitalis 2017.   [10] League of Nations 1933.

would become a cornerstone of the post-World War II social order of refugee protection.

The rise of dictatorships in the 1930s, with their accompanying intolerance and xenophobia almost extinguished the Enlightenment idea of human rights that the convention shakily tried to uphold. But the cloud of dictatorship weakened the practice. A few examples suffice to illustrate: refugees were routinely expelled from their host countries as soon as their Nansen passports expired; the Nansen Office' only option for shielding these refugees from human rights abuse was to establish refugee camps in neutral territory. Furthermore, the ill-fated League refused to protect refugees from fascist Italy and Spain, so as not to suffer the hostility of these governments. Finally, League officials refused to institutionalize permanent refugee aid.

Perhaps the most egregious failure of the League is that it did little to protect Jews from Hitler's reign of terror. Early on the League had attempted to protect Jews: over the objection of the German delegation, the League Council in 1933 had established a "High Commission for Refugees Coming from Germany," and shortly thereafter Hitler left the League. The League Assembly then authorized the new agency to issue identification certificates to *some* Jewish refugees, but otherwise it was starved for funds. But as Jews began to escape the Holocaust, member states quickly closed their doors to them.[11] In 1936 and 1938, the League concluded a "temporary arrangement" and later a treaty to protect refugees who had "lost protection from the Reich" from being sent back to Germany (and later Austria). Both arrangements were weaker than the 1933 convention; the 1938 treaty even stipulated that under certain conditions, Jewish refugees could "be sent back across the frontier of the Reich." The principle of *non-refoulement* was not mentioned.

Horrified by Nazi atrocities, and the League's bumbling,[12] Franklin Roosevelt convened two conferences at Evian, France, outside of the dying organization, to establish what he called an Intergovernmental Committee for Refugees (IGCR)[13] tasked with finding resettlement opportunities for Jews. These meetings represented a step forward in progressive CE: They produced a mandate to provide refugee status to "all persons wherever they may be . . . "[14] and find resettlement for them.

---

[11] Aronson 2004.   [12] Stoessinger 1956, 39.   [13] Sjöberg 1991.
[14] Goodwin-Gill 1996.

Few funds to fulfill the mandate were forthcoming, and, as before, it was left to private NGOs to aid the Jews. The mandate laid dormant, but its universality was a giant step forward in acknowledging our common humanity and became one of the pillars of the modern refugee regime.

All of these efforts to keep alive the flickering light of refuge had been weakened by the ravages of Depression, the undercurrent of anti-Semitism, and weaknesses inherent in the League of Nations. In this milieu, nation-states' superior material deontic power permitted them to ignore universal human rights. Fearful of offending member states, the League had weakened its universal norms. Only voluntary communities of humanitarian practice became the allies of Jewish refugees. Liberal values that recognize our common humanity remained alive, not because nation states espoused belief in universal human rights, but because small communities practiced them: refugees organized their own self-help and advocacy groups; private NGOs allied themselves with refugees and international refugee aid organizations persisted, no matter how weak they became.[15]

Nonetheless, Nansen had initiated practices that opened a new era of international concern with the human rights of refugees and spread new knowledge of their plight. Created out of political necessity, these practices originated in the League of Nations in order to create and regulate harmonious relations among states. But largely as an unintended consequence, they also bolstered refugees' moral worth in the eyes of the international community. Ironically, in the darkest hours of an illiberal era, a new template for protecting refugee rights emerged through a process of CE: the innovative practices, born in the work of Nansen and his cohorts, were selected by the League and by some member states, institutionalized in international organizations, conventions and "arrangements," acknowledged by the president of the postwar world's most powerful nation, and diffused through NGOs and by refugees themselves. These practices would become pillars of a new liberal refugee protection regime.

Two "Cognitive Punches"

Germany's mass deportation of Jews, the Holocaust and the devastation of World War II constituted what Adler called a "cognitive

[15] Skran 1995.

punch." It spurred the creation of "a new liberal international order" promoting freedom and human rights and composed of new international institutions under the umbrella of the League's successor, the United Nations. This liberal order opened "a moral umbrella over the existing Westphalian state system, by creating a universal structure within which national governments could collaborate in the pursuit of progress."[16] The UN's purpose was to help ensure that the conditions that had led to two world wars in the first half of the twentieth century would not rise again. Throughout the last half of the century it had succeeded.

The chaos of the war's aftermath provided a second cognitive punch, spurring the creation of a permanent international refugee protection regime. By 1948, Continental Europe had quickly devolved into violence, famine and dislocation. Jews became refugees again. Poles and Slovaks attacked and killed Jewish survivors of the Nazi genocide; thousands of those who escaped sought to enter Palestine, only to be turned back by the British[17] or held in detention camps – much like the concentration camps they had survived – in Palestine. Furthermore, millions fled to escape newly installed Communist regimes in Eastern Europe, which expelled between twelve and sixteen million Germans. The War had destroyed one-third of Europe's housing stock, and left refugees with no place to find shelter. Allied occupation regimes were overwhelmed. 720,000 Palestinians fled or were expelled from the new state of Israel. All of these groups looked to the new UN organizations for help[18].

The first postwar international organization confronting this crisis was the International Refugee Organization (IRO) founded by the UN in 1946. Twenty-six member states participated in its creation, more than had ever before joined together to aid refugees. With UN funding, the IRO trained refugees for needed professions in potential resettlement countries and expanded the number of displaced persons (DP) camps. It also created an expanding web of refugee allies; by 1948 it had enlisted the help of 128 voluntary organizations. Following Nansen's practice of collaborating with the League Epidemics Committee, the IRO recruited the World Health Organization to

---

[16] Palacio 2017.   [17] Cohen 1970, 172.
[18] Mazower 1999; Judt 2005; Shephard 2011; Lowe 2012.

provide refugees with health services and worked with UNESCO to set up refugee schools.

Each collaboration spread knowledge of the plight of refugees among the members of the new UN organization and beyond and they diffused knowledge about IRO practices to new communities. Reviving the idea of the Nansen passport, the IRO issued a "document in lieu of Passport," which "clarified the refugee's status and enabled him to marry, work, and die legally in host countries." The IRO vetted refugees and initiated a new practice of tracing almost one million missing persons, locating missing children and reuniting families separated during the Holocaust.

The IRO also combed the world for refugee resettlement opportunities. IRO agents cajoled, persuaded and financed states who would agree to accept displaced people for relocation. And unlike its predecessors, it had the financial backing of the United Nations, to fund resettlement worldwide. Resettlement success was unprecedented. Even Nansen had never attempted to resettle refugees in countries outside of the European continent. Nor had any national or international organization tried to resettle refugees overseas. Resettlement was especially successful in those food and labor-starved countries that had lost millions of people during the war and who desperately needed the food rations and refugee labor that the IRO offered. Refugees themselves exercised their agency to make crucial contributions to the countries who resettled them. By the time its doors closed in 1952, the IRO had resettled over one million refugees in sixty-five countries.

The two "cognitive punches" and the IRO's response resulted in historically unprecedented humane treatment of refugees – no matter their religion or ethnic origin. *With the new practices discussed above, the IRO and its many NGO allies saved millions of lives and trained and resettled hundreds of thousands of refugees.* Their practices evidenced successful negotiation between those guided by international norms protecting the rights of refugees and those guided by national norms protecting national interests. The debate was about different prescriptive conceptions of justice, rights and welfare, for example, a competition between different conceptions of how people should relate to one another, how we bind or do not bind together different groups – like aliens and citizens. The compromises they struck brought back into the realm of humanity those whom the Nazi regime had tried its best to dehumanize. As evidenced by their successes, the widespread diffusion of IRO's practices impacted social consciousness of the human plight of refugees and paved the way for a new and comprehensive international refugee protection regime. And as they resettled in far-flung regions and their hosts were compelled to confront and integrate them, refugees themselves again became the vanguard and agents of progress.

1951 Refugee Convention and Beyond

Despite their success, however, three flawed assumptions were embedded in these practices. The first was the widespread belief that the refugee crisis was temporary, a result of World War II and its aftermath. The second was the belief that the crisis was confined to war-torn Europe, whose changing ethno-national and ideological boundaries had produced states that were now persecuting and expelling their minority populations. Third was the assumption that all displaced people were fleeing state persecution. Later I recount how the first two assumptions were put to rest and the third began to disappear as better practices developed with each ensuing refugee crisis.

The 1951 convention Relating to the Status of Refugees abolished the assumption that the refugee crisis was temporary. National and UN officials quickly saw that the Cold War continued to produce a new and larger a flood of refugees from Central and Eastern Europe. While state officials declared their commitment to a permanent solution to the refugee crisis, they also wanted to minimize their obligations toward the refugees. They commissioned a study to help them meet both goals.

The result was entitled "A Study of Statelessness," assessing the previous twenty-five years of national and international practices – both successful and unsuccessful. It assessed the value of practices developed throughout the life of the League and practices of the committees and agencies created in the wake of the League's collapse. It described the evolution of "better practices" that had developed over the past twenty-five years, detailing how situational decisions had led to the "preferential selective survival" of certain practices focused on needs through a process of what Adler calls "endogenous collective learning within" the international community of practice. To write it, younger practitioners joined those who had long worked on refugee issues. The study provided crucial institutional memory and essential background for all involved in building a new international refugee regime. In the process of writing the study, both national and international practitioners, who broadly shared the norms contained in the 1948 Human Rights Convention, contextualized what they knew about the situational plight of refugees and learned to change some of their practices, based on what had and what had not been effective. The study proved to be a crucial piece of background knowledge shaping the 1951 convention.

The study suggested that past practices offered three important lessons for any future regime. First, conferring refugee status upon the displaced was not enough to protect them. The Nansen passport, for example, had been only partially successful and the study recommended that it be dropped. Second, national governments would not offer full human rights to refugees without an international treaty binding them to that offer and binding them particularly to the 1933 principle of *non-refoulement*. Finally, it showed that, states alone would not provide the funds to restore full human dignity to those who were not their own national citizens. It thus recommended creating a permanent *international* organ and a *permanent* Office of a High Commissioner for Refugees that would protect the human rights of refugees and offer them the same services that states provide to their nationals abroad. Relying on the study for guidance, the creators of the convention's final text created a permanent regime to bring refugees into the realm of "common humanity." The study thereby became a key guide to the development of the 1951 convention on the Status of Refugees and an inspiration for the creation of a permanent UN High Commission for Refugees (UNHCR).

The convention and the UNHCR were quickly recognized as an important facet of the new liberal world order and its intent to protect universal human rights. The majority of the world's nations became parties to the convention. UNHCR was not a "go-it-alone" organization required to raise its own funding like its predecessors of the prewar period. It was part of the UN "umbrella" under the auspices of the UN General Assembly. Its funding came directly from the UN budget.

But those who drafted the convention were still limited by their focus on the refugee crisis as a European phenomenon created by World War II and its aftermath. Furthermore, the European Powers did not want the convention to cover the "colored populations" in their colonies.[19]

---

[19] Mayblin 2014.

They thus restricted aid to those refugees from Europe, whose fear of persecution forced them to flee before January, 1951. These restrictions, however, conflicted with the recognition on the part of the drafters that the convention's standards were of universal applicability. And it conflicted with facts on the ground: The convention ignored the exodus of millions from China between 1949 and 1950 and the six million refugees created by the partition of India. Ironically, as the convention was being drafted and ratified, the Korean War was producing millions of refugees as well. But the territorial limitation on who could receive refugee status remained in place.

Written with the knowledge of this limitation, the Final Act of the convention "expressed the *hope* that ... all nations would be guided by [the convention] in granting as far as possible to persons in their territory as refugees and who would not be covered by the terms of the convention the treatment for which it provides." Drawing on this "hope," Gerrit van Heuven Goedhart, the first High Commissioner for Refugees, had wanted to immediately turn his office into a leading *global* agency for refugees, but his hands were tied by the Great Powers and their allies in the UN's General Assembly, which held the authority over the UNHCR and who were blinded by the assumption that the refugee crisis was confined to Europe.

Nonetheless, the hope gradually became a reality. Between 1951 and 1967 UNHCR matured, and the world had changed. The composition of UNHCR's "boss," the General Assembly, changed with it, from an organ of fifty-one members dominated by Western Powers to one of 118 states, whose membership included many non-aligned nations, many who wanted to distance themselves from the Cold War, and an important African-Asian bloc challenging the primacy of the Great Powers. When the General Assembly's majority membership grew to include newly decolonized states in Africa, its focus increasingly shifted away from Europe and toward the refugee crises elsewhere that the wars of "national liberation" had produced. By 1965 the General Assembly had appointed five new members from Africa to UNHCR's executive committee, introducing new elements of practice into the organization and thus strengthening it further. With this shift, UNHCR was granted more resources, and its expertise and its material and organizational capabilities began to outstrip those of its rivals, the Intergovernmental Committee for European Migration (ICEM) and the US "Escapee Program." In Adler's terms, UNHCR had won a competition for the successful institutionalization of its practices. It grew in moral authority and deontic power, and developed into an institution with a long-range strategy that emphasized both protection and material assistance to all forced migrants.[20] Now funded by the General Assembly, it became increasingly autonomous from the member states that created it. With a near monopoly of background knowledge on refugee issues and law, a 1955 Nobel Peace Prize under its belt and the blessing of the United States – whose officials believed it would be useful in dissuading newly liberated states away from the Soviet bloc–UNHCR had become an important vehicle for social learning and a crucial hub for the mobilization of global collective action to aid refugees.

These changes thus led to the abolition of the second assumption of the convention, the assumption that the refugee crisis could be confined to Europe. UNHCR's Executive Committee invited legal experts and NGOs to join it in drafting a Protocol to the 1951 convention which removed its temporal scope as well as the geographic limitation to Europe, giving the convention a global scope and reaffirming its permanence. The United States quickly ratified the Protocol, bringing 145 countries into UNHCR's fold. As UNHCR's practices expanded to include the entire globe, ratification provided evidence that most of the world's nation states and the refugees themselves had found a "better practice," inching toward progress in broadening and deepening acknowledgment of the refugee's right to be acknowledged as human.

The third assumption would prove to be the most difficult to dislodge. Limited by the European experience and Cold War politics, the convention provided a restrictive definition of who could receive UNHCR aid and who it would attempt to resettle as a refugee. Article 1 of the convention, defines a refugee under international law as:

A person who owing to a well-founded fear of being persecuted for reasons of race, religion, nationality, membership of a particular social group or political opinion, is outside the country of his nationality and is unable or, owing to such fear, is unwilling to avail himself of the protection of that country; or who, not having a nationality and being outside the country of his former

---

[20] Loescher 2017.

habitual residence as a result of such events, is unable or, owing to such fear, is unwilling to return to it.

Defenders of the 1951 convention have pointed out that it was never meant to address broader migration issues. Critics argue that clinging to the original definition only allows states to ignore new kinds of persecution refugees are subjected to. Further, they argue, it allows them to manipulate the words of the treaty so that it covers only the refugees they want to accept. The Drafters of the convention assumed that governments were the persecutors and that the reasons cited in the definition were the only ones that obligated states to protect the displaced. But in the ensuing years, millions of people experienced "persecution" in many forms as they fled the carnage of war, gang brutality, communitarian violence, domestic abuse, drought, poverty and natural disaster, all in the absence of protection from their governments. Vast swaths of displaced populations were excluded from refuge. Because they were displaced from their homes by forces other than "state persecution," they lost the right to be treated as human by those states who were able but unwilling to protect them.

Gradually, though, new "background knowledge," accumulated and new communities of practice arose to challenge the old convention and its definition of a "refugee." In 1969, as the wars of independence raging on the African Continent continued to create vast numbers of uprooted people, the Organisation of African Unity (OAU), with the support of UNHCR, created the convention Governing the Specific Aspects of Refugee Problems in Africa, stipulating that the term "refugee" not only applies to those protected by the 1951 convention but:

shall also apply to every person who, owing to external aggression, occupation, foreign domination or events seriously disturbing public order in either part or the whole of his country of origin or nationality, is compelled to leave his place of habitual residence in order to seek refuge in another place outside his country of origin or nationality.

In Latin America similar crises were brewing in the 1970s and 1980s, as governments, particularly in Guatemala and El Salvador murdered and disappeared hundreds of thousands of peasants, indigenous peoples and impoverished urban dwellers. When refugees fled, governments of neighboring countries offered little or no protection. This situation gave rise to a new community of practice in the region, determined to find protection for the new refugees not covered by the 1951 convention or its 1967 protocol. Deeply influenced by 1969 African convention, this community framed the Cartagena Declaration, which called on countries to use the following definition:

the term "refugee" shall also apply to every person who, owing to external aggression, occupation, foreign domination or events seriously disturbing public order in either part or the whole of his [or her] country of origin or nationality, is compelled to leave his [or her] place of habitual residence in order to seek refuge in another place outside his [or her] country of origin or nationality.

This definition, reached by consensus among Organization of American States (OAS) members, not only expands understanding of who can be offered refugee status in a new asylum regime, it also shifts the focus of protection from individuals who feared persecution to *all* of those fleeing "generalized violence, foreign aggression, internal conflicts, massive violation of human rights ... "[21] The Cartagena Declaration, fully supported by UNHCR, was not a legally binding instrument, but it provided an important normative framework promoting humanitarian practices in response to the Central American refugee crisis, and it was incorporated into many national legal frameworks.

Although the narrow definition of refugees was not abolished in refugee law, three significant practices radically enlarged the scope of UNHCR's aid to forced migrants. First, UNHCR broadened its working definition of the term "refugee" far beyond the convention definition[22]: *"Since 2007, the refugee population also includes people in a refugee-like situation."*[23] Second, as globalization enabled forced migrants to more quickly reach safety and news about them to travel rapidly, language was gradually added to signify that UNHCR was prepared to protect new "persons of concern." UNHCR began to speak of people who were "forcibly uprooted," "forcibly displaced" and "people on the move" including stateless people, victims of natural disaster and climate change[24] and people affected by urban displacement.[25] Third, epistemic communities began to link knowledge about climate change, disasters and non-state violence to knowledge about displacement, underlining

---

[21] Reed-Hurtado 2017.   [22] Guterres 2007.
[23] www.unhcr.org/globaltrends2016/.   [24] Guterres 2008b; UNHCR 2009.
[25] Crisp 2009.

the credibility of UNHCR's creeping mission expansion.[26] These three practices gained authority as the UNHCR began to include these populations in its widely diffused annual "Global Reports," later entitled "Global Trends: Forced Displacement." By 2016, 2.6 million refugees, stateless people and "other populations of concern" lived in UNHCR refugee camps, where they were fed, sheltered and educated. Millions more lived in camps set up by allied NGOs. UNHCR also extends protection to over 24 million internally displaced people (IDP) in 24 countries and has over 5,000 urban refugee programs outside the camps.

This evolution of terminology and practice illustrates Adler's claim that "background knowledge is embedded in practices." Each expansion of practice gave rise to normative change as new communities of practice began to value new groups of displaced people as part of "our common humanity." Soon, a "humanitarian marketplace"[27] of competition and cooperation among communities of practice emerged, giving rise to better practices enhancing the human dignity of displaced persons. And UNHCR's practice of producing an annual report of "Global Trends" was gradually endowed with performative power as the "gold standard" of authoritative information on refugees. It informs host government statistics, shapes opinion in the media and provides important data used in academic research.

Cognitive evolution with regard to forced migration occurred through the mechanisms that Adler identified. The postwar international environment and the refugee crises of the period undermined particularistic values of postwar governments and provided fertile ground for the creation of new background knowledge and the nourishing of values based on universal human rights. The genius of the Refugee convention is that it reconciled profoundly different and opposing world views and values: humanist/internationalist and realist/nationalist. In the process of creating UNHCR, national communities "overlapped" with international communities, and their compromises structured social consciousness with regard to the plight of refugees and possible solutions for bringing them into the fold of humanity. Negotiating these compromises resulted in collective learning about new practices and created a new shared understanding of the plight of the displaced and possible solutions to aid them. The decision to institutionalize the offer of refuge came about because of CE in both

[26] Guterres 2008a, b, 2017.   [27] Crisp 2009.

national and international communities and the knowledge they gained from refugees and their allies. Through that same process authorities began to expand their knowledge, and gradually became increasingly convinced that all forced migrants have moral worth and are entitled to full human rights and thus should be given refuge.

Threats to Progress in Refugee Protection in a "Post-Truth" Environment

As Adler warns, however, progress – like that which is detailed earlier – is both contingent and reversible. He cautions that regressive values undermining human interests could arise through the same processes of CE that he describes. Pouliot, Kornprobst and Ish-Shalom (this volume) remind us that actors can "denaturalize" established practices and can thereby dejustify them. When "denaturalized" and "dejustified," progressive practices can be undone. Indeed, refugee protection practices can be undone with the dismissal or abolition of the many "better practices" which have evolved. Which actors want to denaturalize and dejustify these practices? Why? What are their methods of doing so?

Immigration as the Key Battlefield in a Twenty-First Century Culture War

As the twenty-first century opened, the liberal world order began to show signs of retreat from the progress it had achieved. For the first time in a century, a set of large, wealthy and undemocratic or fragile democratic states with governments hostile to liberalism – China, Russia and India – achieved great-power status. They challenged the Western conception of order based on the primacy of liberal post–World War II rules. The retreat of free trade; Russia's invasion of Ukraine; Brexit, the euro crisis, the rise of illiberal European governments, the appearance of anti-liberal non-state actors and their successful efforts to fragment and undermine good governance, the ascendance of authoritarian states, the rise of the extreme right – all combined to put the progress of the postwar liberal order at risk.

The weakening of that order clouded the future of refugee protection.[28] This led to a growing number of asylum seekers crossing

---

[28] Hammerstad 2014.

irregularly into asylum-granting countries and the increasing reluctance of convention parties to host or resettle them. As generalized violence rather than state-sanctioned persecution increasingly became the root cause of refugee flight, asylum-granting countries clung tightly to the narrow convention definition of "refugees" in order to legally eject forced migrants from their territory. UNHCR began to adjudicate fewer asylum decisions and resettle fewer people even as the number of displaced people around the world exploded. Its role was largely reduced to providing aid to those who were forcibly displaced outside asylum-granting countries, mostly (86 percent) in the developing world. Furthermore, anti-immigrant right-wing political movements spread like wildfire throughout the developed world.

Why did these anti-immigrant movements emerge and spread? Other issues like the stability of the dollar, the financial crisis and the rise of income inequality are less visible but more crucial to the well-being of Western populations. Immigrants are a drop in the bucket of Western populations, and the cost to protect them is relatively low while the benefits of migrants in the workforce are likely to be high.[29] But the extreme right recognized that it could gain adherents if they focused on an issue that would strike and intensify fear of "the other" in the hearts of voters. Immigration symbolized the dissatisfaction and anxiety that many felt about their relative economic situation, their life opportunities, their security, their claim to a culture they believe to be slipping away and their declining position in the social hierarchy.[30] These movements and parties provoked and intensified this fear, promising their adherents that excluding aliens would secure their social identity, their jobs and their political power. Migration became the battlefield in a *culture war* between an open conception of society in which migrants could gain status and opportunities and a closed of society in which they are locked out.

Tribalism, "Hot Cognition," and the Spread of "Tribal Epistemology"

The flames of this culture war were fanned in the tinderbox of anti-liberal "tribal practices."[31] These include violent acts against

---

[29] Jaumotte, Koloskova and Saena 2016.   [30] European Parliament 2017.
[31] Chua 2017; Pinker 2018.

immigrants, calls for their expulsion and walls to exclude them and the propagation of false media and social media narratives that stir emotions of intolerance, fear and hatred of foreigners and minorities. Throughout modern history, extreme nativist and atavistic nationalist communities have sought and sometimes gained the political power to wall out migrants and expel minorities. "Tribal" practices today, however, differ profoundly from traditional nationalist practices of the postwar period. Anti-immigrant and other anti-liberal tribal communities today are diverse, often unconnected and include sub-national and transnational practitioners, like members of incel, Qanon, 4Chan, Truth24.net, pop-up alt-right communities and more.

These groups and their practices threaten social stability in liberal democracies where democratic strength has rested on established political parties who traditionally weeded out anti-democratic extremists in order to maintain political compromises that allowed them to govern. It also rested on a strong national identity that was understood to encompass the identity of all citizens. In contrast, modern "tribes" – anti-liberal communities that tout their own superiority and victimhood – are characterized by exclusive collective identities that prevail over individual and national identity. Members may be full citizens of the nation, but their deeper loyalties are to their exclusive ethnic, racial or sectarian tribes which provide them with a sense of belonging. They detest and scorn liberal openness and have vocal disregard for facts; they dismiss scientific methods that produce evidence-based claims. Their opinions call for no verification; they denigrate liberal norms of tolerance, compromise and forbearance; they try to lower the social status of those who adhere to those norms. They mock and attack liberal democratic institutions. They often act to impose their own exclusive identity on the identity of the nation. They believe they are locked in a deadly battle with groups advocating open borders and protection of minority rights, and they loathe them as the enemy. Their battle with institutions that protect forced migrants is part of a larger war with liberal democracy and open society itself, and their numbers are growing.

A hallmark of a "tribal" community is the predominance of "hot cognition" – thinking influenced by emotion over reason and dismissal of methods by which scholars discover and produce factual evidence. "Hot cognition" replaces dispassionate reasoning and has long been present in all political discourse. But its role in producing political outcomes has been underestimated.[32] In right-wing anti-immigrant tribal communities, cognition is on fire: gut feelings of fear, anger and hatred toward "the other" dominate thought. Heightened emotions forge hardened, unsubstantiated opinions. Opinion becomes a sacred value, an affirmation of allegiance to one's community. If the opinion conforms to that of the community, its content, truth or verifiability is irrelevant. This is *"tribal epistemology,"* in which information is evaluated based *not* on conformity to standards of evidence or correspondence to a common understanding of reality, but on whether it supports the tribe's values and goals and is vouchsafed by tribal leaders. "Good is on our side" and "true" blur into one. *Hot cognition can stop cognitive evolution, and tribal epistemology can threaten society's epistemological security.*

Social Sharing

Forged in the furnaces of hot cognition and tribal epistemology, hardened opinion dominates cool, fact-based knowledge and provides fertile ground for the spread of falsehoods through social sharing. People in general are biased toward confirmation: they wish to believe that which endorses what they already consider to be true, and they share information that confirms[33] their values, beliefs and passions. Information is shared, not just to inform or even to persuade but as a *marker of one's identity* and a way to proclaim one's affinity with a particular community.[34]

All communities, liberal and tribal, mark their identity through social sharing. The difference between them is this: with their identity and affinities at stake, liberal communities often cling to the practice of reasoned debate to hone, strengthen and change positions through amassing evidence. But members of tribal communities act first on "hot cognition" and "tribal epistemology," and then tend to double down on their convictions *especially* after being presented with contradictory evidence,[35] that could cause an uncomfortable feeling of cognitive dissonance. "Doubling down" helps resolve the feeling by dismissing the evidence. When "hot cognition" dominates thought,

[32] Anderson 1981; Elster 1999; Redlawsk 2002; McDermot 2004.
[33] Nickerson 1998.   [34] Lee and Ma 2012; Oeldorf-Hirsch and Sundar 2015.
[35] Silverman 2011.

sharing opinions further hardens them and makes them impervious to facts. Several studies suggest that conservatives more strongly avoid dissonance-arousing information about politics and religion than liberals, who assimilate that information more readily into their views.[36]

The nature of tribal sharing means that the practice of fact-checking to gain the upper hand in debate can backfire,[37] because stoking conflict with outsiders strengthens tribal cohesion. When hot cognition prevails, anti-immigrant communities find it easy to spread false information that engenders and maintains fear of "the other." Those who spread falsehoods intentionally play on the fear that criminals, terrorists and disease carriers are hiding among mass groups of immigrants.

Numerous studies demonstrate that anti-immigrant voter attitudes about immigration are *not* driven by facts. A few examples suffice to illustrate: most respondents to extensive surveys believe that levels of immigration in their country are much higher than they actually are. When confronted with that evidence, respondents in Britain rejected official migration figures. The majority of Germans believe that one-third of the people living in Germany are Muslim; the official percentage in 2016 was 6.1 percent. The majority of Americans believe that immigrants do not assimilate into American society and culture, while the bulk of research strongly suggests that the majority do assimilate. Most Americans believe that immigrants commit more crimes per capita than native-born Americans, but they do not. Most believe that immigration increases the risk of terrorism. But more terrorist acts between 2001 and 2015 were committed by right-wing domestic terrorists than by foreign-born jihadists. When confronted with evidence, members of anti-immigrant communities cling ever more tightly to their dogmas. The erroneous beliefs mentioned earlier are the products of the rapid and almost universal spread of misinformation, disinformation and outright falsehoods.

Motivations for Twenty-First Century Post-Truth

Post-truth environments are not new to the twenty-first century. Religious authorities and political regimes since antiquity have used

---

[36] Pew Research Center 2007; Ross, Lelkes, and Russell 2012; Nam, Jost, and Van Bavel 2013.

[37] Nyhan and Reifler 2010.

disinformation campaigns to instill fear and loyalty in their realms. But they were marked by the spread of deceptive propaganda from a *single source for the purpose of achieving or maintaining political domination* – often through the regime's control of the media. The twenty-first century environment is markedly different. In addition to disinformation from above, numerous *unconnected sources* now spread falsehoods from obscure and unknown corners of society *for reasons that often have nothing to do with political domination*. These falsehoods are then "shared" widely through highly decentralized digital communication technologies. In spreading information this way, tribal communities join journalists, scientists, foreign disinformation agencies and political authorities to share what they know, believe, feel and use to manipulate the beliefs of others. Truth is often tinged with falsehood and falsehood tinged with truth. Truth and falsehood become difficult to separate. Bruno Latour even situates the rise of the post-truth era among constructivist academics, arguing that in debunking facts, "a certain form of critical spirit has sent us down the wrong path."[38]

An old proverb claims that "a lie will go round the world while truth is pulling its boots on." The current post-truth environment, characterized by widespread digital communication, ensures the most rapid spread of falsehoods in human history. It facilitates widespread degradation of legitimate information and propagates social distrust in factual knowledge. With digital communication technologies, those who want their voices heard compete for the attention of those who would listen. In that competition, speed of content delivery and entertainment take precedence over truth. Speed blurs the line between information, misinformation and disinformation. As entertainment, exaggeration and lies have more performative power than a dry presentation of facts. Instant "sharing" of information allows social media posts – true, false, distorted and magnified by retweets and "shares" – to dominate media. Both "citizen" and professional journalists vie for a "scoop" and exaggerate their narratives in the hope of attracting attention and advertisers. In this way, mainstream media has become increasingly guilty of purveying misinformation, thus cultivating a general distrust of professional sources of information.

When the ground of distrust is cultivated in this way, conditions are ideal for the germination of falsehoods in the soil of "hot cognition,"

---

[38] Latour 2004.

particularly within the hothouses of information that prevent cross-fertilization of knowledge. With each community ensconced in its own hothouse, there is no chance for opposing communities of practice to debate with each other. Furthermore, digital sharing among tribal communities is more pervasive, both horizontally and vertically, than digital sharing among liberal communities,[39] making their information hothouse larger, but also less visible to liberal communities because of their isolation from one another. Without civil discourse and reasoned debate, the practice of "sharing" within the hothouse can deepen discord between tribal and liberal communities. Tribal communities believe themselves to be in a war in which facts, science and epistemic communities are their adversaries. They often use trolls and bots to "swarm" a factual narrative with inflammatory denunciations.

Liberal communities who depend on facts feel themselves in a losing war with liars. Liberal practices are rarely possible when confronted with hardened intolerance, widespread misinformation, and the absence of civil discourse. Adler quotes Hannah Arendt in a 1967 article: "The result of a consistent and total substitution of lies for factual truth is not that the lies will now be accepted as truth, and the truth defamed as lies, but that *the sense by which we take our bearings in the real world ... is being destroyed.*"[40]

Normlessness

Taken together, the practices described earlier can create a social environment of distrust, confusion and retreat where *normlessness* can shape society's background knowledge and create epistemological insecurity by destroying "the sense by which we take our bearings." Elliot Turiel argues that normlessness implies the negation of any relevant norms in social practices and it signals a *dismissal* of any prescriptive judgments for how people should relate to one another.[41] It normalizes the psychology of "hot cognition," "tribal epistemology," confirmation bias and doubling down in the face of contrary evidence.

Extremist tribal communities with no overt political goal are normless communities. Like other communities of practice, they diffuse their background knowledge through "emergent innovations," such as

---

[39] Benkler, Faris, Roberts, and Zuckerman 2017.
[40] Quoted in Adler 2019, 290.   [41] Turiel 2002.

social media, but unlike liberal communities, they spew disinformation and misinformation to poison institutionalized liberal norms and practices with no goals or values in mind. A normless environment *normalizes* tribal practices of using bots and trolls to "swarm" and "overwhelm" all other voices simply for the sake of being able to do so. The authors of a seminal *article on the spread of* facts and falsehoods through Twitter *found that falsehoods reached far more people than the truth.*[42] Were normlessness to prevail, there would be little possibility of creating a shared reality with opposing communities. The practice of spreading falsehoods endows normless communities with more performative power than the practice of spreading what Adler would call commonsense knowledge.[43] Tribal communities' performative power can lead to deontic power and can become a mortal threat to epistemological security.

In the first decades of the twenty-first century, anti-immigrant rhetoric threatens to destroy epistemological security by fueling the growth of anti-immigrant tribal deontic power. Victor Orban of Hungary, for example, has continually warned that all refugees are potential terrorists. His adherents echo this falsehood. Hungary has seen increased funding channeled to cultural institutions that promote anti-immigrant and extreme ethno nationalist-themed plays, films, music events and art exhibits. Similarly, in the absence of terrorist threats or incidents, the Polish government successfully propagates popular fear of refugee terrorism by spreading false information. To justify its ethnic cleansing of the Rohynga population, the government of Myanmar publishes fake images of Rohynga refugees burning their own huts. The images are shared widely on social media throughout the Buddhist population and continue to be shared long after they are debunked. Falsehoods spread on Facebook brought ordinary Germans to set fire to a refugee shelter.[44] Liberal communities have had slight political power to stop these practices.

Cognitive Devolution?

Adler warns of the danger of post-truth practices to democracy and liberal social orders, but he believes that liberal communities

---

[42] Vosoughi, Roy, and Aral 2018.   [43] Adler 2019, 290.
[44] *New York Times*, August 22, 2018, A1.

successfully contest those practices. An increasingly widespread diffusion and acceptance of normlessness, however, suggests that that success may be tenuous. Liberal communities may not have the power to
oppose post-truth practices when they are spread by tribal communities who have gained deontic power. Once leaders of tribal communities hold power, their post-truth practices can become embedded in the
political system, thereby undermining liberal institutions. The breakdown of truth in this environment is a gateway to the breakdown in the
rule of law that binds us together in a shared reality.

Cognitive evolution leads to progress when *interdependence* gives
birth to new background knowledge and the overlapping of diverse
communities of practice. Led by creative and innovative agents, negotiation and compromise among those communities can lead to the
diffusion of shared background knowledge and to collective learning.
Collective learning, in turn, can lead to the political selection of "better" practices, their successful institutionalization and the wider diffusion and morphing of knowledge. This process, Adler argues, leads to
the shared meanings and restructuring of consciousness that can
expand the boundaries of community.

For this process to lead to progress, however, it must be infused with
humanist-realist norms. The practices that are selected and institutionalized must be repositories of ethical collective knowledge. Recall that
progress in the development of practices to acknowledge the humanity
of refugees was the result of "competition" between national and
international norms. Compromises between these two normative communities allowed practitioners to interact collaboratively; each community traditionally acknowledged the legitimacy of the other's values.
When devising solutions to the plight of displaced people, different
norms have historically guided different answers to the question of
whether, for example, citizens should be treated differently than aliens,
refugees should be treated differently than migrants, stateless people
should be treated differently from citizens. I argued earlier that answers
were found that both communities could live with, and progress was
achieved.

But the same factors that might lead to progress can also lead to
regress. Interdependence can lead to war; its benefits can be unequally
distributed, unequal distribution can give rise to conflict.[45] Indeed, the

---

[45] Keeley 1996.

absence of interdependence could also lead to progress. Kenneth Waltz argued that "[e]ver since Plato, utopias have been set in isolation from other peoples. Island civilizations allowed people to develop unique qualities, uncontaminated by others. The lack of interaction with others prevented conflict and violence."[46] Interdependence does not always lead to the sharing of background knowledge, negotiation, compromise or collective learning.

The same ambivalence holds for the selection of "better" practices. Historically, political and religious authorities selected practices they believed to be "better," and they diffused background knowledge that today would be considered regressive. Michael Servetus was ordered to be executed in the Spanish inquisition for his discovery of pulmonary circulation; he escaped to Switzerland only to be ordered by John Calvin to be burned at the stake. The Catholic Church banned Galileo's evidence that the earth revolves around the sun. In 1662 the British government arrested Henry Oldenburg, who founded the Royal Society in London, and sent him to languish in the tower of London because he corresponded with scientists across Europe seeking out the best articles for publication. Albert Einstein's works were banned and burned in Germany. The ancient process of mummification or a recipe for concrete that gave their structures longevity and strength has been lost and never reproduced. Today, political and religious authorities continue to suggest that people of color are inferior. Refugees seeking asylum are treated as if they were not human.

This regressive treatment of refugees is no longer the dominant norm, and the story told here shows that both interdependence and the diffusion of knowledge facilitated CE that lead to progress in refugee protection. But a glimpse into the future of that protection in a post-truth environment suggests the potential for disassociation and the denigration of collective knowledge. An environment characterized by the rapid spread of misinformation, disinformation and falsehoods engenders distrust in "the other" and an unwillingness to take in a stranger for fear he is a threat. Distrust creates information bubbles and isolation of communities from one another. Isolation prevents the sharing of collective knowledge and collective learning. Post-truth practices create social divisions and conflict and destroy epistemological security. Backed by falsehoods claiming that migrants have

---

[46] Waltz 1999.

less moral worth than native populations, many political authorities and their tribal communities have undermined the progress made in bringing the displaced into the fold of humanity. The lesson is this: when tribal communities gain deontic power in a post-truth environment, practices become *worse*, not better.

Bringing Progress Back In: Refugees and Their Allies as Agents of Progress

Adler suggests indicators of progress to search for in dark times of post-truth and weakened liberal democracy.[47] And there are indeed signs that progress in refugee protection continues: (1) Communities of practice that abhor and oppose post-truth (liberal communities) will fight in the political arena to uphold their values,[48] (2) New practices are developed that counter post-truth practices and (3) "Communities of Action," for example, publics who adhere to liberal democracy and translate their values into actions can weaken tribal practices. In the case of forced migration, examples of each of these signs are abundant.

Indeed, the sixty-five million forcibly displaced people on earth and their allies, "engaged in conscious collaboration,"[49] to develop practices that demonstrate their human worth, may be the most important agents of progress on the planet today. We saw that in the darkest days of the 1930s, with fascism on the march in Germany, small liberal communities continued to initiate and implement new practices to protect refugees: the 1933 convention and the principle of *non-refoulement*, the establishment of refugee protection camps in neutral territory, the League's creation in 1938 of a "High Commission for Refugees," Roosevelt's establishment of an Intergovernmental Committee for Refugees and the creation of the IRO, all of which forged the path for the creation of the current refugee protection regime.

Two examples illustrate current collaboration between refugees and their allies in opposition to the post-truth environment and resistance against illiberal practices. First, since the 1980s, small Communities of Action in the United States and in Europe have created "sanctuary cities" for migrants in defiance of growing national immigration

---

[47] Adler 2019, 285–88.   [48] Ibid., 292–94.
[49] Toulmin, cited in Adler 2019, 278.

restrictions. Second, when the US government spread falsehoods about immigrants and asylum seekers in efforts to stir anti-immigrant hostility, asylum seekers and their allies fought to create opportunities for sustained *contact* between immigrants and host communities who together have created communities of resistance.

Refugees themselves develop resilience and are repositories of the background knowledge required for progress. They rarely travel alone; they must assist one another. They learn to join their voices together to uphold human rights as they protest inhumane conditions in refugee camps. They amass the courage to defy borders. They collectively learn endurance in order to survive hardship, loss, humiliation, hunger, sweltering heat and freezing cold. They are compelled to learn patience and discipline as they cope with failures and languish in refugee camps. They must arm themselves with knowledge of asylum law in order to defend their human rights. They must learn new cultural practices and new languages in places where they find refuge. They must cope with prejudice and hostility in host societies. They become *resilient*, in the sense of Adger's definition, which Adler cites approvingly: "the ability of groups and communities to cope with external stress and disturbances as a result of social political and environmental change."[50] Not all will rise to the challenge of practicing their own humanity. But we can hypothesize that their voices, their memories, their images of refuge, their encounters on the perilous journey to asylum and their encounters in host countries come together to form that knowledge. It is their resilience that leads to the selection of their practices and makes them agents of change.

What I have discovered in my own interviews of refugees who made it to safety[51] is that in their background knowledge they held a special picture of the "promised land" that began the process of creating that resilience. Syrians, Afghans and North Africans felt they had no real choice but to flee. A saying among them was "no risk, no life." It was an image of life that drove them. That picture of life in Europe was lofty and unrealistic but still shaped the practices that helped them endure the journey to refuge. It contained within it a faith that strangers would acknowledge their humanity. They carried that faith with them as they traversed the forbidden space within and between borders in which

---

[50] Adger, cited in Adler 2019, 262.
[51] Conducted in Izmir, Turkey and in Berlin, Germany between 2015 and 2018.

their humanity was not acknowledged. In that space they learned of the inequalities around which humans organize themselves – nation, gender, ethnicity, class – which blind people to a full acknowledgment of others' humanity. They found allies, who, through thousands of acts of kindness, made hostile spaces more humane. Although these refugees now admit that their vision did not conform completely to the realities they encountered when then entered asylum-granting countries, they could build new lives on collective memories and practices of kindness and ingenuity, patience, and endurance as well as the parts of their vision that conformed to and even transformed the reality that they experienced.

Forced migrants and their allies compose communities of practice who possess at least four of Adler's attributes of agency driving CE.[52] First, their agency is relational; the strength of their practices is dependent upon their empathetic relationship with each other. Second, their activities are endowed with meaning. Each act of assistance, of kindness, of generosity, of defiance and of protest is an act of human solidarity, a sign of human equality and worth. Third, they display deft organizational capacity as they journey forward, wait in camps and resettle in new homes. Their use of digital resources has played a crucial role in planning and navigating their dangerous journeys.[53] They and their allies, UNHCR, NGOs and ordinary citizens have encountered obstacles in every corner of the earth that led to creative ways to organize refuge for thousands of vulnerable people. Fourth, their actions are intentional, and the shifting context and constraints of their existence elicits tremendous feats of adaption and creativity, simply to meet basic human needs and keep long-term aspirations alive. Fifth, they are creative. When blocked by a newly built wall, they find new paths to asylum. And because the digital traces phones leave behind make refugees vulnerable to surveillance and other dangers, they have developed encryption technologies that block and erase these traces. Their allies have been equally creative. One NGO collects smartphones from people around the world and distributes them to refugees fleeing conflict. Another provides opensource hot spots for refugees on the move. Croatian engineers who were once refugees themselves hacked a home router and battery, offering free Wi-Fi to refugees traveling through Croatia.[54] Their background

---

[52] Adler 2019, 208–10.   [53] Gillespie, et. al. 2016, 31–35.
[54] https://meshpoint.me/.

knowledge is transformed into creative practices, and these practices are selectively retained, institutionalized and diffused as social practices.

These communities of practice exert power to influence social change.[55] Throughout history, those fleeing bondage, persecution, violence, discrimination and death have exerted a powerful form of practical authority. Their practice of boundary defiance is one of performative power. In the absence of possessing overt political power, refugees and their allies have "moved things" in the direction of a wider acknowledgment of their humanity. Those with deontic power – even those who object to them – have been forced to respond. And, despite current setbacks, they have responded with a flood of treaties, conventions, declarations, laws and agencies all widening the social order of refugee protection, even in the current post-truth environment.

Conclusion

This essay has told the story of how international progress was achieved in alleviating the suffering of forced migrants. CE theory explains why better practices were adopted and how this progress was achieved. The key was the role that refugees and their allies played as agents of change. Their plight ironically gave them the power to elicit a response. Negotiation, compromise and the institutionalization of humanitarian practices was vital to the diffusion of a changing social consciousness and the creation of a new social order for refugee protection. Throughout the post-World War II period, liberal internationalist protection practices gained ground while satisfying the nationalist demands of the state parties to the Refugee convention. Creators of the UNHCR proved to be realistic partners in agency, belonging to both national and international communities, selecting better practices from the past, innovating new practices that satisfied state parties, successfully competing for the institutionalization of their practices, diffusing their knowledge and allying with other communities who defended the value of human worth. This represented progressive CE that "changed the quality of outcomes"[56] for millions of displaced people by alleviating their suffering and – through law and practice – bringing them into the realm of our common humanity.

---

[55] Guzzini, this volume.   [56] Reus-Smit, this volume.

A crucial test of Adler's CE theory is the "post-truth" tribal environment of the twenty-first century, with the effort to dismantle refugee protection at its center. As the number of refugees on earth multiplied, the number of countries shutting their doors to them increased and the number of new tribal communities of anti-immigrant practice grew. As the centerpiece of their recruitment strategies, extreme right-wing communities successfully seized upon post-truth practices that deepened fear of refugees as terrorists and criminals. I have shown how the psychological power of confirmation bias, doubling down, and "sharing" as an identity marker, have created and magnified the falsehoods that drive voters to extreme right-wing political parties and create a toxic environment for the future of CE. Each of these features of a post-truth environment calls for further investigation in future research.

To elaborate CE theory under post-truth conditions, scholars must investigate whether and how *cognitive devolution might be possible*. They could explore how interconnectedness can unravel to become disassociation, how the absence of negotiation and compromise can lead to *collective unlearning* and lost knowledge, how "worse practices" such as border closures and illegal deportations are selected, and how institutions now fail to protect the displaced. Scholars should also explore the phenomenon of *normless* practices. Although CE theory claims that all practices are normative; a post-truth environment contains a strong element of *normlessness*. Adler makes a cogent argument that post-truth practices could undermine progress but does not entertain arguments identifying the characteristics of normlessness put forth by psychologists of moral development. I would suggest that *normlessness* not only undermines progress but *could pose a challenge to cognitive evolution theory itself*.

Despite crushing disappointments of the post-truth environment for the social order of refugee protection, I conclude on a positive note. In the final chapter of *Cognitive Evolution*, Adler posits two important conditions under which collapse of a social order can be averted: the level of social *homeorhesis* (stability of change over time that permits or hinders better practices to come to the fore) and the level of *resilience* of communities of practice. Although the post-truth environment is one of greatly weakened homeorhesis, putting at risk the continuous selection of communities that practice refugee protection and endangering the survival of their practices, we are also witnessing great resilience and creativity among refugees themselves, their allies, and those communities that constitute the refugee protection regime. Immigrants and their allies have fought and will continue to fight for the acknowledgment of their humanity. And the international social order that protects refugees is still providing safety and refuge to millions of uprooted people. The social order of refugee protection is resilient and creative, even in a post-truth environment. This is progress.

References

Adler, Emanuel. 1991. Cognitive Evolution: A Dynamic Approach for the Study of International Relations and Their Progress. In *Progress in Postwar International Relations*, edited by Emanuel Adler and Beverly Crawford, 43–88. New York: Columbia University Press.

Adler, Emanuel. 2019. *World Ordering: A Social Theory of Cognitive Evolution*. Cambridge: Cambridge University Press.

Anderson, Norman. 1981. *Foundations of Information Integration Theory*. New York: Academic Press.

Aronson, Shlomo. 2004. *Hitler, the Allies, and the Jews*. Cambridge: Cambridge University Press.

Barnett, Michael. 2009. Evolution without Progress? Humanitarianism in a World of Hurt. *International Organization* 63 (4): 621–63.

Barnett, Michael and Janice Stein. 2017. Pragmatism, Meaning, and Suffering: Evolutionary Callings and Exhaustions. Paper Presented at the Workshop *A Celebration of Emanuel Adler's Scholarship and Career*. Toronto, 12 May.

Benkler, Yochi, Robert Faris, Hal Roberts and Ethan Zukerman. 2017. Study: Breitbart-led Right-wing Media Ecosystem Altered Broader Media Agenda. *Columbia Journalism Review*. www.cjr.org/analysis/breit bart-media-trump-harvard-study.php. Accessed March 18, 2018.

Carr, Edward Hallet. 1939, 1964. *The Twenty Years Crisis 1919–1939: An Introduction to the Study of International Relations*. Reprint of the 2nd ed. New York: Harper and Row

Chua, Amy. 2017. *Political Tribes: Group Instinct and the Fate of Nations*. London: Penguin.

Cohen, Aharon. 1970. *Israel and the Arab World*. New York: Funk and Wagnall.

Crawford, Beverly. 2018. Refugees and their Allies as Agents of Progress: Knowledge, Power and Action in Forbidden and Dangerous Boundary Regions. Working Paper. Berkeley: University of California Berkeley, Institute of European Studies. https://escholarship.org/uc/item/7t86g05f.

Crisp, Jeff. 2009. Refugees, Persons of Concern, and People on the Move: The Broadening Boundaries of UNHCR. *Refuge* 26(1): 73–76.

Deudney, Daniel and Elizabeth Mendenhall 2016. Green Earth: The Emergence of Planetary Civilization. In *New Earth Politics: Essays from the Anthropocene*, edited by Simon Nicholson and Jinnah Sikina, 43–72. Cambridge, MA: MIT Press.

Douglass, Frederick. 1857. If There Is No Struggle, There Is No Progress. West India Emancipation Speech, Canandaigua, New York, August 3. www.blackpast.org/african-american-history/1857-frederick-douglass-if-there-no-struggle-there-no-progress/. Accessed February 4, 2018.

Elman, Colin and Miriam Elman eds. 2003. *Progress in International Relations Theory: Appraising the Field*. Cambridge, MA. MIT Press.

Elster, Jon. 1999. *Alchemies of the Mind: Rationality and the Emotions*. Cambridge: Cambridge University Press.

European Parliament. 2017. Attitudes towards Immigration in Europe: Myths and Realities. *European Social Survey*. www.europeansocialsurvey.org/do cs/findings/IE_Handout_FINAL.pdf. Accessed March 21, 2018.

Gillespie, Marie, Lawrence Ampofo, Margaret Cheesman, et al. 2016. *Mapping Refugee Media Journeys Smartphones and Social Media Networks*. Research Report. Paris: The Open University/France Médias Monde. www.open .ac.uk/ccig/sites/www.open.ac.uk.ccig/files/Mapping%20Refugee%20Media %20Journeys%2016%20May%20FIN%20MG_0.pdf. Accessed March 3, 2018.

Goodwin-Gill, Guy. 1996. *The Refugee in International Law*. Oxford: Clarendon Press.

Guterres, Antonio. 2007. People on the Move. *The Guardian*, December 11. www.theguardian.com/commentisfree/2007/dec/11/peopleonthe move. Accessed June 18, 2021

Guterres, Antonio. 2008a. *Climate Change, Natural Disasters and Human Displacement: A UNHCR Perspective*. Geneva: UNHCR.

Guterres, Antonio. 2008b. Millions Uprooted: Saving Refugees and the Displaced. *Foreign Affairs* 87(5): 90–99.

Guterres, Antonio. 2017. *Remarks at the High-level event at COP23*, November 15. www.un.org/sg/en/content/sg/speeches/2017-11-15/secre tary-general-cop23-remarks Accessed March 22, 2018.

Hammerstad, Anne. 2014. *The Rise and Decline of a Global Security Actor: UNHCR, Refugee Protection and Security*, Oxford: Oxford University Press.

Ikenberry, G. John. 2018. End of the International Order? *International Affairs* 94 (1): 7–23.

Jaumotte, Florence and Ksenia Koloskova, Sweta C. Saxena. 2016. *Impact of Migration on Income Levels in Advanced Economies*. Spillover Notes. Washington DC: International Monetary Fund.

Judt, Tony. 2005. *Postwar: A History of Europe since 1945*. London: Penguin.

Keeley, Lawrence. 1996. *War before Civilization*. New York: Oxford University Press.

League of Nations. 1933. *Convention of 28 October 1933 relating to the International Status of Refugees*. www.refworld.org/docid/3dd8cf374 .html. Accessed March 6, 2018.

Lee Chai and Long Ma. 2012. News Sharing in Social Media: The Effect of Gratifications and Prior Experience. *Computers in Human Behavior* 28 (2): 331–39.

Linklater, Andrew. 2010. Global Civilizing Processes and the Ambiguities of Human Interconnectedness. *European Journal of International Relations*. 16(2): 155–78.

Linklater, Andrew. 2011. *The Problem of Harm in International Politics*. Cambridge: Cambridge University Press.

Loescher, Gil. 2017. UNHCR's Origins and Early History: Agency, Influence, and Power in Global Refugee Policy. *Refuge* 33(1): 77–86.

Latour, Bruno. 2004. Why Has Critique Run out of Steam? From Matters of Fact to Matters of Concern. *Critical Inquiry* 30(4): 225–48.

Lowe, K. 2012. *Savage Continent: Europe in the Aftermath of World War Two*. New York: Viking Press.

Mayblin, Lucy. 2014. Colonialism, Decolonisation, and the Right to be Human: Britain and the 1951 Geneva Convention on the Status of Refugees. *Journal of Historical Sociology* 27(3): 423–41.

Mazower, Mark. 1999. *Dark Continent: Europe's 20th Century*. New York: Alfred A. Knopf.

McDermot, Rose. 2004. The Feeling of Rationality: The Meaning of Neuroscientific Advances for Political Science. *Perspectives on Politics* 2 (4): 691–706.

Nam, H. Hannah, John T. Jost and Jay J. Van Bavel. 2013. "Not for All the Tea in China!" Political Ideology and the Avoidance of Dissonance-Arousing Situations. *PLoS ONE* 8(4): e59837.

Nickerson, Raymond. 1998. Confirmation Bias: A Ubiquitous Phenomenon in Many Guises. *Review of General Psychology* 2(2): 175–220.

Nyhan, Brendan and Jason Reifler. 2010. When Corrections Fail: The Persistence of Political Misperceptions. *Political Behavior* 32(2): 303–30.

Oeldorf-Hirsch, Anne and S. Shyam Sundar. 2015. Posting, Commenting, and Tagging: Effects of Sharing News Stories on Facebook. *Computers in Human Behavior* 44(2): 240–49.

Palacio, Ana. 2017. The Twentieth Century Ended in 2017. Nobody Knows What Era We're in Now. *World Economic Forum/Project Syndicate*,

January 26. www.weforum.org/agenda/2017/01/twentieth-century-2017/. Accessed January 4, 2018.

Pew Research Center: Journalism and Media Staff. 2007. Cable News. *Pew Research Center*, May 25. www.journalism.org/2007/05/25/cable-news/. Accessed January 4, 2018.

Pinker, Stephen. 2018. *Enlightenment Now: The Case for Science, Reason, Humanism, and Progress*. New York: Viking.

Price, Richard, ed. 2008. *Moral Limit and Possibility in World Politics*. Cambridge: Cambridge University Press.

Redlawsk, David. 2002. Hot Cognition or Cool Consideration? Testing the Effects of Motivated Reasoning on Political Decision Making. *Journal of Politics* 64(4): 1021–44.

Reed-Hurtado, Michael. 2017. The Cartagena Declaration on Refugees and the Protection of People Fleeing Armed Conflict and Other Situations of Violence in Latin America. In *In Flight from Conflict and Violence: UNHCR's Consultations on Refugee Status and Other Forms of International Protection*, edited by Volker, Türk, Alice Edwards and Cornelis Wouters, 141–80. Cambridge: Cambridge University Press.

Ross, Lee, Yphtach Lelkes and Alexandra Russell. 2012. How Christians Reconcile Their Personal Political Views and the Teachings of Their Faith: Projection as Means of Dissonance Reduction. *Proceedings of the National Academy of Sciences of the Unites States* 109(10): 3616–22.

Sachar, Howard. 1979. *A History of Israel*. New York: Alfred A. Knopf.

Shephard, Ben. 2011. *The Long Road Home: The Aftermath of the Second World War*. New York: Alfred A. Knopf.

Sjöberg, Tommie. 1991. *The Powers and the Persecuted: The Refugee Problem and the Intergovernmental Committee on Refugees (IGCR) 1938–1947*. Lund: Lund University Press.

Silverman, Craig. 2011. The Backfire Effect. *Columbia Journalism Review*, June 17. https://archives.cjr.org/behind_the_news/the_backfire_effect .php. Accessed March 1, 2018.

Skran, Claudena. 1995. *Refugees in Inter-War Europe: The Emergence of a Regime*. Oxford: Oxford University Press.

Stoessinger, John. 1956. *The Refugees and the World Community*. Minneapolis: University of Minnesota Press.

Tate, Merze. 1943. The American Negro in World War I and World War II. *The Journal of Negro Education* 12(3): 521–32.

Turiel, Elliot. 2002. *The Development of Social Knowledge: Morality and Convention*. Cambridge: Cambridge University Press.

United Nations Ad Hoc Committee on Refugees and Stateless Persons. 1949. *A Study of Statelessness: United Nations: Lake Success*, August 1. www .refworld.org/docid/3ae68c2d0.html. Accessed February 5, 2018.

UNHCR. 2009. *2008 Global Trends: Refugees, Asylum-seekers, Returnees, Internally Displaced and Stateless Persons*. Geneva: UNHCR.

Vitalis, Robert. 2017. *White World Order, Black Power Politics: The Birth of American International Relations*. Ithaca: Cornell University Press.

Vosoughi, Soroush, Deb Roy and Sinan Aral. 2018. The Spread of True and False News Online. *Science* 359(6380): 1146–51.

Waltz, Kenneth. 1999. *On Interdependence*. Forli: Lecture presented at the Bologna Center and the International Relations Program of the University of Bologna.

Wendt, Alexander 1992. Anarchy Is What States Make of It: The Social Construction of Power Politics. *International Organization* 46(2): 391.

8 | Holding the Middle Ground
Cognitive Evolution and Progress

CHRISTIAN REUS-SMIT

In a field long structured by interparadigm debates, seizing the middle ground between polarized theoretical positions has been an attractive "third way." Martin Wight famously cast the rationalism of the English School as a "via media" between realism, on the one hand, and revolutionism, on the other. Robert Keohane positioned liberal institutionalism between neorealism and his earlier transnationalism. And constructivists have commonly located themselves between the rationalism and materialism of neorealism and neoliberalism and the radical interpretivism of poststructuralism. The immediate attractions of such strategies are easy to see. Seizing the middle ground clears the log jams of interparadigm debates, promising theoretical paths forward that take the best from the poles and leave behind the obstructive but ultimately superfluous. It also promises to galvanize scholarly support, creating an innovative theoretical space for both newcomers to the field and jaded adherents of existing theoretical poles. And, finally, seizing the middle ground, dramatic as it may sound, conveys an aura of utter reasonableness.

Beyond these immediate attractions, seizing the middle ground serves political, sociological, ethical and epistemic purposes. Politically, it is an intellectual practice that makes sense only in polarized disciplinary terrains, and while tracking any middle way assumes the existence of poles, it is an act of intellectual resistance, a refusal to reproduce the rituals of antagonistic debate. Sociologically, it is more than an intellectual maneuver; it is an attempt to constitute a new community of theoretical practice, to give a theoretical endeavor an identity and to foster new axes of debate. Ethically, seizing the middle ground is always about forging new intersections between empirical and normative theory. If, as I have argued elsewhere, all empirical theories have normative dimensions and all normative theories depend on empirical assumptions, then seizing the middle ground disrupts these intersections (which we see clearly in Wight's, Keohane's and Emanuel Adler's writings). Finally,

208

seizing the middle ground serves epistemic purposes. All theoretical positions rest on meta-theoretical assumptions: ontological and methodological, as well as epistemological. And it is not surprising that efforts to navigate between polarized theoretical positions involves, at a minimum, the artful navigation between rival meta-theoretical positions, and more ambitiously, the reformulation of underlying meta-theoretical commitments.

Emanuel Adler's 1997 article "Seizing the Middle Ground: Constructivism in World Politics" is the most highly cited effort to position constructivism on a terrain between the dominant mainstream theories of neorealism and neoliberalism and their critical theoretic challengers.[1] More than this, it is a constellation point for ideas Adler had advanced in earlier writings, and that he would develop to great effect over the coming two decades, most notably in his recent magnum opus, *World Ordering: A Social Theory of Cognitive Evolution* (henceforth *World Ordering*).[2]

Holding the middle ground may be harder than seizing it, though. This is partly because the theoretical poles of contending paradigms may rest on incommensurable ontological or epistemological assumptions. The idea that material forces make the world go around is not easily reconciled with the notion that ideas go all the way down. Similarly, the assumption that legitimate knowledge is a description or representation of reality sits uncomfortably with the proposition that ideas construct or constitute that reality. The challenge of holding the middle ground is further complicated, however, by the distinctive nature of International Relations (IR) as a theoretical project. Duncan Snidal and I have argued elsewhere that IR is best understood as a practical discourse, concerned at a fundamental level with questions of how individuals, states, institutions, the "international community" should act.[3] Yet addressing such questions draws IR scholars onto particularly challenging terrain, not just between contrasting ontological or epistemological positions, but between these and normative theory. Answering the question of how we should act requires both an understanding of the domain of action *and* a set of normative purposes to animate action.

This chapter explores the difficulties of holding the middle ground through a reading of Adler's writings over the past three decades.

[1] Adler 1997. [2] Adler 2019. [3] Reus-Smit and Snidal 2008.

I draw a distinction between two different approaches to seizing the middle ground, which I term, for want of better words, *singular* and *dualist*. The former, as part one details, is found in Martin Wight's tripartite distinction between realism, rationalism and revolutionism. This distinction is noteworthy because it is at once a typology of different ontological positions, arraying theories with very different assumptions about the nature of the political universe, and a classification of different views of the potential for normative change, or progress.[4] The second, dualist approach separates questions of ontology from those of progress, imagining two middle grounds. Exemplified in Adler's work, the first middle ground, familiar to us all, is between the ideal and the material and the individual and structural (easily presented in a neat two by two) (see Drieschova, Chapter 3, this volume, for a more critical and materialist perspective). But when Adler discusses progress, which is a prominent and enduring theme in his work, he introduces a second, less remarked upon, middle ground. He calls this position "humanist realism," locating it between stasis, on the one hand, and utopianism, on the other (my terminology). The difficulties of holding the middle ground in singular approaches is apparent in Hedley Bull's constant back and forth over the relative priority of the values of order and justice, a relationship central to rationalism's location between realism and revolutionism. The difficulties of the dualist approach are evident in Adler's shifting reconciliations between his two middle grounds. In his early work, reconciliation was to come through a condominium between constructivism and communitarian normative theory, but later this shifted to an emphasis on practices as a bridge between the analytical and the normative (see also Chapter 1 of this volume). Neither of these earlier reconciliations is sufficient, I argue, and I suggest three possible solutions found in existing literatures. In *World Ordering* Adler pursues a variant of one of these, and I conclude with a brief discussion of the enduring tensions within such an approach.

Before proceeding, it is important to note that Richard Price and I have ploughed much of the same terrain as Adler. We too have tried to nudge constructivism onto the middle ground between the ontological and normative, and we too have moved from an early argument about a division of labor with normative theory toward a more integrated

---

[4] See also Crawford, this volume.

argument (emphasizing, in our case, the structure of ethical reasoning). Much of what I say here about the difficulty of holding the middle ground applies not just to Adler's work, but to ours as well.[5]

The Singular Approach

Few schools of thought in IR have devoted as much energy to narrating their identity and place in the field as the English School. And central to this narrative is Wight's oft-quoted distinction between three great traditions of international thought: realism, rationalism and revolutionism. For Wight, these constitute the principal ideas about international relations, evolving as consistent and coherent strands of thought from the time of Machiavelli. At one extreme lies revolutionism, which Wight saw as the oldest of the three traditions. Revolutionists "believe so passionately in the moral unity of the society of states or international society, they identify themselves with it, and therefore claim to speak in the name of its unity, and experience an overriding obligation to give effect to it, as the first aim of international politics."[6] At the other extreme lies realism, expressing a profound skepticism about the very existence of international society and emphasizing "in international relations the element of anarchy, of power-politics, and of warfare."[7] Between the two lies the "broad middle road" of rationalism, a tradition Wight considered "specially representative of Western values."[8] This view neither denies the condition of anarchy between states, nor the moral standing of states as valid political authorities. But it sees states as rational, as capable of establishing and maintaining social relations without a central authority. It

does not derogate from the moral claims of states, conceding that they are, in Suarez's phrase, *communitates perfectae* (exercising valid authority); but it sees them as relatively, not absolutely perfect. It does not see international society as ready to supersede domestic society; but it notes that international society actually exercises restraints upon its members.[9]

While there is some debate about whether the core insight of the English School is that international society is a key structuring condition of international relations, or somewhat differently, that

---

[5] See Price and Reus-Smit 1998; Reus-Smit 2008.   [6] Wight 1992, 8.
[7] Ibid., 15.   [8] Wight 1966a, 91.   [9] Ibid., 95.

international relations always exhibit realist, rationalist and revolutionist dynamics, the School has laid special claim to the rationalist middle ground, holding true to the core insight of society under anarchy.

Wight's typology is complex, however, mapping at least two things at once: the ontological and the normative. The three traditions express deep-seated assumptions about the nature of the political universe beyond the state. Foundational for realists is the assumption

that there is no such thing as international society: that international relations constitute an anarchy whose social elements are negligible. The doctrine that the state is the ultimate unit of political society entails the doctrine that there is no wider society to embrace states.[10]

By contrast, revolutionists assume not only that international society exists, but that it is pregnant with the potential for its own transcendence. "On this view, international society is none other than the community of mankind, half glimpsed and groping for its necessary fulfillment."[11] Between these extremes, rationalists assume a world of states, sufficiently rational to maintain a minimal framework of institutional norms and practices that enable coexistence under anarchy. Wight identified these assumptions in a long line of thinkers, from Suarez and Grotius to Lincoln, Gladstone and Churchill, but also in the recurrent practices of states. "This pattern of ideas is persistent and recurrent. Sometimes eclipsed and distorted, it has constantly reappeared and reasserted its authority, so that it may even seem something like a consensus of Western diplomatic opinion."[12]

The distinction between realism, rationalism and revolutionism is not just ontological, though: it is also normative. I mean this in two senses. First, the three traditions were not simply different accounts of international reality, but also prescriptions for how political actors should act within those realities. As Hedley Bull put it in his Martin Wight Memorial Lecture, "[e]ach pattern or tradition of thought embodied a description of the nature of international politics and also a set of prescriptions as to how men should conduct themselves in it."[13] For realists this was the prudent pursuit of the national interest, for revolutionists it was the realization of the community of humankind and for rationalists it was the preservation of the society of

[10] Ibid., 92.   [11] Ibid., 93.   [12] Ibid., 90.   [13] Bull 1976, 106.

states. Second, in addition to these prescriptions, the three traditions offer different accounts of the potential for normative change, or progress. The realist account was expressed succinctly by Wight himself in his essay, "Why is there no international theory?" While progress may be possible within the state, "[i]nternational politics is the realm of recurrence and repetition."[14] At the other extreme, revolutionists, whether Kantian or Marxist, see progress as not only possible, but immanent within the society of states – international society, in Wight's words, is considered "the chrysalis of the community of mankind": cosmopolitanism born of internationalism.[15] Between these positions, on the broad middle ground, rationalists express a guarded, incrementalist view of progress, in which progress is animated and contained by the constant negotiation, and unstable reconciliation, of two key values: order and justice.

As this brief discussion shows, Wight's account of the rationalist via media, and the English School's seizure of this terrain, is singular in form. Not only is a single spectrum from realism to revolutionism imagined, with a single via media between, but the spectrum is at once ontological and normative, as is the rationalist middle ground. This is a direct consequence of Wight's approach to international theory. As Bull observed, "[w]hile the behaviouralists sought to exclude moral questions as lying beyond the scope of scientific treatment, Wight placed these questions at the centre of his inquiry."[16] From this perspective, ontology alone would never do: the normative had to occupy the same stage. Yet this has rendered the rationalist middle ground particularly unstable. A degree of instability is already there at the ontological level. Imagining the international universe as a society of states has never been able to shake the realist critique that the struggle for power under anarchy is the ultimate determinant of world politics. Equally, it has never been able to counter, in any definitive sense, the claim that international society, to the extent it exists, always has universalist dynamics (whether it is the connection between absolutist sovereignty and Christian universalism, or popular sovereignty and the universal rights of the individual). This instability is compounded, though, by the vagaries of rationalism as a normative space. To be sure, Bull sees the values of order and justice as reconcilable if order is conceived in social terms and justice is confined to the

---

[14] Wight 1966b, 26.   [15] Wight 1966a, 95.   [16] Bull 1976, xi.

preservation of the rights of states. But realists also lay claim to order as cardinal value of international relations, and revolutionists assert the priority of human over international justice. The constant negotiation of order and justice, thus, pulls debate toward the poles.

The Dualist Approach

In "Seizing the Middle Ground" Adler locates constructivism in the ontological and epistemological space between "rationalist" and "relativist interpretive" approaches. Ontologically, he follows Alexander Wendt in mapping the terrain of debate on two axes: whether theories give causal priority to ideational or material forces, and whether they emphasize individual agents or structures. Some rationalists, like neorealists, are structuralists and materialists; others, like neoliberals, lean toward individualism and idealism (but only thinly so, seeing ideas as individual motives or intervening variables). Constructivism, by contrast, occupies the middle ground between both axes. It is structurationist, in Anthony Gidden's ungainly terminology. Social structures constitute individuals as knowledgeable agents, and these agents produce and reproduce structures (see also Pratt, Chapter 4, this volume). Similarly, rejecting crude materialist arguments that attribute political outcomes to underlying physical forces, and also radical interpretive claims that the material world has no independent reality, constructivists seek to understand how intersubjective meanings and material contexts interact to shape social and political outcomes. In Adler's words,

[c]onstructivism seizes the middle ground because it is interested in understanding how the *material*, subjective, and intersubjective worlds interact in the social construction of reality, and because, rather than focusing exclusively on how structures constituted agent's identities and interests, it also seeks to explain how *individual agents* socially construct these structures in the first place.[17]

While Adler's mapping privileges ontology, it is also epistemological. The debate over the causal priority of ideas or material forces is not just about what the world is made of, or what makes it go around, but about what we can know about this world. This dimension is captured

---

[17] Adler 1997, 330.

in Adler's distinction between reflective, constitutive and mediative epistemologies. Rationalists hold the first of these, assuming that "reality is independent of cognition but can be accurately represented in true descriptions."[18] Constructivists acknowledge material reality, but claim that it can only be known through human language (see Sondarjee, Chapter 5, this volume, for a discussion of the importance of narratives). Taken to the extreme, this leads to an exclusive focus on discourses, and a denial that the material world has any significance outside these discourses. The mediative position lies between these poles, insisting that "social reality emerges from the attachment of meaning and functions to physical objects; collective understandings, such as norms, endow physical objects with purpose and therefore help constitute reality."[19] Moreover, regardless of the meanings attached to physical objects, the material world has a reality that is both constraining and enabling. As Martin Hollis observed with an artful turn of phrase, "life in a desert full of oil differs from life in a tundra full of bears."[20]

Unlike the middle ground identified by Wight and claimed by the English School, Adler's middle ground lacks a normative dimension: it is an ontological and epistemological domain. One can read into it differing positions on the possibility of normatively inspired change. A heavily structural and materialist position is likely to be skeptical of such change, just as a position that emphasizes ideas and individual agency could be more optimistic. A middle ground position might admit the possibility of change, but see it as heavily constrained. All of this is implied, though: it is not a primary axis in Adler's mapping. Nor do we see in this mapping any substantive normative values. Each of Wight's traditions was both an account of the nature of the international universe and a prescription for how states should act in that environment. Yet such prescriptions are nowhere to be found in Adler's two by two.

Yet Adler has long been interested in understanding the nature and possibility of progress in world politics, and has always conceived progress as inherently normative, as the advancement of the human condition toward the realization of a given set of values. Indeed, he steadfastly denies "that constructivists are blind to ideas of progress in international relations or that they do not care about improving the

---

[18] Ibid., 323.   [19] Ibid., 324.   [20] Hollis 1977, 26.

world just as much as Habermas and other critical theorists do."[21] His own writings on progress, which predate "Seizing the Middle Ground" and carry through to *World Ordering*, testify to this. But where do the values and dynamics of normative change inherent to progress fit in Adler's account of the middle ground?

Put simply, they appear in a second, explicitly normative mapping, and occupy an altogether different middle ground from the first. In Adler's early writings on progress, he imagines a spectrum of positions on the possibility of normative change in international relations. At one extreme there is the position I term "stasis," which is akin to Wight's realist view that international relations is "the realm of recurrence and repetition": progress doesn't occur. At the other extreme is utopianism, where the possibility of change is unconstrained by material forces or political dynamics. Between the two, on a second middle ground, lies "humanist realism," which

blends power structures, interests, and pessimism with bounded optimism, a dynamic view of international politics, and the conviction that some choices do exist and that change can, at times, lead to the enhancement of human interests across borders.[22]

It is clear that Adler sees constructivism occupying both middle grounds: the ontological/epistemology, and the normative-progressive. To occupy only the first would lead to a purely "analytical" constructivism, a form he considers impoverished. In a 2005 article on the relationship between constructivism and Barry Buzan's reformulation of the English School, he criticizes Buzan's attempt to recast the School in purely analytical terms, and argues that "Buzan's theory will be strengthened if after methodologically distinguishing analytical from normative theory, he reintroduces critical and normative features." It is imperative, he writes, that "an IR theoretical synthesis must bridge not only between constructivists and rationalists, but also between analytical and normative IR theory."[23]

Two Bridges

The existence of two middle grounds in Adler's work – one ontological/epistemological, the other normative-progressive – begs a crucial

---

[21] Adler 1997, 334.   [22] Adler 2005b, 84.   [23] Adler 2005a, 181.

question: How are these grounds to be bridged? The challenge is twofold. First, a connection needs to be established between how Adler wishes to develop the ontological middle ground (his theory of cognitive evolution) and the humanist realist proposition that progress is possible but constrained (which I take to be an empirical–theoretic proposition). In other words, the theory of cognitive evolution needs to show how progress, understood as the positive advancement of the human condition, is possible. Second, an account is needed of what the values are that give progress substantive content and how these values are justified normatively. If progress means anything, it is movement toward some normative ends (see Crawford, Chapter 7, this volume). Not only does Adler acknowledge this, he defines such ends in universalist terms. A key condition for progress, he writes, is "the emergence of new values, the redefinition of old values, and a change in the context of valuing that advances human interests across national borders without creating an unbearable harm to other values or human interests."[24] These are clearly cosmopolitan ends – advancing *human* interests *across* borders – but why these values and not others? Where, theoretically, do these values come from, and how can their priority be justified normatively?

Over the course of his writings, Adler has set out two ways of bridging the ontological and normative middles grounds and meeting the above-mentioned challenges. The first, which might be termed the "alliance approach," sees an early articulation of cognitive evolution theory explain the possibility of progress, and communitarian normative theory enlisted as the source of substantive values. As noted earlier, progress occurs for Adler when new values that advance human interests emerge and take hold, and when expectations change about "the quality of outcomes for individual agents."[25] These changes come about through processes of cognitive evolution, understood in early statements as "the process of innovation and political selection, occurring mainly within and between institutional settings, that creates the 'objective' collective understanding that informs the interests of government."[26] Such evolution entails three sequential processes: innovation, through which new values and expectations are created; political selection, which determines which values are privileged and perpetuated and diffusion, whereby values and expectations spread to

[24] Adler 2005b, 78.   [25] Ibid.   [26] Ibid., 72.

other nations.[27] The existence of these evolutionary processes makes progress possible, as they offer pathways and mechanisms through which values that advance human interests can emerge, be selected and then spread. There is nothing in this schema, however, that guarantees progress, or even makes it a likely possibility (see Chapter 1, this volume). Regressive values that undermine human interests might also arise through the very same processes of cognitive evolution. The key question, which Adler rightly poses, is "what causes expectations and values that enhance human interests across national borders to be politically selected, maintained, and spread at the domestic and international levels."[28] In his early writings, Adler offers only a tentative answer, suggesting that interdependence, in economic, security and environmental domains, may undermine old particularistic values and create space for the innovation, selection, and diffusion of values that "veer away from war, poverty, and human rights violations."[29]

But if the theory of cognitive evolution provides an account of the possibility of progress, it does not provide a normative justification for the universalist values that give progress its substantive content. In this first way of bridging the ontological and normative middle grounds, Adler seeks such a justification in an alliance between constructivist social theory and communitarian normative theory. These bodies of thought share much in common, not the least their emphasis on the constitutive effects of community specific intersubjective meanings. Communitarian ethicists have long challenged the deontological nature of cosmopolitan universalism, arguing that all moral values emerge and gain purchase within concrete, historically and culturally located communities. From this perspective, cosmopolitan ethics are ethics from nowhere. At first blush, constructivist theory would seem to reinforce these claims, holding, as it does, that values are salient not because individuals exercise right reason, but because they exist intersubjectively within a concrete community. Despite these similarities, though, Adler is at pains to stress the differences between these bodies of thought. Constructivism takes no position on which is more important, the community or individual interest; it does not prioritize the good over the right; it offers systematic insights into the mechanisms and dynamics of change; it has a more sophisticated account of power; it takes seriously the possibility of expanding community through moral

---

[27] Ibid., 73.   [28] Ibid., 78.   [29] Ibid.

dialogue and communication; and, more importantly, constructivism adopts a more variegated and dynamic conception of community, highlighting "the dynamic attributes of community, which may lead to the creation of transnational identities and security communities."[30] Where communitarian normative theory has traditionally imagined communities as homogeneous and bounded, often taking the nation as the model, constructivism sees multiple, overlapping communities, with individuals navigating the intersubjective terrains of different communities simultaneously.

By focusing on the dynamics of change, showing how moral dialogue can expand the bounds of community, and highlighting the existence of multiple, overlapping communities, Adler sheds further light on how progress might be possible. Furthermore, in doing these things, constructivism brings to an alliance with communitarian normative theory a more sophisticated ontology. It is not clear, however, that this alliance gives Adler what is needed to meet the second challenge, to provide a normative justification for the cosmopolitan values that give his conception of progress substantive content. Indeed, while constructivism and communitarianism converge at the level of ontology, they part company when constructivism is wedded to a cosmopolitan conception of progress. Communitarianism is morally particularist not universalist, and can no more justify the privileging of the pursuit of human interests across borders than constructivism itself.

Adler's second, more recent way of bridging the ontological/empirical and normative middle grounds relies not on an alliance with an established body of normative theory but on the concept of practice. When Adler argues that individuals live simultaneously in multiple, overlapping communities, one of his early innovations was to understand these as communities of practice. Like other constructivists, he understands communities as intersubjective realms; as groups of individuals bound together and constituted by shared meanings. But where many constructivists locate these meanings in language and communication, and see them as produced and reproduced through argument and persuasion, Adler locates them in social practices, in things people do as much as say. As he puts it in *World Ordering*, practices "translate structural background intersubjective knowledge into intentional acts and endow those acts with social meaning."[31]

---

[30] Ibid., 13.   [31] Adler 2019, 110.

Importantly for our purposes, Adler argues that practices have normative content. His writings contain two different versions of this claim, however, both of which find expression in *World Ordering*. The first is that all practices contain within them an intersubjective notion of what constitutes "the better" practice.

In most cases, practitioners not only value their performances, which they would like to improve, but also value solving problems and doing things better than in the past, better than others, and better than alternative communities of practice, not only for efficacy reasons, but also because what they do is deemed to be appropriate.[32]

From this perspective, practices are always normative: they always embody and enact conceptions of the good or better practice. This insight challenges the all-pervasive dichotomy between instrumental and normative action, and because practices depend on reciprocal understandings of their normativity, it may also be a basis on which "a minimalist and pragmatist perspective on 'better practices' can be defended."[33] But despite these strengths, this argument struggles to meet the second of our two challenges: to provide a normative justification for the cosmopolitan values Adler sees animating progress.

The second version of the claim that practices have normative content focuses on the intersubjective background knowledge that informs practices. Adler argues that such knowledge can be technical and normative. Because technical knowledge addresses "how to" questions, its role in shaping practices is clear. And Adler's earlier work on epistemic communities focused on how such knowledge is mobilized, and how, under certain conditions, it affects the nature of social practices. The role of normative knowledge – understood as intersubjective beliefs about the good and the right – is less clear, however. Technical knowledge consists of cause and effect propositions about the contexts in which practices are performed, and about the efficacy of the practices themselves. By contrast, the normative knowledge discussed here concerns the values practices are meant to achieve, or values that determine practices' legitimate scope and domain. For example, with regard to climate change, technical knowledge includes propositions about the effects of human action on global warming and the relative efficacy of market and non-market responses, whereas

[32] Ibid., 131.   [33] Ibid., 133.

normative knowledge includes things like the principle of common but differentiated responsibilities. Such a principle rests on values of fairness and equity, and when combined with technical knowledge, these values have shaped climate-change practices (see Hass, Chapter 6, this volume, for a defense of epistemic communities in the context of climate change).

In the end, although this element of Adler's theory explains how cosmopolitan values might come to animate and inform practices, contributing further to our understanding of how progress might be possible, it does not provide a normative justification for these values. To be sure, once embedded within practices, they may well become integral to the normative value actors attach to those practices. But the same value might accrue to particularistic values embedded in practices. The fact that they are constitutive of extant practices may provide those engaged in the practices with normative reasons for their continued performance, but offers no broader normative defense. The fact that slave owners attached value to the practice of slavery does not establish the normative superiority of slavery over anti-slavery – such a defense would require a different kind of argument.

Other Strategies

Once Adler laid claim to two middle grounds – one ontological/epistemological, and one normative – the unity of his theory depended on him bridging these terrains. A connection had to be built between his version of constructivism, which stresses cognitive evolution in communities of practice, and his humanist realism. For a bridge to be robust it would have to meet two challenges: it would have to show how progress was possible (which the theory of cognitive evolution arguably does), and it would need to provide a normative defense of the cosmopolitan values that give substantive content to "humanist" realism. As we have seen, over the course of Adler's writings two bridges are imagined: the first seeking an alliance with communitarian normative theory, the second giving normative content to practices. The first fails because although constructivism and communitarianism share an ontology, the latter's normative prescriptions are particularist not universalist, leaving Adler's humanism decidedly vulnerable. The second bridge abandons the alliance strategy and seeks an answer in the theory of practices. Yet the propositions that practices are always normative and that normative background knowledge can shape practices, cannot alone provide a normative defense of the cosmopolitan values inherent to his humanist realism.

Existing literatures suggest three possible strategies for resolving the problem, for bridging Adler's analytical and normative middle grounds.

The first is to follow Hedley Bull and ground the values that undergird progress in the imperatives of international order building. As noted in my discussion of Wight's via media, the distinction between realism, rationalism and revolutionism is not only an ontological mapping but also a normative one: the typology differentiates between different accounts of the possibility of progress, and different prescriptions about how actors ought to act in the international universe. On the latter, Wight confined normative action to the preservation of the society of states, but as Bull later argued this involved the ongoing reconciliation of the values of order and justice. Order was essential to the pursuit of higher values, but without justice order was forever precarious. Two things are notable about this strategy. The values are cast broadly, leaving actors scope to define and redefine their content through argument and practice. They are universal, in the sense that Bull sees them as cardinal values in any international order, but they are not universal in an enlightenment sense. In addition to this, the values of order and justice can be plausibly grounded in the preservation of the society of states – in other words, they can be linked to the primary interests of actors, and to production and reproduction of the order on which their ontological status and well-being depends. It is not hard to see how some version of this argument could be enlisted in Adler's project, especially if international society is recast as a community of practice. At present Adler is caught between maximal and minimal accounts of progress: the former tied to the pursuit of human interest across borders, the latter to the realization of highly localized, practice specific ends. Recasting progress at the achievement of values essential to the production and reproduction of international society, understood as a product of community of practice, and seeing these values as standing in a dynamic tension (like order and justice), may be a way of giving humanist realism substantive and sustainable content.

A second strategy would be to strike an alliance with cosmopolitan theorists who are grounding their universal values in collective practices. Take, for example, recent work in the field of human rights. The conventional way of justifying human rights normatively has been to link such rights to the moral integrity of the individual. Human beings are particular kinds of moral beings, distinguished by their capacities to imagine a good life and seek its realization. Human rights, it is argued, exist to protect these capacities, to protect a particular kind of moral personhood.[34] Naturalist arguments such as this have been subjected to sustained criticism, despite the fact that they undergird many of the claims made internationally in defense of human rights. In response, several scholars have sought to ground human rights not in the moral integrity of the individual but in the established practices of states. Jack Donnelly made this move some years ago, arguing, as one part of his defense of human rights, that core norms codified in the Universal Declaration of Human Rights are now "principles that are widely accepted as authoritative within the society of states."[35] More recently, Charles Beitz argues that human rights now constitute a global practice, and that the nature of this practice should exercise some "authority" over how we answer key questions about the nature, status and function of human rights. More specifically, he holds that understanding the practice can help determine "what an ordinarily competent participant in the discourse of human rights would understand herself to be committed to if she were to acknowledge that a human right to such and such exists."[36] This work is instructive because it is explicitly concerned with the moral status of cosmopolitan values, but seeks to ground this status in international practices. Moreover, scholars such as Beitz very carefully distinguish between the kinds of moral questions that a practice approach can answer and those it cannot. Such an approach may also offer insights into how cosmopolitan values are seeded and institutionalized within communities of practice.

Finally, a third strategy might be to embrace the unthinkable and give processes of cognitive evolution a universalist dynamic. This would be akin to what Habermas did with the theory of communicative action, in which universalist imperatives (freedom from domination, and the need to reach an understanding) underlie the argumentative processes of reaching agreement about social norms. For constructivists who focus on the linguistic and discursive constitution of society, these arguments are but a step away: indeed, Habermas's theory has often been employed by constructivists as an empirical theory, its

---

[34] Griffin 2008, 32.   [35] Donnelly 2002, 38.   [36] Beitz 2009, 11.

normative dimensions quietly ignored. Translating these insights to the theory of cognitive evolution would be a larger step, however. Yet one can imagine what such a path might look like. Although communities of practice are primarily realms of doing, they too involve processes of understanding, processes that are produced and reproduced through nonverbal forms of communication. To what extent, it might be fruitful to ask, do these processes exhibit similar universalist dynamics to those identified by Habermas? If they differ, how and in what way? As noted earlier, at one point in Adler's evolving argument, the importance of political, economic and security interdependence is highlighted. It is suggested that such interdependence brings to the fore, and increases the salience of, values that promote human interests across borders. But what is it about communities of practice born of interdependence that has this normative effect? Might a practice version of the theory of communicative action be at work in these kinds of contexts?

Adler's Chosen Bridge

Of these three possible strategies, it is a version of the Habermasian that Adler ultimately adopts in *World Ordering*. In addition to arguing that practices are always normative and that normative knowledge always shapes practices, Adler sees in certain practices a universalist moral dynamic. These practices are distinctive because they acknowledge "our common humanity," by which Adler means that they embody a minimalist "golden rule": value other human beings' lives as you value your own.[37] This value, Adler holds, undergirds other core human values, such as "[e]quality, liberty, fraternity, and mutual self-respect."[38] Crucial to his argument is the proposition that practices embodying this golden rule are not random or entirely contingent. Indeed, Alder sees the proliferation of such practices as a product of human cognitive evolution, in particular of the evolution produced by ever greater human interconnectedness. In contrast to Rawlsian international ethicists, who held that practical global interdependence demanded the formulation of global principles of justice,[39] Adler sees interconnectedness producing practices that actually embody cosmopolitan values. "Interconnectedness," he writes,

[37] Adler 2019, 280.   [38] Ibid.   [39] Beitz 1999.

promotes the sharing of practices that enhance our common humanity, thus enhancing the propensity for the evolution of social orders based on horizontal systems of rule, rather than exclusively or mainly hierarchical systems of rules, in which domination and coercion are more likely.[40]

Adler is careful to stress the contingency that still attends such evolutionary processes: progress, he argues, is only ever "bounded."

Being contingent, partial, reversible, and constituted through practice and politics in transactions – including learning and contestation, in and among communities of practice – the notion of bounded progress stops short of the enlightenment idea of progress but goes beyond normative relativism.[41]

The reversibility of processes the engender practices that embody the value of common humanity is all too apparent in today's retreat from global institutional projects and turn inward to exclusionary forms of ethno-nationalism. Here Adler sees the flaunting of one of the key conditions required for the development of progressive practices, which "practitioners need to take responsibility for what they practice." This involves "judgement and normative understanding of the situation," Adler argues, as "[n]ormative understandings are constitutive of, and happen in, practice".[42] Instead of this, we see too many leaders using "post-truth practices," "undermining collective *epistemological security* for the sake of political domination."[43] The impact of epistemological insecurity is profound. It "literally does away with interconnectedness and with horizontal systems of rule; how else would people stay connected without a common social epistemic background."[44] All is not lost, however. Adler sees hope in "practical democracy," which "encourages shared action, negotiation, and deliberation in a public political space." In such democratic contexts, it may be that "dialectically" peoples come to "contest post-truth politics," encouraging once again the development of practices that embody the value of common humanity.[45]

Conclusion

Seizing the middle ground in IR theory is easier than holding it, especially when the middle ground sought is normative as well as

---

[40] Adler 2019, 281. [41] Ibid., 276. [42] Ibid. [43] Ibid., 290.
[44] Ibid., 292. [45] Ibid., 294.

epistemological and ontological. There are many constructivists with lesser ambitions, who seek only the terrain between epistemological and ontological extremes. Constructivism, for them, is an analytical project: nothing more, nothing less. There is an important strand of constructivism that has never been satisfied with this, however: that has seen in constructivism valuable resources for normative theorizing about IR, not just for theorizing norms. Much of this work has centered on the claim that all normative theorizing makes assumptions about the parameters of possible moral change, and constructivism contributes by providing powerful insights into these parameters.[46] Critics argue that even if this is true constructivism remains an empirical theory; it cannot, on its own, justify the cosmopolitan values many of its exponents favor. Emanuel Adler's *World Ordering* goes much further than previous constructivist efforts, however. His theory of human cognitive evolution locates progress toward the minimalist cosmopolitan value of common humanity in practices born of interconnectedness, and thus makes the case for the reality of bounded moral progress. This argument will undoubtedly be challenged, but it forces critics onto new terrain. It will no longer be sufficient to claim that constructivism has no resources to justify cosmopolitan values; it will also need to be shown that Adler's central claim is wrong: that interconnectedness has engendered practices that embody the value of common humanity, and that this constitutes bounded yet meaningful progress.

References

Adler, Emanuel. 1997. Seizing the Middle Ground: Constructivism in World Politics. *European Journal of International Relations* 3(3): 319–63.

Adler, Emanuel. 2005a. Barry Buzan's Use of Constructivism to Reconstruct the English School: "Not All the Way Down." *Millennium: Journal of International Studies* 34(1): 171–82.

Adler, Emanuel. 2005b. *Communitarian International Relations: The Epistemic Foundations of International Relations*. London: Routledge.

Adler, Emanuel. 2019. *World Ordering: A Social Theory of Cognitive Evolution*. Cambridge: Cambridge University Press.

Beitz, Charles. 1999. *Political Theory and International Relations*. Princeton: Princeton University Press.

---

[46] See, in particular, Price 2008.

Beitz, Charles. 2009. *The Idea of Human Rights*. Oxford: Oxford University Press.

Bull, Hedley. 1976. Martin Wight and the Theory of International Relations. *Review of International Studies* 2(2): 101–16.

Donnelly, Jack. 2002. *Universal Human Rights in Theory and Practice*, 2nd ed. Ithaca: Cornell University Press.

Griffin, James. 2008. *On Human Rights*. Oxford: Oxford University Press.

Hollis, Martin. 1977. *Models of Man: Philosophical Thoughts on Social Action*. Cambridge: Cambridge University Press.

Price, Richard, ed. 2008. *Moral Limit and Possibility in World Politics*. Cambridge: Cambridge University Press.

Price, Richard and Christian Reus-Smit. 1998. Dangerous Liaisons? Critical International Theory and Constructivism. *European Journal of International Relations* 4(3): 259–94.

Pogge, Thomas, W. 1989. *Realizing Rawls*. Ithaca: Cornell University Press.

Reus-Smit, Christian. 2008. Constructivism and the Structure of Ethical Reasoning. In *Moral Limit and Possibility in World Politics*, edited by Richard Price, 53–82. Cambridge: Cambridge University Press.

Reus-Smit, Christian and Duncan Snidal. 2008. Between Utopia and Reality: The Practical Discourses of International Relations. In *The Oxford Handbook of International Relations*, edited by Christian Reus-Smit and Duncan Snidal, 3–40. Oxford: Oxford University Press.

Wight, Martin. 1966a. Western Values in International Relations. In *Diplomatic Investigations: Essays in the Theory of International Politics*, edited by Herbert Butterfield and Martin Wight, 89–131. London: George Allen and Unwin.

Wight, Martin. 1966b. Why Is There No International Theory? In *Diplomatic Investigations: Essays in the Theory of International Politics*, edited by Herbert Butterfield, and Martin Wight, 17–34. London: George Allen and Unwin.

Wight, Martin. 1992. *International Theory: The Three Traditions*. New York: Holmes and Meier.

9 | Conclusion

On World Ordering's New Vistas and a Rough Sketch of Cognitive Evolution's Theory of Politics

EMANUEL ADLER

World Ordering: A Social Theory of Cognitive Evolution's cover depicts the "Tale of the Heike," which I use as a thought experiment to capture the book's crux. [1] For those who have not read the book, the "Tale of the Heike" refers to a Japanese legend about a six-year-old Japanese emperor from the Heike clan of Samurais who was drowned during a naval battle in 1185. Years after the battle, a crab with samurai-like markings on its back appeared on the shores of Japan. Heike fisherman, believing that the drowned emperor's spirit "lived" in those crabs, threw them back to the sea, thus promoting their preferential survival. As told by Carl Sagan,[2] the story features *artificial natural selection*, according to which a myth played a role in the natural selective retention of "samurai crabs" genes. To me, the story also suggests something profound, *cognitive evolution*, a social, thus nonnatural, theory of evolutionary change. It shows not only how and why a particular type of crab species preferentially survived, but also how a particular kind of social order, symbolically represented by the drowning of a Japanese emperor, evolved and was sustained across time by a community of practice whose members, because of what they knew and who they were, threw samurai crabs back into the sea. As a case of collective creative variation, the myth was selectively retained not only in the minds of individuals (if the myth existed only there it would have died together with those individuals), but also in the recurrent practice of throwing samurai crabs back into the sea. Cognitive evolution theory thus shows the futility of ontologically separating material objects, practices, meaning, ideas and knowledge

---

[1] I thank Patricia Greve for her invaluable research assistance.   [2] Sagan 1980.

when explaining change and stability of any kind of social order, be it Japanese fisherman, nation states or humanity.

I began thinking about cognitive evolution almost forty-five years ago, when I first started my graduate studies at UC Berkeley with Ernst Haas. In addition to immensely stimulating conversations with Haas over strong cappuccinos, I read several books that played a catalytic role, mainly Robert Pirsig's *Zen and the Art of Motorcycle Maintenance*,[3] Ludwik Fleck's *Genesis and Development of a Scientific Fact*,[4] Stephen Toulmin's *Human Understanding*,[5] Ilya Prigogine's *From Being to Becoming*[6] and finally Carl Sagan's *Cosmos*.[7] I also was lucky to attend lectures by Jürgen Habermas and Michel Foucault. Berkeley, during those days, was bursting with new ideas about nature, culture, knowledge and learning, what Marilyn Ferguson called *The Aquarian Conspiracy*.[8] In a matter of only a couple of years, the essential concepts and ideas about cognitive evolution came together in a rough form. In the following years, I traversed side roads such as constructivism, epistemic communities, security communities, progress in postwar international relations, and, more recently, social practices and communities of practice, until the analytical and normative features of cognitive evolution theory finally came together – and so did *World Ordering*.

The most exciting experience I have had with cognitive evolution theory, other than the meaning it gave to my academic life, is witnessing the theory's own evolution into uncharted territory but auspicious directions, driven by curious and knowledgeable colleagues and students. *Theorizing World Orders: Cognitive Evolution and Beyond*, therefore, is the "Nobel Prize" I could only dream about receiving for my work. Rather than taking a congratulatory approach, the book engages in constructive criticism while pushing cognitive evolution theory forward with new insights, theoretical innovations and suggestions on whether and how the theory works, or should work, in practice.

The book's editors and other contributors have amply and accurately described cognitive evolution theory, thus saving me the trouble of having to describe again the theory's main arguments, mechanisms, processes and normative analysis. I will therefore engage with how

---

[3] Pirsig 1974.   [4] Fleck 1979.   [5] Toulmin 1972.   [6] Prigogine 1980.
[7] Sagan 1980.   [8] Ferguson 1980.

contributors interpret cognitive evolution theory and will then refer to its future with new vistas in mind. In the first section, I will briefly address some of my colleagues' general and critical points. I say some because, for the most part, I agree with their criticisms and suggestions, which I am very grateful for. In section two, I will make the case for framing IR theory around the concept of world ordering. Before I am accused of vanity, let me clarify that I do not mean necessarily doing so from a cognitive evolution perspective but from any theoretical perspective, irrespective of its "ism." World ordering is not only vital to understanding much of what is puzzling about world politics these days, but it can also help us think in new ways about IR's most important subjects. In section three, I take up the gauntlet thrown down by the editors in their introduction and suggest a preliminary sketch of a cognitive evolution theory of politics. In the last section, I will briefly apply this sketch to how politics could and should play a key role on confronting issues that make world order, and the human condition more generally, most vulnerable.

Reading Your Reading

I appreciate that the suggested "new vistas" not only open the theory's ontology and mechanisms at work, but also pave the road for a research program with indeterminate but scientifically progressive directions. Therefore, I am grateful to Pouliot, Kornprobst and Ish-Shalom for outlining and describing cognitive evolution theory in such a clear way, to the point that I kept saying: "Cool, did I write that?" Particularly illuminating is the comparative section that juxtaposes my theory of world order with leading world order theories, such as John Ikenberry's[9] and Hedley Bull's.[10] The comparison speaks for itself, but most importantly it conveys the message to IR scholars that *World Ordering*, above and beyond the social theory that informs it, suggests an IR theory on world order change and stability, and as such should be judged by IR scholars.

I also find the introduction's critical questions and agenda for further research to be very useful. In the following section, I will come back to several critical issues the editors of this volume asked. In the spirit of clarification, however, I would like to make a few minor points

---

[9] Ikenberry 2011.   [10] Bull 1977.

upfront. First, the editors often refer to my "meta-theory," namely, cognitive evolution's ontological, epistemological and social theoretical foundations. While the concept of meta-theory is widely used in IR theory to demarcate clear boundaries between IR theory and social theory, when it comes to a theory of change and stability of international social orders based on cognitive evolution, *social theory is IR theory*. While this comment may be read as a tedious semantic point, it is not; neither cognitive evolution theory nor evolutionary constructivist theory more generally make sense without grounding them in process ontology and evolutionary epistemology. Especially IR scholars who work in the sociological tradition need at times to integrate social theory into their IR theories. Often, they (we) do this implicitly, thus blurring the boundaries between the two.

Second, the editors read my concept of meta-stability as involving evolution.[11] This is not the way I see it. Meta-stability involves constant fluctuations, permanent change. Evolution, however, occurs only after changes build up to a critical mass, reach an intersubjective threshold, and tip, resulting in a new social order that replaces the old one. While this may happen at times quite suddenly (take, for example, the fall of the Berlin Wall), changes building up toward a threshold often are characterized by liminality, according to which the old and new social orders overlap; the old social order is still not gone and the new has yet to evolve.

Before continuing, let me raise a point that applies to several of the volume's contributors: Throughout my career I have built on the work of eminent scholars, in my case, for example, John Searle, Karl Popper, John Dewey, Etienne Wenger and to a lesser extent Pierre Bourdieu, and in IR, Ernst Haas, Karl Deutsch and John Ruggie. Because my use of their work has been "unorthodox" – borrowing from their work what I find useful, but seldom buying into their entire corpus of work, and almost always combining what I borrowed with other scholars' approaches to produce my own gestalt – this approach sometimes got me in trouble: "Aha! Adler is a pragmatist rather than a scientific realist" (I am a pragmatic realist); "he buys into Popper's 'positivist approach'"; "he follows Bourdieu"; namely, some of my readers interpreted that I followed a particular "guru" wholesale. Rather than following "gurus," I discriminately take ideas that serve my theoretical

---

[11] Pouliot, Kornprobst and Ish-Shalom, this volume.

purpose, detach them from their entire opus and blend them into my own theoretical construct, hoping that the product of this endeavor will be original and useful. Two examples I draw from Pratt's chapter will suffice. In my book, I rely considerably on Searle's arguments on collective intentionality, which I assign to communities of practice. As I mentioned explicitly in Chapter 2, however, I disagree with Searle's representational approach and thus with his argument that background knowledge is pre-intentional. When it comes to cognitive evolution's subjective "micro-foundations," however, I take a position closer but not identical to Bourdieu's phenomenological approach (see Chapter 4). I argue at length about why and under what conditions background knowledge becomes reflexive and migrates to the "foreground."[12] Or take, for example, Dewey. His work had a deep influence on mine. Unlike Dewey[13], however, I do not use the concept of habits but replace it with the concept of practices, and while I recognize that cognitive evolution may be conditioned by the environment, for instance, international crises, I take endogenous factors, such as learning and contestation, to also drive practice change.

Keeping on with Pratt's chapter, Pratt's phenomenological approach is original, methodologically plausible, thus, worth pursuing. There are, however, different ways to theorize how the range of human lived experience can provide insights and evidence on how social cognitions evolve in communities. Psychology suggests ways to theorizing cognitive evolution further, for example, focusing on how emotions affect practical performance.[14] I, for one, chose to focus on practitioners' dispositions and expectations for it opens a window into people's ways of experiencing the past and imagining the future. The methodological value of referring to dispositions and expectations is that we can study human experience without getting inside "others' minds."

My only disagreement in this volume with Drieschova's argument on the importance of material factors and technology for cognitive evolution is that the mechanisms she suggests, particularly regarding selective retention, seem to rely on a functionalist Darwinian analogy. In my

---

[12] Stein 2011.   [13] Dewey 1922.

[14] On psychology and cognitive evolution, see Campbell 1960; Cosmides and Tooby 1987; Lopez, McDermott and Peterson 2011; Buss 2016. On emotions and political behavior, see McDermott 2004; Mercer 2013; Hutchinson and Bleiker 2014.

view, as shown clearly by the evolution of the QWERTY typewriter keyboard,[15] the most efficient technology will not always be selectively retained, and seldom do purposeful individuals "select" social order according to what works. Apart from this, I acknowledge the important role that material factors, particularly technology play in cognitive evolution. Thus, for example, in a recent article,[16] in which Drieschova and I study the post-truth phenomenon (we relabel it as "truth subversion,") we show how the interaction between practices, knowledge, norms and technology can destroy liberal orders and democracy. As a distinctive form of politics and "communicative action," truth subversion practices can only be understood when looking at the coevolution of practices, knowledge and technology. Hitler and Mussolini mastered the politics of truth subversion, mostly using radio and public rallies. Today's state of the technological art, including the Internet, artificial intelligence (AI) and social network platforms enables political domination and surveillance of entire populations to the extent that Hitler and Mussolini could only have dreamt about.

When considering material factors, however, I find less useful the variant of the so-called "new materialism" literature that highlights "assemblages," abstract structural unities of things and sayings that become something else, namely, different "wholes."[17] Supporters of this theory first need to avoid functionalism by explaining how the "wholes" concretize, thus, why they acquire one form rather than another. However, Action-Network Theory (ANT),[18] which endows objects with agency, can be useful to researching cognitive evolution, for instance, on world-ordering topics, such as climate change.

I entirely agree with Sondarjee that narratives – stories that people tell about themselves – coevolve with practices. What is the Tale of the Heike if not a narrative the Heike told about themselves, which shaped their identity and constituted their community of practice? Following the thought experiment, however, the narrative constitutes natural reality (the selective retention of the samurai crab) by, first, becoming embedded in a crab's shell, which bears a pattern that resembles a samurai warrior, and, second, by retaining the practice of throwing the samurai crab back to the sea. In other words, narratives play a crucial role as part of practices and communities of practice's

---

[15] David 1985. [16] Adler and Drieschova 2021.
[17] De Louze and Gauttari 1987; Delanda 2006. [18] Latour 2005.

background knowledge. This is particularly true when narratives are "viewed as part of communities of practice, [because] narratives can be expected to act as other shared resources, be they discourses or activities."[19] I should have made this point more explicit in my book and thank Sondarjee for emphasizing it. As the story of the samurai crab shows, stories that people tell about themselves and others, both through language and material representations, may help enrich research on the sources of cognitive evolution's creative variation processes. We may also be able to study selective retention processes by focusing on the role narratives play as a source of communication through action and practice, thus, helping practices and knowledge spread more widely.

Peter Haas and I collaborated when developing the concept of epistemic communities in IR,[20] thus, we agree on the importance of the concept when studying global governance and world ordering. We probably agree to disagree, however, first on definitions of social order: whereas P. Haas takes social order as a synonym for governance, I, although acknowledging the role governance plays in world order, take the latter as an arrangement of practices and background knowledge within and between communities of practice. Second, my approach of not adopting concepts wholesale, regardless of what their designers first meant by them[21] also becomes a source of misunderstanding and perhaps also disagreement between us. P. Haas refers to the meanings that extant literatures – I believe the literature on environmental governance is crucial in his case – gave to the concepts of epistemic communities and communities of practice. These literatures not only reify the concepts, but also compare both communities in terms of their nature, differences and similarities, and their policy impact.[22] I, on the other hand, depart from the concepts' first meanings and widespread use. As I argued in my book, I conceive of communities of practice as part of a mechanism or mechanisms aimed at explaining world ordering. Thus, I understand communities of practice as a more encompassing category than epistemic communities (they are constituted by knowledge after all), whose practices emerge not only from consensual scientific knowledge, but also from all types of background

[19] De Fina and Georgakopoulou 2008, 384. See also Faizullaev and Cornut 2017.
[20] Adler 1992; Adler and Haas 1992.
[21] In IR, see Ruggie 1975 and Haas 1982.
[22] See, for example, Cohendet et al. 2001.

knowledge, including normative and ideological. Identifying epistemic communities as epistemic communities of practice, as I do now,[23] enables me to understand the effect of scientific background knowledge on the conditions of possibility for the emergence of world-ordering practices, their selective retention, and the conditions for their long-term survival. The arms control epistemic community, which I studied several decades ago,[24] played a major role in the Cold War because arms control's social scientific knowledge was performed in practice. The concept of epistemic communities of practice offers a useful way to understanding not only the relationship between knowledge and power, but also between knowledge and practices. Studying epistemic communities of practice, however, does not mean abandoning the concept of epistemic communities when studying global ordering. Rather, we should study epistemic communities and world ordering not only from a policymaking perspective, but also as sources and mechanisms of world ordering.

I learned much from Crawford's chapter. Her tracing of the trajectory of the refugee international social order is equal to none, and I appreciate that cognitive evolution theory was a catalyst for applying it so successfully in this case. In turn, I learned a lot not only about refugees but also about cognitive evolution, progress and its discontents and how and why truth subversion, by threatening democracy, market economy and multilateralism, poses a threat to the current liberal international order.[25] Crawford's chapter, in short, shows how to rigorously apply empirically cognitive evolution with attention to the theory's analytical and normative perspectives.

Crawford arrives at two conclusions, however, which I do not entirely share, but I am open to be persuaded. First, she argues that multiple people spread falsehoods from different sources. While I agree, it is mainly populist leaders who manipulate the truth-subversion practice to their benefit and for political domination. America and truth-subversion would be different had Trump not been elected as US president. Second, Crawford questions cognitive evolution theory because it does not explain the "normlessness" nature of the refugee social order. As I mentioned in chapter 10 of *World Ordering*, however, all practices are normative but not all normative

---

[23] Adler 2014, 2019; Adler and Faubert forthcoming.   [24] Adler 1992.
[25] For a different account see Adler and Drieschova 2021.

practices are ethical. Thus, I prefer to read Crawford's concept of "normlessness" as ethical normlessness. But although the relative lack of progress of the refugee social order shows that IR practices have a long way to go for serving our common humanity, bounded progress may still occur one day. Moreover, the refugee social order's poor ethical success does not challenge my theory's analytical argument about how cognitive evolution takes place.

I group Chris Reus-Smit's and Stefano Guzzini's chapters together because earlier versions had a large impact on revising my book for publication. I wrote *World Ordering*'s chapter 10 to a large extent because of Reus-Smit's early draft of his chapter. In turn, Guzzini taught me some lessons on power and epistemology, which are subjects he knows better than I do. In different ways, they identified some choices I may need to make; addressing them improved the book but also established important paths to pursue in studying cognitive evolution and world ordering.

Reus-Smit cleverly shows that I was pursuing two "middle grounds," the analytical middle ground I suggested in my 1997 article and a rough account of a normative middle ground on progress and an IR humanist realist approach, which I suggested as early as 1991. Asking "where do the values and dynamics of normative change inherent to progress fit in Adler's account of the middle ground" (this volume), Reus-Smit suggested three alternative strategies. The first was to follow Hedley Bull.[26] His distinction between realism, rationalism and revolutionism was not only ontological but also normative. The second alternative was to "strike an alliance" with cosmopolitan theorists, particularly Charles Beitz,[27] and ground "their universal values in collective practices," such as human rights. Reus-Smit's third strategy was to give processes of cognitive evolution "a universalistic dynamic," such as Habermas[28] did with the theory of communicative action, when grounding normative agreements in an analytical theory based on argumentative processes.[29] Behind these three alternative strategies there are large and rich literatures in international political theory, which I review in *World Ordering*, chapter 10, and have no room to properly discuss here.

---

[26] Bull 1977.   [27] Beitz 2009.   [28] Habermas 1996.
[29] See, also, Linklater 1998.

Briefly, however, I chose to follow Reus-Smit's third strategy but with a twist. Arguing that the main ethics discussed in international political theory literatures are not mutually exclusive,[30] particularly cosmopolitanism[31] and communitarianism,[32] I grounded a normative theory of cognitive evolution in the latter two ethics with the addition of American pragmatist ethics, particularly John Dewey's.[33] Instead of following Habermas' "discursive principle,"[34] I suggested a "practical principle." A normative middle ground based on a practical principle identifies some practices as the repositories of ethical collective knowledge that gain ground by communities of practice. While as I said all practices are normative, only practices that carry "common humanity" values[35] may, but do not necessarily must, lead to better practices and progress. The minimal and contingent conception of common humanity entails valuing other human beings' lives as we value our own. All other values, such as freedom and equality follow this "golden rule." While the world is characterized by ethnic and cultural diversity, a common humanity is grounded on human beings' *worth*.[36]

Guzzini's chapter discusses two "choices" that I made in the book, one on epistemology and the other on power. Pointing out that there are two kinds of constitutive theory, a limited one that refers to the constitution of social facts, and an expansive one about explaining conditions of possibility, helped me clarify that cognitive evolution theory is mostly about the constitution of possibility of social orders, about the propensities of social orders to become. At the same time, however, cognitive evolution also suggests mechanisms and processes that explain, for instance, how practitioners causally change the world to match their intentional acts – think about how a myth changed the course of natural evolution of a species of crabs. Thus, the expansive notion of constitutive explanations and causal explanations are not mutually exclusive.[37] In accordance with cognitive evolution theory's process-oriented ontology and evolutionary epistemology, they are retrospective rather than predictive.

---

[30] Frost 1996; Linklater 1998; Erskine 2008.
[31] See, for example, Rawls 1971; Beitz 1979.
[32] See, for example, MacIntyre 1981; Walzer 1990.
[33] Dewey 1983. See also Cochrane 1999.   [34] Habermas 1984, 1987.
[35] Stuurman 2017.   [36] Plato 1968; Pirsig 1974; Boltanski and Thévenot 2006.
[37] For a seminal discussion of constitution and causation in IR, see Wendt 1998.

Guzzini's second contribution to *World Ordering* rests on his argument that horizontal systems of rule, on which I rely heavily for my theory, are no less about power, albeit informal, than vertical systems of rule and domination, a point I adopted. Horizontal systems of rule, however, bring people to act together[38] because the knowledge and practices they share promote reciprocity and the need for justification.[39] Vertical or hierarchical systems of rule, on the other hand, tend to be formal and often based on coercive practices. I show in my book that vertical systems of rule also play an important role in cognitive evolution both within and among contesting communities of practice. Most often, however, international social orders have been characterized by the overlap between both systems of rule. There is, however, a normative choice between them. Horizontal systems of rule are *better*, neither only because of their informal nature, nor only because systems of rule in which power is spread among individuals and institutions, such as in democracies, can achieve better results. Rather, horizontal systems of rule are better primarily because they surpass vertical systems of rule, let alone authoritarian ones, in enhancing our common humanity; vertical systems of rule may dialectically lay the seeds of their own destruction.[40]

Both Reus-Smit and Guzzini not only help improve cognitive evolution theory with new vistas, but also suggest choices scholars need to make when pursuing these new vistas. Reus-Smit shows what alternatives may be available when integrating normative theory to cognitive evolution theory. Guzzini, in turn, points to choices between constitutive theory and causal theory and among different types of domination, which, of course, brings us back to the kind of normative theorizing that Reus-Smit's supports.

World Ordering

Framing IR Theory as World Ordering

Building on *World Ordering*, and looking forward, I suggest a broad agenda for IR theory: *studying world politics as dynamic processes of*

---

[38] Arendt 1958. See, also, Bernstein, 2018.   [39] Kornprobst 2012.
[40] I borrow my concept of horizontal systems of rule from Hannah Arendt (1958). For systematic discussions of power in IR see Barnett and Duvall, 2005; Guzzini 2013.

social ordering. In the past, the study of international order produced an abundant, important, theoretically driven and empirically rich literature,[41] but which did not have the resonance it deserved, as compared, for example, to literatures that relied on the concept of international systems. Only in the past few years, after scholars and pundits realized that the seemingly stable liberal international order was threatened, did a rapidly growing literature appear in the West, which tried explaining the challenges. Some scholars argue that the liberal international order has already failed;[42] others say that the liberal order can endure,[43] while still others argue that if the liberal international order is not fixed it probably will be replaced.[44] In my view, the recent challenge to the Liberal International Order is sufficient for turning the study of world ordering into IR theory's cornerstone for years to come. There are, however, more conceptual reasons.

I am neither calling for changing the themes that world politics' scholars research, nor am I promoting cognitive evolution theory or constructivism more generally. Instead, I am calling for the study of world ordering from a variety of theoretical perspectives with the use of multiple methodologies. Concerning the latter, I do not mean for individual scholars necessarily adopting a range of methods and analytical eclecticism[45] in a single piece of research, although with some caveats I adopt analytical eclecticism, but for multiple scholars to experiment with a variety of methodologies and test their power and effectiveness. Concerning my own pragmatist methodological preference, I have two points to make on analytic eclecticism. First, constructivist evolutionary research eschews variance-type predictive explanation and replaces it with a historical reconstructive explanation of change and stability processes based on the uncovering of constitutive pragmatist mechanisms,[46] abduction[47] and practice tracing.[48] We need to start "near 'the end' of a process ... asking how it could have been produced"[49] although it could have been produced otherwise.

---

[41] For a review of the literature see chapter five in *World Ordering*.
[42] Haass 2018; Mearsheimer 2019.
[43] Deudney and Ikenberry 2018; Ikenberry 2018.
[44] Colgan and Keohane 2017.
[45] An "intellectual stance that supports efforts to complement, engage, and selectively utilize theoretical constructs embedded in contending research traditions." Sil and Katzenstein 2010, 411.
[46] Gross 2009.   [47] Reasoned inference to the best explanation.
[48] Pouliot 2014.   [49] Dennett 1995, 62.

Second, unlike Sil and Katzenstein, I believe that meta-theory, such as evolutionary epistemology, helps guide theory making and doing rigorous empirical research.

We should continue to study what we may call *first-order themes*, such as war and peace, diplomacy, international institutions, foreign-policy decision-making, power, national interests, global issues and so on, in search of improved (and if possible consensual) knowledge. We should study these themes, however, as building blocks of a *second-order theme* in mind (such as "international systems" was in the past), namely, the development, maintenance, stability and change of world order and its normative attributes.

I also propose focusing on the topic of world ordering anew while remaining mindful of the interpenetration between global and international political, economic, and technological challenges and attributes and domestic and local politics and policies. We should avoid, however, the ontological and epistemological straitjacket imposed by the "levels of analysis'" conception.[50] World ordering should be understood, I suggest, neither exclusively like IR scholars often do: namely, as something that takes place "up there" because of balances of power, international and world institutions, norms and practices, which subsequently reverberate "down here"; such as, for example, the effects of globalization and immigration waves on domestic and local politics. Nor should world ordering be understood exclusively as a phenomenon that takes place "down here" involving domestic and local institutions and public policies, which end up reverberating "up there." I mean, for example, the effects of democratic recessions and the upsurge of populist and authoritarian leaders on international and global norms, institutions and practices. Abandoning the level-of-analysis conception means, therefore, *theorizing and empirically researching world ordering as simultaneous and interactive top-down and bottom-up processes, social structures, and agents.*

Take, for example, the effect of technological development on world ordering from an interactive top-down and bottom-up perspective. Artificial intelligence, to focus on an illustration to which I will return later, is beginning to impact international politics, international economic relations and global governance. Robot-based manufacturing and learning machines and algorithms, which cause unemployment

---

[50] See Singer 1961.

and domestic public opinion discontent within Western countries, are already influencing international institutions, norms and practices, for example, on free trade and multilateral cooperation. At the same time, international power competition and international balance of power changes – which are the product of how states use social networks to influence people's beliefs and desires in other states to affect the outcomes of their elections – are influencing domestic and local orders resulting in, for example, political polarization, democratic recession and the growth of populism.

As this illustration shows, it would be of limited use to focus exclusively on either top-down or bottom-up processes. The study of global ordering, and of *global "multistakeholder" multilateral governing*,[51] therefore, should consist of explaining the dynamic, simultaneous sets of global, international, transnational, national and local processes, involving multiple interconnected and interpenetrated social structures as well as international and domestic social orders.[52] One implication of my argument is the need to study world ordering synchronically, distributed across multiple agents, namely, performed not only by foreign and security practitioners and by diplomats posted in international organizations, but also by national and local public-policy and corporate practitioners. Due to its dynamic nature, however, world ordering should also be studied diachronically as ongoing activities, where relatively minor decisions may have long-range consequences, and vice versa. The challenge, however, is theorizing world ordering as parsimoniously as possible, which is why I will suggest a sketch of a cognitive evolution theory of politics below.

Cognitive evolution theory may be useful for studying world ordering as simultaneous and interactive top-down and bottom-up political processes, first, because, combining a "meta-theory," a "constitutive theory of world order," an "explanatory theory of how social order evolves," and a "normative theory" about the "nature of better orders,"[53] it advocates inclusivity without compromising clarity.[54] As I mentioned before, this program encourages IR scholars, such as

---

[51] For example, by communities of practice including state, transnational civil society and corporate agents. See, Slaughter 2019.
[52] On global governance more generally, see Rosenau, and Czempiel 1992; Hurrell 2007; Avant, Finnemore and Sell 2010; Zürn 2010, 2018.
[53] Guzzini's endorsement in Adler 2019.   [54] Lawson 2019.

Habermas did in Sociology, to ground normative theory in analytical explanatory theory.

Second, cognitive evolution theory should encourage constructivist researchers to adopt an evolutionary research program, which, not resting on naturalist analogies, is consistent with constructivism's dynamic and emergent nature. Third, cognitive evolution theory "removes" ideational phenomena, such as norms and "ideas," from being exclusively in the human mind and locates them where politics rests, namely, human agency and social practices. Fourth, cognitive evolution theory suggests an alternative and more dynamic and reflexive approach on practices than Pierre Bourdieu's theory and language. Fifth, it places communities of practice center stage as the site of agency and social structure and as the backstage of politics and political practice. Thus, cognitive evolution theory reimagines IR by observing it through the lens of "software" (practices, knowledge) rather than exclusively of "hardware" (states and institutions).

Sixth, cognitive evolution theory invites scholars to explore world ordering as a multiplicity of separate yet overlapping regional and functional international social orders.[55] It thus suggests a complementary approach to studying multi-level global governance. Seventh, an additional payoff of cognitive evolution theory, which can enliven debates over where political authority lies, is locating social power in the collective assignment of status-functions, and in social performances. Eight, focusing on time, creativity and variation and selection processes and mechanisms, the theory suggests a socially emergent approach to world order, to the point that it associates order with flux rather than stability. Methods for retroactively tracing emerging processes and evolutionary trajectories, and for qualitatively identifying the propensities of world orders' resilience, and intersubjective thresholds and tipping points, will help scholars empirically research flux and meta-stability. Ninth, by examining contestations between competing communities of practice, world ordering theory is exceptionally well located to understanding, tracing and explaining the contemporary world-order's puzzling fluctuations along a continuum between, on the one hand, growing extreme and xenophobic nationalist and disassociation processes and, on the other hand, liberal-international interconnectedness. Finally, cognitive evolution theory should help identify

---

[55] For excellent books on regional orders see Katzenstein 2005; Hurrell 2007.

where and when societies adopt better practices; thus, what, realistically, contingently and reversibly, it would take for better world orders to evolve.

A Theoretical New Vista on Cognitive Evolution

Exploring world ordering from a top-down, bottom-up, rather than a level-of-analysis, perspective may help addressing world vulnerability threats, such as climate change, AI, and nuclear war, which endanger our planet and common humanity, better than other approaches. These problems have only global solutions, but lack of trust between states prevents seeking global solutions, even when leaders are aware – some are not – of the conundrum. Neither global government and global neo-functional integration, nor multilateral global governance, are likely to produce the trust needed to adopt global solutions.[56] Overcoming global vulnerabilities may require a major catastrophe to shake peoples' identities, unless, before it is too late, states begin learning to frame their national interests (understood as what advances their power, influence, security, wealth and citizens' well-being) as depending on global solutions, which, in turn, depends on interconnectedness. What I call *"embedded globalism"* (to be distinguished from embedded globalization), which relies on reframing national interests, requires the simultaneous involvement of, on the one hand, domestic and local political actors and processes, and, on the other hand, *global "multistakeholder"* communities of practice, which cut across and combine practitioners from state institutions, international organizations, transnational civil society, scientific organizations and business corporations.

Anchoring global practices in new definitions of national interests should help establish dispositions for, and constitutive expectations of, solutions that rest on global interconnectedness. Trust may thus develop neither by coercion of a global government nor because of the functional influence of global institutions and policy coordination at the international level. Rather it can, but not necessarily will, end up developing because of the ongoing mutual accountability that grows from sharing global practices, and from transaction processes, including learning, contestation and coalition-building taking place within

[56] Zürn 2010, 2018.

and between communities of practice at the global level. Take, for example, the Airbnb community of practice, which consists of millions of people who came to blindly share their home – one of their more precious possessions – with millions of renters who are uncertain whether the house they rented over the Internet is real and "nice," rather than fake, or a dump.[57] What explains the community of practice's trust, and helps keep the Airbnb social order metastable is mutual accountability, the shared identity that develops within communities of practice and the distribution of social power among the practitioners involved. Therefore, limited regional integration processes, such as the European Union (EU), have led to some measure of regional interests in solving global vulnerabilities. Their shared practices, mutual accountability and the identity that goes with them, predisposes (so far, unfortunately, only some western) EU members to reframe their national and regional interest as an imperative of solving global problems globally.

The concept of embedded globalism does not mean that states must share national interests, but rather only implies anchoring the need of addressing global vulnerabilities, by means of reciprocated mutual help, in their notion of national interest. Embedded globalism incorporates nationalism, but of the kind that seeks cultural distinction, rather than ethnic and/or religious superiority and exclusion. It also incorporates *practical democracy*, which I will have more to say about later. Within nation-states that practice practical democracy, deontic power is horizontally distributed among practitioners who occupy a variety of status positions and functions, such as prime ministers, diplomats, legislators, local leaders, corporate practitioners, scientists, journalists or NGOs. It is no coincidence that in the EU it is mainly democratic states that promote regional and global solutions to global vulnerabilities.

This section, I believe, provides tentative answers to the concerns the editors raised in the introduction. It indicates, for example, how local, domestic and international social orders can overlap and interpenetrate each other; the latter requires communication of knowledge, rules, values and practice standards across local, domestic and international social orders and the constellation of communities of practice that constitute them. My illustration of AI earlier also shows how technology becomes an intrinsic factor in cognitive evolution, and how it

---

[57]   Gebbia 2019.

becomes a trigger for the motivation and purpose to order social life, thus for the development of communities of practice to protect life and our common humanity.

A Sketch of Cognitive Evolution's Theory of Politics, and of the Relevance of Practical Democracy

Responding to the editors' call to suggest a constructivist theory of politics, I will make a more modest attempt to offer a rough, tentative and unfinished sketch. First, I will briefly describe what I mean by cognitive evolution politics, explain why it is crucial for the theory and argue that practical democracy may play an important role in it. Second, I will briefly show that world ordering efforts to confront global vulnerabilities should rest largely on the politics of cognitive evolution.

Politics, Cognitive Evolution and World Ordering

Politics is the oil that lubricates cognitive evolution. It takes place in and between communities of practice, which is where practices develop, through which practices and knowledge spread, and because of which selective retention of practices takes place. Without politics, therefore, there is no cognitive evolution. Cognitive evolution, rather than being processes occurring exclusively in people's minds, between individual people, and exclusively within and between people's institutions, such as political parties, states, diplomatic representatives and international organizations, is a quintessentially political process. Without cognitive evolution, and processes such as practices' and background knowledge's creative variation and selective retention, people would not know their political struggles' purposes, how and when to act, with whom, and in response to what. People and institutions would not take political action seeking control or, alternatively, freedom and coexistence.[58]

It is a paradox of politics that a similar configuration of political practices, which agents use to organize the meaningful aspects of their communal life thus keeping their social orders together, also play a role

---

[58] Arendt 1958. For an excellent short review of the literature on politics, see Ish-Shalom 2019: 19–20.

in conflicts that bring about the evolution of social orders. Political practices help constitute communities' shared epistemic and normative meanings and identities. Yet they also play a role in challenging, and promoting change of, political orders.[59]

I briefly define politics as a constellation of practices practitioners use to collectively generate, organize, govern and challenge social orders. For more detail and nuance, I stand by my definition of politics in *World Ordering* as:

> a constellation of practices through which agents govern societies; manage and resolve conflict; organize, guide, and control interconnectedness and disassociation processes; and strive either to keep social orders metastable or to bring about their evolution. [It is also] about the conditions of possibility of better social orders that flow not only from interconnectedness, communities of practice's spread, and practices' reciprocity but also from humans' will to perform 'better' in terms of both their performance and the ethical quality or value of their practices.[60]

Cognitive evolution politics requires power. Material power, such as physical, technological and institutional resources, but particularly social (deontic and performative) power is productive of interconnectedness and disassociation. As properties of communities, rather than of single individuals, power is decentralized, productive and relational,[61] enabling agents to be mutually accountable and act in concert.[62] Power is, however, a term we should use to describe the convergence of forces that enable contestation within and between communities and resistance[63] to practices and their background knowledge.

Power is, therefore, analogous to *fields of forces* that, constituted by the contestation of complementary or opposing tendencies,[64] keep communities of practice metastable, enable world ordering, and help some communities of practice to overcome competing communities or, alternatively, succumb to them, thus bringing about world order evolution. Fields of forces – material, technological, institutional and social (deontic and performative) – are therefore structurally and ontologically real propensities (see *World Ordering*, chapter two) for

---

[59] According to Wenger (1998: 91–92), the politics of communities of practice include influence, personal authority, charisma, ambition and argumentative demonstrations.
[60] Adler 2019, 21; 300.   [61] Foucault 1980, 1984.   [62] Arendt 1958.
[63] Foucault 1980, 1984.   [64] Popper 1959, 37–38.

politics; they are needed for the creative variation and selective retention of political practices in and between communities of practice. Fields of forces, to some extent such as what Peter Katzenstein and Lucia Seybert[65] call "protean power" (the structural potential for innovation and experimentation that produces unexpected and uncertain outcomes), constitute the conditions of possibility for the creative variation of practices and background knowledge. Understood as fields of forces, power also structures convergent and competing tendencies that are at play in political, economic and social selective retention processes.

Take, for example, what Shoshana Zuboff[66] calls "Surveillance Capitalism," "a new economic order that claims human experience as free raw material for hidden commercial practices of extraction, prediction, and sales." The resulting behavioral data "is fed into advanced processes known as 'machine intelligence,' and fabricated into *prediction products* that anticipate what you will do now, soon, and later. Finally, these prediction products are traded [for profit] in a new kind of marketplace for behavioral prediction."[67] This recently evolved economic social order, which consists of innovative practices, the background knowledge bound up within them, and a constellation of communities of practice, rests on and is held together by a convergence of a field of (material and social) forces. It begins with an ingenious (but perverse) social-economic innovation by Google for "mining" people's minds to predict their future dispositions and expectations and subsequently sell these predictions for profit in a global information market. The social and economic innovation, however, is not enough; it requires new material technological advances, such as AI; machine platforms and social networks (another social and economic innovation), through which people participate in surveillance capitalism; corporations' (such as Google and Facebook) material economic power, their deontic power to create social reality by shaping our knowledge and practices "toward others' ends,"[68] and their performative power to persuade audiences that they are working for the public good.

The field of forces I just described is decentralized, relational and productive of "surveillance capitalism." It is distributed among

---

[65] Katzenstein and Seybert 2018. [66] Zuboff 2019, 8; 14. [67] Ibid.
[68] Ibid., 8; 187.

machine intelligence corporations; billions of people who become hooked to machine intelligence and vote with their fingers; states that do not regulate machine intelligence, or worse, states that use it for political gain and international domination; and scientists and technologists who engage in the innovation of algorithms and hardware for profit, for advancing their careers and prestige, and just for the thrill of producing new knowledge and technological innovations. The selective retention of surveillance capitalist practices and knowledge, therefore, is not a choice that a few individuals, states, or economic firms make, but the result of the fields of forces that constitute the conditions of possibility for surveillance capitalism to exist, for its practices and knowledge to spread within and between communities of practice, to the point that it has now become a nearly global phenomenon.

Surveillance capitalism's cognitive evolution, however, would not have been possible, and cannot keep spreading, without politics within and between communities of practice. Some of these communities comprise tech corporations, scientists and governments that do nothing to control it. Other communities, which are comprised of different governments and scientists, civil society and corporate practitioners, oppose surveillance capitalism communities of practice, either because of privacy concerns, economic reasons, political reasons or ethical reasons, and negotiate the terms of the economic order's evolution and whether to control or arrest its spread. From a normative ethical perspective, surveillance capitalism, together with the technological and social practices that make it up, threatens to rob humans of their common humanity, thus becoming a source of vulnerability not only for our lives, well-being, political systems, and economic welfare, but also for our very humanity.[69] Thus, the pushback – so far is ineffective.

Politics, of course, is integral to the main contestation now taking place in world ordering between liberal internationalist communities of practice and ethnic, often racist, communities of practice. In recent years, we have witnessed a movement from interconnectedness-type liberal politics to disassociation-type extreme nationalist politics. But we also witness a political pushback in the other direction, for example, in the United States, Hong Kong, Poland, Hungary and Israel, which is led by liberal practitioners that contest populist authoritarian leaders and regimes and their ethnic and/or religious nationalism. As Larry

[69] Harari 2018; Bostrom 2019; Zuboff 2019.

Diamond reports, "in recent surveys, 69 percent of respondents in Latin American countries, 89 percent in East Asia, 72 percent in Africa and 81 percent of Middle Eastern Arabs agreed with some version of the Winston Churchill-inspired precept that democracy might have its problems, but it's still the best form of government."[70] Moreover, as Crawford explained and illustrated with the case of refugees, it is usually small communities of practice that carry the burden of politically pushing back against antidemocratic, illiberal practices. These communities may remain small but through politics they may spread and affect other communities of practice, for example, anti-racist, anti-xenophobic, and pro-human rights' communities.

Practical Democracy

I introduced the concept of practical democracy in *World Ordering*'s chapter 10 because democracy is central to the normative features of world ordering and cognitive evolution politics.[71] I build my understanding of practical democracy mainly on John Dewey's pragmatist conception of democracy, which transcends needless dichotomies.[72] Dewey considered that democracy is not only a system of government embodied in institutions but also a social order or configuration of practices that individuals routinely accept as part of their identity. Moreover, it is a mode of collective identity and community association. Individuals learn and develop their civic skills, such as negotiation, compromise and building consensus, in communities. Democratic practitioners practice democracy in interaction with all sectors of society.

According to Dewey, democracy should hold moral liberal values, such as freedom, equality and fraternity, and be based on practices of pluralistic participation and cooperation. At the same time, however, it should be republican, or represent a moral community where individuals, for the sake of improving democracy, learn political virtues, such as reflecting, negotiating and experimenting. The state plays an important role to ensure, through legal practices, the social conditions that all citizens have equal opportunities and can fulfill their interests without restrictions.

---

[70] Larry Diamond paraphrased in Diehl 2019.   [71] See also Frega 2017.
[72] Dewey 1916.

Perhaps most importantly, democracy should be both direct and representative. Unlike elitist concepts of democracy, according to which masses are ignorant, Dewey considered that which he called "the public" must be heard, because it carries the practical knowledge and experience of a democracy based on cooperation. This means that the quality of democratic knowledge partly relies on public experience and practice. At the same time, democracy depends on representative practices, such as the rule of law and representative institutions, such as political parties, the parliament and the courts.

Learning and education are crucial to Dewey's concept of democracy. Background knowledge that constitutes democratic practices obtains and spreads through education. As Christopher Ansell[73] argued, experimental knowledge acquired by learning is habitual. In times of decision and crisis, however, it becomes reflective. Democratic knowledge thus must reconstitute itself, and democracy must be renewed through experimental reflexivity. Practical democracy, therefore, must create a negotiation public space, which is reproduced through experiential learning.

The concept of practical democracy has several advantages. First, its ontology is broader than Jürgen Habermas' concept of deliberative democracy, which rests on a "discourse principle," according to which the normative imperative of overcoming domination relies on a discourse where everyone is making a good-faith attempt to evaluate claims based on reason rather than self-interest. Although I do not dispute Habermas' deliberative democracy's conditions as an ideal type, I regard the concept of "practical democracy" to be more comprehensive and more realistically achievable than Habermas' "deliberative democracy"[74] concept. Practical democracy rests on practices and values of a common humanity, beginning with humans' minimum common denominator, regardless of their diversity, which is life's "worth" or "good," and on which other values, such as liberty and equality, rest. Common humanity values and practices depend on epistemological security, namely, collective trust in a common-sense factual reality. Deliberative democracy, on the other hand, which is based on truth validity claims, sets a higher standard than epistemological security, thus making it much more difficult to confront truth subversion practices.

[73] Ansell 2011, 9–10.   [74] Habermas 1996.

Second, the concept of practical democracy builds on the politics of learning, contestation, experimentation and negotiation within and across communities of practice, and by extension within and between domestic and international institutions that consist of reified practices. This kind of politics aims first and foremost at promoting national interests that sustain values of common humanity. Thus, for example, to confront climate change, global challenges require practical democratic politics, which rests on changing national interests because of practices that rely on the interaction in public spaces between science and expertise and public common-sense knowledge.

Third, practical democracy relies on horizontal accountability, which is "associated with engagement in joint activities, negotiation of mutual relevance, standards of practice, peer recognition, identity and replication, and commitment to collective learning" and who gets to qualify as competent.[75] A minimalist normative understanding of mutual accountability, as constituted in communities of practice, is related to competent performances.[76] A more ambitious and ethical meaning, which I associate with the politics of practical democracy, is that practitioners should be mutually accountable to engage in better practices, for example, contest and fight against environmentally harmful practices. The latter meaning not only constitutes and strengthens reciprocity of practitioners in communities of practice, but it also encourages reciprocity endowed with normative ethical meanings and purposes.

Fourth, practical democratic politics requires epistemological security, not only trust in consensual scientific knowledge, for example, about climate change, but on publics' common sense as collectively experienced by people in practice,[77] for instance, weather patterns, flooding of cities, extreme drought and much more. In other words, the backlash against, the apathy, irrationality and inaction that characterizes climate change politics requires *not only the "elite supply"* of scientific knowledge and public policy proposals, *but also the "public's demand"* for arresting and redressing climate change. Combining, coordinating and rationalizing supply and demand requires practical democratic politics within and between communities of practice. The combination of "supply" and "demand" is the foundation of legitimate "epistemic practical authority," namely, legitimate power to rule

[75] Wenger 2010, 195.　[76] Adler and Pouliot 2011, 6.　[77] Rosenfeld 2019.

according to reliable sources of knowledge and practices, and, by extension, of "practical meaning fixation," the authoritative ascription of practical meaning to material and social reality, on which domestic and global public policies to confront climate change must rest.

Politics must rely, therefore, on practical democracy for the protection against truth subversion and epistemological insecurity. Epistemological security has always been fragile, and since the evolution of the Enlightenment and later of democratic practices, it has relied *either* on elite and later expert knowledge, *or* people's common-sense understanding of reality.[78] I agree, however, with John Dewey[79] that, while publics should inform political judgments, the latter should be based on facts and when possible on science.[80] Practical democracy requires the understanding that the few have been elected over the many to rule on their behalf in a transparent way, and that this requires experts to uncover facts that become democratically and practically legitimate when they are accepted and corroborated by publics' common sense via elections and support for public policies.[81] In recent years, however, due to a mixture of economic resentment against globalization and immigration and the development of social networks, such as Facebook and Twitter, and AI-based algorithms, people increasingly have ceased

putting any stock in expert voices of any kind, seeing all of them as hacks or phonies speaking only for themselves and their partisan, financially interested cronies. That's when facts start to look indistinguishable from opinions or beliefs, the former appearing as just a disguised manifestation of the latter. That's also when the way becomes clear for a demagogic outsider who, with the help of alternative media like far right news sources that spring up to aid the process with conspiracy theories and vituperation directed against enemies, promises to elevate "the people" over all sources of knowledge, from universities to major newspapers to beholden politicians, who can be said to be complicit in elite, technocratic rule.[82]

Epistemological insecurity may therefore present a severe threat to democracy. For people to be able to evaluate their government's performance there needs to be a shared understanding of what is real and

---

[78] Holst and Molander 2019; Rosenfeld 2019. We should be careful, however, not to confuse this argument with populism, which rests on demagogues' critique of elite expertise and on praise of people's expertise to dominate them.
[79] Dewey 1927.   [80] Müller 2019.   [81] Adler and Drieschova 2021.
[82] Rosenfeld 2019, 97.

true.[83] Only by promoting and empowering democratic *practices* elites and publics will be able to confront the truth subversion problem and restore epistemological security.[84] Because practical democracy politics partly rely on publics' common sense, it may help put a wedge between the public and its reliance on tribal group loyalty and populist leaders' "straight" (truth subversion) talk. Education of truth-telling, such as about the relationship between information technologies and democracy and good citizenship[85] may help restoring some of the enraged people's dignity and respect, regain their trust in scientific expertise, and develop an ethical commitment in public life.[86] The above, together with practical public policies to address the sources of people's economic predicament, while not sufficient, can and should play a necessary role in reducing polarization and "echo chambers," and overcoming populist leaders' truth subversion practices. Practical democracy politics can help, therefore, closing the gap between the currently increasing chasm between expert knowledge and popular participation, and between traditional politics – which is mostly blind to how technological changes are affecting the world – and the kind of politics and new practices that are required to dealing with new information technologies, "echo chambers," and truth subversion.

Finally, do nation-states have realist reasons (both in a general and in an IR sense) to believe that collective moral responsibility will prevent global catastrophes because of climate change, AI and nuclear war threats to earth and humanity? At a time when global vulnerabilities cannot be dealt without global solutions, world ordering is moving in the disassociation-led extreme nationalism. Thus, we should not expect world government, global integration, international organization and our narrow measure of global governance to solve global-vulnerability problems any time soon. Yet time is of the essence. Rather, nation-states, let alone great powers, will move forward only when dictated by their national interests and security dilemma concerns. It would take only one state not adopting rules and practices for preventing catastrophe to start a race to the bottom (of the precipice).

Only by making the prevention of global catastrophe a part of the national interest will states adopt what E. H. Carr[87] called "enlightened interests." But will national communities and their people feel

---

[83] Adler and Drieschova 2021.   [84] Rosenfeld 2019.   [85] Peters 2017.
[86] Rosenfeld 2019.   [87] Carr 2001.

responsibility for the fate of other national communities, let alone the fate of the earth? *Only when they believe that taking responsibility for other communities' survival will assure their own national survival.* Practical democratic politics can encourage mutual moral responsibility by empowering communities of practice, which, consisting of government, corporate and civil society practitioners, particularly scientists, become the vehicle of learning to address global vulnerabilities by adopting better practices of embedded globalism, namely, by embedding global problems and solutions in national interests. The road to hell may be paved with good intentions, but also the road to paradise may often be paved with egoistic intentions.

Relying on practical democratic politics to address world vulnerabilities is a tall order but, paraphrasing Winston Churchill, it may be the worst option except for all others. More specifically, Nick Bostrom, a Swedish philosopher who founded the "Future of Humanity Institute" at Oxford University to explore a nontheological and realistic exploration of existential risks for humanity arising from anthropogenic climate change, the development of AI's superintelligence, and nuclear war, recently suggested "the Vulnerable World Hypothesis":[88] namely, "there is some level of technological development at which civilization almost certainly gets devastated by default."[89] More specifically, Bostrom analyzed future vulnerabilities, particularly the development of a technology that destroys the civilization that invented it,[90] and ways to escape destruction by exiting what he calls the world's "semi-anarchic default condition." Regarding the latter, he considers (a) effective policing and surveillance capabilities (which, to prevent a few individuals from bringing about global catastrophe, may de facto lead to a world of surveillance totalitarian states), and (b) reliable global-governance mechanisms for solving global coordination problems and protecting global commons, leading to a de facto world government or something closely resembling it.[91]

In my view, tight world surveillance medicine would kill the patient, and it would run against common humanity values (I would not like my children to live in such a world). Developing global governance

---

[88] Bostrom 2019.   [89] Ibid., 1.
[90] Bostrom (2019 p. 4) defines "civilization devastation" as "any destructive event that is at least as bad as the death of 15% of the world population or a reduction of global GDP by >50% lasting for more than a decade."
[91] Ibid.

mechanisms for solving global coordination problems, in turn, would require eliminating nationalism, wars and human conflict in general, which, short of a world government, would be close to impossible to achieve before catastrophe hits. World government is, however, a chimera that could also become a nightmarish world totalitarian state. At the same time, there are no, or only partial, technological solutions to reducing world vulnerabilities. World ordering vulnerabilities arise not only from natural but primarily from social reasons, which therefore can only have social and political solutions. Technological solutions, moreover, usually have all kind of unintended physical, economic and political consequences, some of which can be dire for the planet and humanity.

Bostrom's approach relies on risk assessment, which assumes that all future possibilities already exist and that we just do not know which one will end up materializing. But as I recently argued elsewhere,[92] people calculate risks under the illusion of control. We live in a world of radical uncertainty characterized by propensities rather than calculable probabilities and risk. If risk calculus is, however, suspect, how can leaders and publics be persuaded that world vulnerabilities are not stories and conspiracies made-up by (mostly liberal) elites and experts who are losing political, economic and social control? How can mutual trust develop not only among leaders and peoples around the world to change their interests, but also in scientific epistemic authority that cannot rely on accurate predictions and scientific-risk calculation?

At least partially escaping this dilemma implicates bringing science and scientists to the people so that people's common-sense understandings of reality remains attuned to scientific experimentation, empirical facts and reasoned common sense. By this I do not mean sending epistemic communities to teach scientific models to the people, but empowering democratic practices that show in practice why populist authoritarianism, truth subversion practices and echo chambers, hurt people and are self-defeating. We should remember that people's recent distrust of expertise does not mean divine epistemic authority has become superior to science in their minds (although for some it has). Instead, most anti-science attitudes, for example, on anthropogenic climate change theories and data, have to do with identity polarization and tribal group loyalties.

---

[92]   Adler 2020.

Democratic politics' challenge, thus, is to invest epistemic authority, as Dewey argued, in both scientific experimentation and the publics' common sense. More than a rational, mathematically calculating and deterministic concept of scientific truth, we need practical democracy political practices to address world vulnerabilities. Horizontally organized constellations of communities of practice, cutting across physical, identity and functional boundaries, which contest disassociation-driven authoritarian populist communities of practice, may help empower and diffuse embedded globalism practices around the world to address world vulnerabilities. Legislators, judges, Google programmers, industry scientists and university researchers need to mobilize on behalf of our common humanity as well as of their personal, business, scientific and national interests to create the local, national and international political energy required to address global vulnerabilities before it is too late. They will require performative power that combines reason and emotion, as well as deontic power for attaching new meanings and functions to nation states' security interests, and to the interests and sense of responsibility of business, civil society, science and international institutions' practitioners.

Artificial Intelligence and "World Vulnerability"

AI, particularly Artificial General Intelligence (AGI), which has been identified as one of today's main sources of world vulnerability,[93] offers an excellent illustration of my arguments earlier. In contrast to narrow AI, which applies to specific functions, such as self-driving cars, "AGI (...) can reason across a wide range of domains, and thus could replicate many human intellectual skills, while retaining all of the advantages of computers, such as perfect memory recall. Run on sophisticated computer hardware, AGI could outpace human cognition."[94] As it stands right now, however, most AI is narrow, which helps feed optimistic expectations, for example, that it will help us live longer and healthier lives, as opposed to expectations that AGI and superintelligence one day could replace "homo sapiens."[95]

The two camps of optimistic- and pessimistic-leaning scientists talk past each other, because they look at different time and space dimensions of the same problem. Optimists say that worrying about AGI now

---

[93] Bostrom 2019.   [94] Baum 2018.   [95] Harari 2018.

is like worrying about overpopulation on Mars.[96] Pessimists argue, however, that superintelligence is coming to your neighborhood soon and that, when it does, the challenge will be not only about being replaced by machines, but also about what the machines' values are going to be: "Up to now, AI research has focused on systems that are better at making decisions, but this is not the same as making better decisions."[97] AI poses, of course, other threats to world ordering, such as the development of autonomous weapons and a global arms race, "surveillance capitalism,"[98] digital authoritarianism, gene editing and a massive loss of jobs across the world, especially medium-skill jobs.

At a time when optimistic and pessimistic scientists continue to disagree about the risks posed by AGI, a constellation of communities of practice with a horizontal system of rule, which is aimed at addressing AGI's and other AI's world vulnerabilities, is slowly beginning to take shape.[99] To a large extent, the initiatives have been led by the scientific community, and the leader, if not pioneer, has been the "Asilomar" community, which for some has become the "shorthand for the responsibility of science."[100] In 1975, a Conference on Recombinant DNA Molecules, which was funded by the National Institute of Health (NIH) and the National Science Foundation, was held at Asilomar, California. It lifted a scientific moratorium on bio-engineering research, which had been agreed on a few years before, but set guidelines for excessively dangerous experiments, such as cloning, for example. The recommendations became the basis of NIH funding and for rules adopted around the world that are standing until today. Asilomar did not only create an effective safety regime, but it also meant that participants "gained the public's trust" – not least of all because around 15 percent of the participants were from the media.[101]

---

[96] See Andrew Ng quoted in Garling 2015.   [97] Russell 2019, 32.

[98] Zuboff 2019.

[99] Anne-Marie Slaughter and Fadi Chehadé have similarly suggested that, since "the Internet is a network of networks, its governing structures should be, too," and that we need a "digital co-governance order that engages public, civic, and private leaders." While they conceive of the suggested regime using network theory rather than a community of practice approach, we both emphasize politics, ideas, institutions, and horizontal co-governance. Slaughter and Chehadé, 2019.

[100] Capron 2015.

[101] Even *Rolling Stone* published an article about the conference, which they titled "The Pandora's Box Congress." http://libgallery.cshl.edu/items/show/85616. Last accessed October 11, 2019.

In 2017, The Future of Life Institute[102] organized a "Conference on Beneficial AI" at Asilomar, explicitly alluding to and inviting comparisons to the 1975 conference. More than 100 AI researchers from academia and industry as well as economists, lawyers, ethicists and philosophers took part in discussions to come up with "principles of beneficial AI."[103] To date, more than 3,800 AI researchers and others have signed the declaration of twenty-three AI principles arrived at by the conference.[104] In July 2018, during the International Joint Conference on Artificial Intelligence in Stockholm, in a letter published online, "2,400 researchers in 36 countries joined 160 organizations in calling for a global ban on lethal autonomous weapons. Such systems pose a grave threat to humanity and have no place in the world, they argue." The Future of Life Institute drafted and circulated the letter.[105]

At the same time, tech giants such as Microsoft, Google and Amazon, as well as smaller companies, drew up corporate principles to ensure the ethical design and use of AI. The Partnership on AI, as it came to be called, meant to guide industry practices, but it has remained "largely toothless."[106] Activists, employees, but also some companies themselves, however, are calling for government regulation to ensure ethical practices; "the most significant changes have been driven by employee protests."[107] In June 2018, Google CEO Sundar Pichai, after an employee backlash against Google's role in a US Air Force research project that critics considered a step toward autonomous weapons, outlined the company's AI principles, "which make clear that the company will not develop any tools for weapons designed primarily to inflict harm."[108] Likewise, after Amazon employees protested the sale of facial recognition services to police departments and various academic studies highlighted the bias that plagues these

---

[102] The non-profit Institute was founded in March 2014 by MIT cosmologist Max Tegmark, Skype cofounder Jaan Tallinn, DeepMind research scientist Viktoriya Krakovna, Boston University Ph.D. candidate in Developmental Sciences Meia Chita-Tegmark, and UCSC physicist Anthony Aguirre. It is partly funded by Elon Musk, who sits on the scientific advisory board.
[103] See https://futureoflife.org/bai-2017/. Last accessed October 11, 2019.
[104] See https://futureoflife.org/ai-principles/ and https://futureoflife.org/principles-signatories/. Last accessed October 11, 2019.
[105] McFarland 2018.   [106] Metz 2019.   [107] Ibid.
[108] McFarland 2018. Project Maven is a "Pentagon effort to develop artificial intelligence, to be used in military drones, with the ability to make distinctions between different objects captured in drone surveillance footage." Jenkins 2018.

services, Amazon and Microsoft called for government regulation in this area.

Scientists and corporate leaders have also joined forces. In July 2015, over 1,000 experts in AI signed a letter warning of the threat of an arms race in military AI and calling for a ban on autonomous weapons. The letter was presented in Buenos Aires at the 24th International Joint Conference on Artificial Intelligence (IJCAI-15) and was cosigned by Stephen Hawking, Elon Musk, Steve Wozniak, Noam Chomsky, Skype cofounder Jaan Tallinn and Google DeepMind cofounder Demis Hassabis among others.[109] NGOs have also been active in the same field. The "Campaign to Stop Killer Robots" is a coalition of NGOs formed in 2013 and includes 100 organizations from fifty-four countries.[110]

The constellation of AI communities of practice in-the-making for dealing with AI's world vulnerability has had to contend with states racing to develop AI for security, economic and world-domination reasons, or as Russian President Vladimir Putin said in 2017, "the nation that leads in the development of artificial intelligence will become the ruler of the world."[111] That view has become common-place in global capitals. Already, more than a dozen governments have announced national AI initiatives. In 2017, China set a goal of becom-ing the global leader in AI by 2030. In 2019, the White House released the American AI Initiative, and the U.S. Department of Defense rolled out an AI strategy.[112] Canada was one of the first countries to have one.[113]

Most of the AGI R&D is carried out in the United States, Europe and China. So, establishing standards and ethical ground rules is ultimately a job for the entire international community.[114] At a UN meeting in Geneva in March 2019 (under the Convention on Certain Conventional Weapons, CCW) potential restrictions under inter-national law to lethal autonomous weapons systems (LAWS) were discussed.[115] A majority of states taking part supported either a total ban or strict legal regulation. States that objected to legal regulation

[109] Zakrzewski 2015; Gibbs 2015.
[110] See https://autonomousweapons.org/. Last accessed October 11, 2019.
[111] Scharre 2019.   [112] Ibid.   [113] McBride, Mouallem and Semeniuk 2018.
[114] Baum 2018.
[115] There were earlier Governmental Expert meetings in 2017 and 2018 at the UN in Geneva.

included the United Kingdom, Australia, Israel, Russia and the United States.[116] At the 2019 annual meeting of the World Economic Forum in Davos, Japan, South Africa, China and Germany called for global oversight of the technology sector. Japan wants to use the G20 to highlight data governance. Germany's Chancellor Angela Merkel called for a "common digital market" in the EU, and international oversight of data usage.[117] The European Commission issued, at the end of 2018, "draft ethics guidelines for a trustworthy AI." The European model "aspires to shape the creation of human-centric AI with an ethical purpose"[118] and "ensure trust based on EU values."[119] In June 2018, the European Commission appointed fifty-two experts to a High-Level Expert Group on Artificial Intelligence, comprising representatives from academia, civil society as well as industry.[120] Yet, the preliminary guidelines the EU drew do not address where ownership of the AI sector and responsibility for it and its related technologies actually lie.

Do all of the above activities and best practices that have been suggested – for example, mandatory transparency and accountability for any party that touches the data[121] and aligning AI to values – mean that the preliminary efforts for setting a horizontal constellation of communities of practice to regulate and control AI, particularly AGI, are bearing fruit? If they are, they are only nascent. While there is mutual engagement, and government, industry and scientists who participate in the aforementioned efforts share a joint enterprise, the repertoire of power resources they use is too limited, there is not enough alignment and coordination, and most importantly, few if any practices have been institutionalized. Moreover, the resistance is massive: it is comprised both of powerful states that aim to develop AI "to rule the world," and of corporate leaders looking to AI to rule the world economy.

---

[116] Gayle 2019; United Nations 2019.   [117] Bradsher and Bennhold 2019.
[118] Amico 2019.
[119] See the EU Commission's Press Release at https://europa.eu/rapid/press-release_IP-19-1893_en.htm and its "fact sheet" on AI at http://ec.europa.eu/n ewsroom/dae/document.cfm?doc_id=51610. Last accessed October 11, 2019.
[120] See https://ec.europa.eu/digital-single-market/en/high-level-expert-group-artificial-intelligence. For a critique of the guidelines, see www.accessnow.org /laying-down-the-law-on-ai-ethics-done-now-the-eu-must-focus-on-human-rights/. Last accessed October 11, 2019.
[121] Kelly 2019.

However, totalitarian surveillance practices should be out of the question, a world state is improbable, and likely undesirable, and purely technological fixes are insufficient for addressing AI's vulnerabilities. Future crises may improve the chance of embedded globalism politics and practices to advance our common humanity. But we should not count on crises; they may be catastrophic and happen after it is too late. The politics of cognitive evolution must be put at the service of reducing world vulnerabilities, and world ordering and practical democracy should play a big role. Practices, their epistemic background and communities of practice have a crucial role to play in our journey toward bounded progress.

Conclusion

A cognitive evolution-based world ordering approach is a work in progress. Whether it will find a broad reception depends, in my view, on IR scholars willing to contemplate IR from outside the box. First, cognitive evolution theory requires escaping paradigmatic and methodological constraints by understanding and explaining world politics truly dynamically, to some extent as what Karl Deutsch called the "nerves of government."[122] By this concept, Deutsch meant the cybernetic communication processes lying beneath all politics, which can be modeled and can therefore help political actors to control their destinies. His seminal book was not very successful veering scholars' minds away from "bones" and "muscles," namely, states, oil, balances of material power and international organizations, toward the information processes that control human and state behavior.

Such as Deutsch, but with a different understanding of what "the nerves of government" mean – the knowledge encoded in communally empowered practices that constitutes polities' and societies' organization and governance through time – I suggest a social evolutionary theory for exploring how the flow of knowledge in and across political structures regulates and normalizes world politics' modus operandi. Cognitive evolution theory can therefore be useful not exclusively for constructivist scholars, in general, and for constructivists focusing on practices and communities of practice, more particularly. Rather, it may open new ways of theorizing and doing empirical research for

---

[122] Deutsch 1963.

scholars of different traditions interested on, for example, (a) the benefits and pitfalls of conceiving international order as multiple and overlapping rather than being only one, (b) network analysis highlighting knowledge rather than information transmission, (c) bridging across level-of-analysis and (d) overcoming macro-micro, and ideas versus material interests, straightjackets. Cognitive evolution theory also provides a fertile ground for (e) exploring how technological development engenders new international practices and why certain technology-triggered practices take hold rather than others, (f) the dialectical processes involved in simultaneous tribal and globalist currents, (g) the politics of expertise by state actors, corporations and scientists dealing with global threats to humanity and (h) breaking the walls that artificially separate between normative and analytical theorizing. As the aforementioned subjects exemplify, a social epistemology of world politics, meaning how knowledge flows through the nerves of world politics and become collectively institutionalized, can benefit not only one but all IR theoretical traditions. I do not mean, however, that cognitive evolution theory can explain everything in world politics. Scholars of different theoretical persuasions may therefore consider joining debates about cognitive evolution and world ordering's limitations and potential, such as this volume is doing.

Second, future critiques and analyses of cognitive evolution theory must engage with IR's "hardware," for instance, material factors, particularly technology, nation-states and governmental and non-governmental international institutions, business corporations, domestic and regional organizations and more. This volume is a good start, but there is more to do to show how "software" and "hardware" work together.

Third, although it does not require normative theorizing, a cognitive evolution world ordering research program can nevertheless be enriched by it. As I mentioned in my book, cognitive evolution normative theorizing gives a normative meaning to "the middle ground." It buys neither into realism's pessimism that nothing changes, nor into idealism's optimism that the world is inexorably moving toward a cosmopolitan society, both of which are "unrealistic." Since the dawn of time, humans have been expanding the array of social practices at their disposal, moved by greed and fear yet also by imagination, inventiveness and attempts to prevent people's worst instincts and actions. Technological innovation is but a servant to humans' worst and best intentions. Most important for understanding world ordering, organized into communities of practice, people have been contesting through the ages not only the efficacy and efficiency of means to achieve their purposes, but also how to get better purposes by performing better practices. But if better practices become institutionalized, progress is, however, always limited, contingent and, reversible; at best it means escaping the abyss.

When looking at what appears to be our present world disorder, but which reveals, really, a worldwide contestation between opposing communities of practice, whose members hold different visions of what a better world order could become, it is imperative to imbue politics, namely, practices deployed to govern society, with values that can be ethically defended as being better. Cognitive evolution theory suggests the lowest common denominator that humans, regardless of their allegiances and their cultural diversity, possess, namely, life's value, which is thus worth defending. Defeating what seem to be world order's worst tendencies today, such as the move toward populist authoritarianism, and preventing environmental, AI and nuclear war-triggered catastrophes may thus depend less on brute power, and practicing domestic and international politics under the illusion that technology, human passions and events can be controlled. Rather it may depend largely on the widespread adoption of practical democracy and on creative human agency directed at mobilizing peoples to embrace and practice common humanity values.[123]

References

Adler, Emanuel. 1991. Cognitive Evolution: A Dynamic Approach for the Study of International Relations and Their Progress. In *Progress in Postwar International Relations*, edited by Emanuel Adler and Beverly Crawford, 43–88. New York: Columbia University Press.

Adler, Emanuel. 1992. The Emergence of Cooperation: National Epistemic Communities and the International Evolution of the Idea of Nuclear Arms Control. *International Organization* 46(1): 101–45.

Adler, Emanuel. 2014. Epistemic Communities of Practice. Paper presented at the annual meeting of the American Political Science Association, August 30, Washington, DC.

[123] See also Adler 2020.

Adler, Emanuel. 2019. *World Ordering. A Social Theory of Cognitive Evolution*. Cambridge: Cambridge University Press.

Adler, Emanuel. 2020. Control Power as a Special Case of Protean Power: Thoughts on Peter Katzenstein and Lucia Seybert's Protean Power: Exploring the Uncertain and Unexpected in World Politics. *International Theory*, 12(3): 422–34.

Adler, Emanuel and Alena Drieschova. 2021. The Epistemological Challenge of Post-Truth to the International Liberal Order. *International Organization* 75(2): 359–86.

Adler, Emanuel and Michael Faubert. forthcoming. Epistemic Communities of Practice. In *Conceptualizing International Practices: Directions for the Practice Turn in International Relations*, edited by Christian Bueger, Alena Drieschova and Ted Hopf. Cambridge: Cambridge University Press.

Adler, Emanuel and Peter Haas. 1992. Conclusion: Epistemic Communities, World Order, and the Creation of a Reflective Research Program. *International Organization* 46(1): 367–90.

Adler, Emanuel and Vincent Pouliot. 2011. International Practices: Introduction and Framework. In *International Practices*, edited by Emanuel Adler and Vincent Pouliot, 3–35. Cambridge: Cambridge University Press.

Amico, Alissa. 2019. The AI Governance Challenge. *Project Syndicate*, March 15. www.project-syndicate.org/commentary/artificial-intelligence-governance-standards-by-alissa-amico-2019-03.

Ansell, Christopher. 2011. *Pragmatist Democracy: Evolutionary Learning as Public Philosophy*. New York: Oxford University Press.

Arendt, Hannah. 1958. *The Human Condition*. Chicago: University of Chicago Press.

Avant, Deborah D., Martha Finnemore and Susan K. Sell, eds. 2010. *Who Governs the Globe?* New York: Cambridge University Press.

Barnett, Michael and Raymond Duvall, eds. 2005. *Power and Global Governance*. Cambridge: Cambridge University Press.

Baum, Seth. 2018. Preventing an AI Apocalypse. *Project Syndicate*, May 16. www.project-syndicate.org/commentary/preventing-artificial-intelligence-apocalypse-by-seth-baum-2018-05.

Beitz, Charles R. 1979. *Political Theory and International Relations*. Princeton: Princeton University Press.

Beitz, Charles R. 2009. *The Idea of Human Rights*. Oxford: Oxford University Press.

Bernstein, Richard J. 2018. *Why Read Hannah Arendt Now*. Cambridge: Polity.

Boltanski, Luc and Laurent Thévenot. 2006. *On Justification: Economies of Worth*. Princeton, NJ: Princeton University Press.

Bostrom, Nick. 2017. Strategic Implications of Openness in AI Development. *Global Policy* 8(2): 135–48.

Bostrom, Nick. 2019. The Vulnerable World Hypothesis. *Global Policy*. https://doi.org/10.1111/1758-5899.12718.

Bourdieu, Pierre. 1977. *Outline of a Theory of Practice*. Translated by Richard Nice. Cambridge: Cambridge University Press.

Bradsher, Keith and Katrin Bennhold, 2019. World Leaders at Davos Call for Global Rules on Tech. *The New York Times* 10(4): 455–76.

Bull, Hedley. 1977. *The Anarchical Society: A Study of Order in World Society*. New York: Columbia University Press.

Buss, David. 2016. *Evolutionary Psychology: The New Science of the Mind*. New York: Routledge.

Campbell, Donald T. 1960. Blind Variation and Selective Retention in Creative Thought as in Other Knowledge Processes. *Psychological Review* 67(6): 380–400.

Capron, Alexander M. 2015. The Lessons of Asilomar for Today's Science. *The New York Times*. www.nytimes.com/roomfordebate/2015/05/28/scien tists-curbing-the-ethical-use-of-science/the-lessons-of-asilomar-for-todays-science.

Carr, E. H. 2001. *The Twenty Years' Crisis, 1919–1939*. New York: Palgrave.

Cochrane, Mollie. 1999. *Normative Theory in International Relations*. Cambridge: Cambridge University Press.

Cohendet, Patrick, Fredric Creplet and Oliver Dupouët. 2001. Communities of Practice and Epistemic Communities: A Renewed Approach of Organisational Learning within the Firm. Retrieved from ResearchGate www.researchgate.net/publication/228587324_Communities_of_Practic e_and_Epistemic_Communities_A_Renewed_Approach_of_Organizatio nal_Learning_within_the_Firm.

Colgan, Jeff D. and Robert O. Keohane. 2017. The Liberal Order Is Rigged: Fix It Now or Watch It Wither. *Foreign Affairs* 96(3): 36–44.

Cosmides, Leda and John Tooby. 1987. From Evolution to Behavior: Evolutionary Psychology as the Missing Link. In *The Latest on the Best: Essays on Evolution and Optimality*, edited by John Dupre, 277–306. Cambridge, MA: MIT Press.

David, Paul A. 1985. Clio and the Economics of QWERTY. *The American Economic Review* 75(2): 332–37.

De Fina, Anna and Alexandra Georgakopoulou. 2008. Analyzing Narratives as Practices *Qualitative Research* 8(3): 379–87.

DeLanda, Manuel. 2006. *A New Philosophy of Society: Assemblage Theory and Social Complexity*. London: Continuum.

Deleuze, Gilles and Félix Guattari. 1987. *A Thousand Plateaus: Capitalism and Schizophrenia*. Minneapolis: University of Minnesota Press.

Dennett, Daniel C. 1995. *Darwin's Dangerous Idea: Evolution and the Meaning of Life*. New York: Simon and Schuster.

Deudney, Daniel and G. John Ikenberry. 2018. Liberal Order: The Resilient Order. *Foreign Affairs* 97(4): 16–24.

Deutsch, Karl. 1963. *The Nerves of Government: Models of Political Communication and Control*. New York: The Free Press.

Dewey, John. 1916. *Democracy and Education*. New York: Macmillan.

Dewey, John. 1922. *Human Nature and Conduct*. New York: Henry Holt.

Dewey, John. 1927. *The Publics and Its Problems: An Essay in Political Inquiry*. New York: Henry Holt.

Dewey, John. 1983. *John Dewey: The Middle Works, 1899–1924*, edited by Jo Ann Boydston. Carbondale: Southern Illinois University Press.

Diehl, Jackson. 2019. Yes, Dictators Are Ascendant. But People All Over the World Are Fighting Back. *The Washington Post*.http://www.washington post.com/opinions/global-opinions/yes-dictators-are ascendant-but-people-all-over-the-world-are-fighting back/2019/07/21/f4139be4-a960-11e9-86d d-d7f0e60391e9_story.html.

Erskine, Toni. 2008. *Embedded Cosmopolitanism: Duties to Strangers and Enemies in a World of Dislocated Communities*. New York: Oxford University Press.

Faizullaev, Alisher and Jérémie Cornut. 2017. Narrative Practice in International Politics and Diplomacy: The Case of the Crimean Crisis. *Journal of International Relations and Development* 20(3): 578–604.

Ferguson, Marilyn. 1980. *The Aquarian Conspiracy: Personal and Social Transformation in the 1980s*. New York: St. Martin's Press.

Fleck, Ludwik. 1979. *Genesis and the Development of a Scientific Fact*. Chicago: University of Chicago Press.

Foucault, Michel. 1980. *Power/Knowledge: Selected Interviews and Other Writings, 1972–1977*. New York: Vintage.

Foucault, Michel. 1984. *The Foucault Reader*. New York: Pantheon Books.

Frega, Roberto. 2017. Pragmatism and Democracy in a Global World. *Review of International Studies* 43(4): 720–41.

Frost, Mervyn. 1996. *Ethics in International Relations: A Constitutive Theory*. Cambridge: Cambridge University Press.

Garling, Caleb. 2015. Andrew Ng: Why "Deep Learning" Is a Mandate for Humans, Not Just Machines. *Wired Magazine*. www.wired.com/bran dlab/2015/05/andrew-ng-deep-learning-mandate-humans-not-just-machines/.

Gayle, Damien. 2019. UK, US and Russia among Those Opposing Killer Robot Ban. *The Guardian*, March 29. www.theguardian.com/science/20 19/mar/29/uk-us-russia-opposing-killer-robot-ban-un-ai.

Gebbia, Joe (cofounder of Airbnb). 2016. How Airbnb Designs for Trust. *TED2016*. www.ted.com/talks/joe_gebbia_how_airbnb_designs_for_ trust. Last accessed October 11, 2019.

Gibbs, Samuel. 2015. Musk, Wozniak and Hawking Urge Ban on Warfare AI and Autonomous Weapons. *The Guardian*.

Gross, Neil. 2009. A Pragmatist Theory of Social Mechanisms. *American Sociological Review* 74(3): 358–79.

Guzzini, Stefano. 2013. *Power, Realism and Constructivism*. Abington: Routledge.

Haas, Ernst B. 1982. Words Can Hurt You; Or, Who Said What to Whom about Regimes. *International Organization* 36(2): 207–43.

Haass, Richard. 2018. Liberal Order R.I.P. *Project Syndicate*, March 21. www .project-syndicate.org/commentary/end-of-liberal-world-order-by-richard-n- -haass-2018-03.

Haass, Richard. 2019. *How a World Order Ends. Foreign Affairs* 98(1): 22–30

Habermas, Jürgen. 1984. *The Theory of Communicative Action*, vol. 1. Boston: Beacon Press.

Habermas, Jürgen. 1987. *The Theory of Communicative Action, vol. 2: The Critique of Functionalist Reason*. Boston: Beacon Press.

Habermas, Jürgen. 1996. *Between Facts and Norms: Contributions to a Discourse Theory of Law and Democracy*. Cambridge, MA: MIT Press.

Harari, Yuval Noah. 2017. *Homo Deus: A Brief History of Tomorrow*. Toronto: Signal.

Harari, Yuval Noah. 2018. *21 Lessons for the 21st Century*. Toronto: Signal.

Holst, Catherine and Anders Molander. 2019. Epistemic Democracy and the Role of Experts. *Contemporary Political Theory* 18(4): 541–61.

Hurrell, Andrew. 2007. *On Global Order: Power, Values, and the Constitution of International Society*. Oxford: Oxford University Press,

Hutchinson Emma and Roland Bleiker 2014.Theorizing Emotions in World Politics. *International Theory* 6(3): 491–514

Ikenberry G. John. 2011. *Liberal Leviathan: The Origins, Crisis, and Transformation of the American International Order*. Princeton, NJ: Princeton University Press.

Ikenberry G. John. 2018. The End of the Liberal International Order? *International Affairs* 94 (1): 7–23.

Ish-Shalom, Piki. 2019. *Beyond the Veil of Knowledge: Triangulating Security, Democracy, and Academic Scholarship*. Ann Arbor: University of Michigan Press.

Jenkins, Ryan. 2018. When It Comes to AI and Weapons, the Tech World Needs Philosophers. *Washington Post*, June 12. www.washingtonpost.com /news/posteverything/wp/2018/06/12/when-it-comes-to-ai-and-weapons-the -tech-world-needs-philosophers/.

Katzenstein, Peter J. 2005. *A World of Regions: Asia and Europe in the American Imperium*. Cornell, NY: Cornell University Press.

Katzenstein, Peter J. and Lucia A. Seybert, eds. 2018. *Protean Power: Exploring the Uncertain and Unexpected in World Politics*. Cambridge, UK: Cambridge University Press.

Kelly, Kevin. 2019. AR Will Spark the Next Big Tech Platform – Call It Mirrorworld. *Wired*, February 12. www.wired.com/story/mirrorworld-ar -next-big-tech-platform/.

Kornprobst, Markus. 2012. From Political Judgments to Public Justifications (and Vice Versa): How Communities Generate Reasons upon Which to Act. *European Journal of International Relations* 20(1): 192–216.

Latour, Bruno. 2005. *Reassembling the Social: An Introduction to Actor-Network Theory*. Oxford: Oxford University Press.

Lawson, George. 2019. Emanuel Adler, World Ordering: A Social Theory of Cognitive Evolution. *International Sociology Reviews* 34(5): 642–52.

Linklater, Andrew. 1998. *The Transformation of Political Community: Ethical Foundations of the Post-Westphalian Era*. Columbia: University of South Carolina Press.

Lopez, Anthony C., Rose McDermott and Michael Bang Petersen. 2011. States in Mind: Evolution, Coalitional Psychology, and International Politics. *International Security* 36(2): 48–83.

MacIntyre, Alasdair. 1981. *After Virtue: A Study in Moral Theory*. Notre Dame: University of Notre Dame Press.

McBride, Jason, Omar Mouallem and Ivan Semeniuk. 2018. *The Globe and Mail*, March 26. www.theglobeandmail.com/report-on-business/rob-magazine/canadas-ai-explosion-visit-three-labs-where-machines-are-being-taught-to-think-likepeople/article38336675/.

McDermott, Rose. 2004. *Political Psychology in International Relations*. Ann Arbor: University of Michigan Press.

McFarland, Matt. 2018. Leading AI Researchers Vow to Not Develop Autonomous Weapons. *CNN Business*, July 18. https://money.cnn.com/ 2018/07/18/technology/ai-autonomous-weapons/.

Mearsheimer, John J. 2019. Bound to Fail: The Rise and Fall of the Liberal International Order. *International Security* 43(4): 7–50.

Mercer, Jonathan. 2013. Emotion and Strategy in the Korean War. *International Organization* 67(2):221–52.

Metz, Cade. 2019. Is Ethical A.I. Even Possible? *The New York Times*, March 1. www.nytimes.com/2019/03/01/business/ethics-artificial-intelligence.html.

Müller, Jan-Werner. 2019. The Pre-History of Post-Truth. *Project Syndicate*, April 26. www.project-syndicate.org/onpoint/the-pre-history-of-post-truth-by-jan-werner-mueller-2019-04.

Peters, Michael A. 2017. Education in a Post-Truth World. *Educational Philosophy and Theory* 49(6): 563–66.

Pirsig, Robert M. 1974. *Zen and the Art of Motorcycle Maintenance.* New York: Bantam Books.

Plato. 1968. *The Republic*, 2nd ed. Translated with notes and an interpretive essay by Allen Bloom. New York: Basic Books.

Popper, Karl R. 1959. *The Propensity Interpretation of Probability. British Journal for the Philosophy of Science* 10(37): 25–42.

Pouliot, Vincent. 2014. Practice Tracing. In *Process Tracing: From Metaphor to Analytic Tool*, edited by Bennett, Andrew and Jeffrey T. Checkel, 237–53. Cambridge, UK: Cambridge University Press.

Prigogine, Ilya. 1980. *From Being to Becoming: Time and Complexity in the Physical Sciences.* San Francisco: W. H. Freeman.

Rawls, John. 1971. *A Theory of Justice.* Cambridge, MA: Harvard University Press.

Rosenau, James N. and Ernst-Otto Czempiel. 1992. *Governance Without Government: Order and Change in World Politics.* Cambridge: Cambridge University Press

Rosenfeld, Sophia. 2019. *Democracy and Truth: A Short History.* Philadelphia: University of Pennsylvania Press.

Ruggie, John G. 1975. International Responses to Technology: Concepts and Trends. *International Organization* 29(3): 557–83.

Russell, Stuart. 2019. The Purpose Put into the Machine. In *Possible Minds: Twenty-Five Ways of Looking at AI*, edited by John Brockman, 20–32. New York: Penguin Press.

Sagan, Carl. 1980. *Cosmos.* New York: Random House.

Scharre Paul. 2019. Killer Apps. The Real Dangers of an AI Arms Race. *Foreign Affairs.* www.foreignaffairs.com/articles/2019-04-16/killer-apps.

Sil, Rudra and Peter J. Katzenstein. 2010. Analytic Eclecticism in the Study of World Politics: Reconfiguring Problems and Mechanisms across Research Traditions. *Perspectives on Politics* 8(2): 411–31.

Singer David D. 1961. The Level-of-Analysis Problem in International Relations *World Politics* 14(1): 77–92.

Slaughter, Anne-Marie. 2019. A New Kind of Multilateralism is on the Horizon. *Financial Times*, September 18. www.ft.com/content/dae8bbd6-d930-11e9-9c26-419d783e10e8.

Slaughter, Anne-Marie. and Chehadé, Fadi. 2019. How to Govern a Digitally Networked World. *Project Syndicate*, March 25. www.project-syndicate.org/commentary/global-digital-governance-system-by-anne-marie-slaughter-and-fadi-chehade-2019-03.

Stein, Janice Gross. 2011. Background Knowledge in the Foreground: Conversations about Competent Practice in "Sacred Space." In *International Practices*, edited by Emanuel Adler and Vincent Pouliot, 87–107. Cambridge: Cambridge University Press.

Stuurman, Siep. 2017. *The Invention of Humanity: Equality and Cultural Difference in World History*. Cambridge, MA: Harvard University Press

Toulmin, Stephen. 1972. *Human Understanding: The Collective Use and Evolution of Concepts*. Oxford: Clarendon.

United Nations. 2019. Autonomous Weapons That Kill Must Be Banned, Insists UN Chief. *UN News*, March 25.

Walzer, Michael. 1990. The Communitarian Critique of Liberalism. *Political Theory* 18(1): 6–23.

Wenger, Etienne. 1998. *Communities of Practice: Learning, Meaning, and Identity*. Cambridge, UK: Cambridge University Press.

Wenger, Etienne. 2010. Communities of Practice and Social Learning Systems: The Career of a Concept. In *Social Learning Systems and Communities of Practice*, edited by Chris Blackmore, 179–98. London: Springer.

Wendt, Alexander. 1998. On Constitution and Causation in International Relations. *Review of International Studies* (24)5: 101–17.

Zakrzewski, Cat. 2015. Musk, Hawking Warn of Artificial Intelligence Weapons. *The Wall Street Journal*, July 27. www.wsj.com/articles/BL-DGB-42790.

Zuboff, Shoshana. 2019. *The Age of Surveillance Capitalism: The Fight for a Human Future at the New Frontier of Power*. New York: Public Affairs.

Zürn, Michael. 2010. Global Governance as Multi-Level Governance. In *Handbook on Multi-Level Governance*, edited by Henrik Enderlein, Sonja Wälti and Michael Zürn, 80–102. Northampton: Edward Elgar.

Zürn, Michael. 2018. *A Theory of Global Governance: Authority, Legitimacy, and Contestation*. Oxford: Oxford University Press.

Milton Keynes UK
Ingram Content Group UK Ltd.
UKHW020839110324
439289UK00018B/123